# Restless Fires

MERCER
UNIVERSITY PRESS

*Endowed by*
**Tom Watson Brown**
*and*
**The Watson-Brown Foundation, Inc.**

# RESTLESS FIRES

## YOUNG JOHN MUIR'S THOUSAND-MILE WALK TO THE GULF IN 1867–68

*James B. Hunt*

MERCER UNIVERSITY PRESS

MACON, GEORGIA

MUP/ H855 // P457

© 2012 Mercer University Press
1400 Coleman Avenue
Macon, Georgia 31207
All rights reserved
First Edition

Books published by Mercer University Press are printed on acid-free paper that meets the requirements of the American National Standard for Information Sciences—Permanence of Paper for Printed Library Materials.

Mercer University Press is a member of Green Press Initiative (greenpressinitiative.org), a nonprofit organization working to help publishers and printers increase their use of recycled paper and decrease their use of fiber derived from endangered forests. This book is printed on recycled paper.

Library of Congress Cataloging-in-Publication Data
Hunt, James B., 1943-
  Restless fires : young John Muir's thousand-mile walk to the Gulf in 1867/68 / James B. Hunt. -- 1st ed.
      p. cm.
   "MUP/ H855"--T.p. verso.
   Includes bibliographical references and index.
   ISBN 978-0-88146-392-7 (hbk. : alk. paper) -- ISBN 0-88146-392-2 (hbk. : alk. paper) 978-088146-393-4 (pbk. alk. paper)-- 0-88146-393-0 (pbk. alk. paper)
  1. Muir, John, 1838-1914--Travel--Southern States. 2. Southern States--Description and travel. 3. Southern States--Environmental conditions--History--19th century. 4. Natural history--Southern States. 5. Muir, John, 1838-1914--Travel--Cuba. 6. Cuba--Description and travel. 7. Cuba--Environmental conditions--History--19th century. 8. Natural history--Cuba. 9. Naturalists--United States--Biography. 10. Naturalists--United States--Diaries. I. Title.
   QH31.M9H86 2012
   508.75--dc23
                           2012021867

*John Muir, c.1863 at around 25 years of age.*

# CONTENTS

# PREFACE

In an undated journal entry John Muir wrote, "I only went out for a walk, and finally concluded to stay out till sundown, for going out, I found, was really going in."[1] John Muir's thousand-mile walk of 1867 when he was 29 was, indeed, a deep "going in." Throughout my professional life as a professor of history I have sought to fathom the impact of youthful travel on a young person's worldview.

In my previous writings on historical figures such as John Quincy Adams, Frederick Douglass, and Jane Addams, I have discovered how critical youthful travel is to a young person's worldview and sense of self. Some of these leaders kept diaries, such as John Quincy Adams, and others wrote autobiographies close to the experience such as Frederick Douglass.

Muir's journal is exceptional in the ways he reflects on his lived experiences: while there are daily jottings of flowers, plant life, sunsets, habitations, and encounters with people, there are also original and powerful ideas, sharply written. Muir's journal addresses the universal problems of death; a human being's relationship with nature; how God can be viewed through the glory of a palmetto, the delicacy of a flower, or the behavior of a predatory animal; and, his critique of conventional, orthodox thinking on nature. Far in advance of his time, Muir rejects a utilitarian view of nature, preferring a view that sees nature governed by laws of its own design, independent of human self-interest.

---

[1] Linnie Marsh Wolfe, ed., *John of the Mountains, the Unpublished Journals of John Muir* (Madison: University of Wisconsin Press, 1979) 439.

In his journal, young Muir is both delighted and challenged by what he sees and experiences. He is traveling through a tough time in the South—just two years after the Civil War. He is a witness to its devastation, Muir's encounters with suspicious villagers sprinkle across the pages much like the debris of war. It is no wonder he has little regard for human communities as he desires to flee to nature for comfort and solace, as he did for five days in a cemetery teeming with life outside Savannah, Georgia.

Muir's journal was a work in progress. Close readers of his manuscript note numerous revisions, cross-outs, and re-writes. He re-wrote sections while on the walk, probably shortly after the walk while in California, and well after the walk when he worked with his journals while dictating and writing his autobiography from 1908 to 1910. The journal also appears to be an assemblage of some pages from other journals and sketchbooks. Still, his experiences and his thoughts ring with a tone true to the moment.

This work places John Muir's thousand-mile walk within the historical framework of Reconstruction. He bears witness to the war's devastation, the suspicious feelings of some Southerners to strangers, and the economic hardships felt among mountain folk, African American freedmen, and the planter class. He also receives Southern hospitality, including a family in Florida that most likely saved his life by nursing him back to health from a deadly bout with malaria.

This book also traces the development of Muir's environmental thought from his background in Scotland and Wisconsin, through his reading interests and preferences, his studies at the University of Wisconsin, and his reflections on his walk through the South to the Gulf of Mexico in 1867 and 1868. Key figures loom large in Muir's life including his father, a foil against whom he rebelled, and Jeanne C. Carr, the wife of a Wisconsin professor who befriended Muir and encouraged his independent thinking and decisions. Muir blended his life experience, his reading, his studies, and his friendships into new channels of thought due to his lived experiences on the walk to the Gulf.

It has been a joy to read Muir, to follow his journey, to engage in his thinking. His insights provide a radical critique that nature simply does not exist only for human use and exploitation. Muir teaches us to be more humble in our self-estimation and self-interest. All of nature, in Muir's view, has intrinsic worth; each part plays an important role. Muir gives voice to this perspective through this remarkable walk and his record of it. My contribution is to unpack the circumstances, context, and experiences that gave Muir the opportunity to see anew and think anew.

# ACKNOWLEDGMENTS

Historians stand upon the shoulders of those who precede them in their work. Almost every book is the work of a collaborative effort of librarians, researchers, editors, copy-editors, and early readers of the first drafts. For all this assistance, I am grateful.

I am indebted to the many fine libraries and special collections that assisted me in this journey, funded through a 2007 research and development grant from Whitworth University. Muir scholars have a rich repository in the John Muir Papers available in the Holt-Atherton Special Collections at the University of the Pacific in Stockton, California. I wish to thank its Director, Shan Sutton and his able assistant, Trish Richards, who provided a congenial setting and easy access to materials necessary for this research on John Muir. Digitized versions of Muir's photographs, journals, drawings, and correspondence are now available online through the Holt-Atherton Collection Web site, which allows convenient access for scholars and the general public.

Other libraries, such as the University of California, Berkeley, Stanford University Library, Inter-Library loan services at the Whitworth University Library, and the University of Montana Library in Missoula provided helpful bibliographical assistance and access to Muir's papers on microfilm. The Huntington Library's collection of Muir Family Papers, along with the Jeanne C. Carr Papers, provided useful insights and material.

My own journey from Louisville, Kentucky, to Cedar Key, Florida, began on 1 September 2007 and led to my discovering major and minor libraries and research institutions along the route. These included the University of Louisville Library's

Special Collections Department, the Filson Historical Society of Louisville, the William T. Young Library at the University of Tennessee at Knoxville, the collections at the University of Georgia in Athens and the Georgia Historical Society in Savannah, and the Special Collections Department at the Smathers Library of the University of Florida. All of these collections provided maps, diaries, newspapers, local histories, and material relevant to the social, political, and economic contexts of the communities through which Muir passed in 1867. Librarians at smaller libraries, such as the Fentress County Historical Society in Jamestown, Tennessee, the Roane County Archives and Library in Kingston, Tennessee, Union County Historical Society in Blairsville, Georgia, and the Cedar Key Public Library at Cedar Key, Florida, were very helpful in uncovering details about local communities or obscure 1867 narratives that enhanced Muir's story within the context of Reconstruction.

I am deeply appreciative of scholars and writers who took their time and energy to read drafts of this work. Dr. Ronald C. White, an outstanding writer and historian of Abraham Lincoln, read an early draft and offered generous encouragement for this project. The advice and counsel of Bonnie Gisel, who read an early draft of this manuscript, was invaluable in providing suggestions for improving content and style. Other readers of early draft who provided helpful ciriticim include: Harold Wood of the Sierra Club's John Muir Exhibit website, Dr. Dennis Williams, Dr. Larry Daloz-Parks, and Dr. Richard Baldwin. Terry Mitchell's initial proofreading showed care and accuracy. I also want to express special appreciation to Marc Jolley of Mercer University Press for his support and assistance with this book.

Finally, I express my heart-felt thanks to my wife and fellow historian, Linda Lawrence Hunt. She wrote about a Norwegian woman who walked across America in 1896 on a wager to save her family farm—a distance much greater than that walked by young John Muir. Linda offered consistent support, encouragement, and an occasional kick to move this project along. Together, we had great fun following intrepid walkers across the continent and through the South, working together on our research projects and reading each other's work. An excellent critic, Linda provided just the right balance between criticism and encouragement—sometimes in the same sentence. Because of her enthusiastic support, I can, with confidence affirm this work as a labor of love.

# INTRODUCTION

John Muir, environmentalist and leader of the American conservation movement in the late nineteenth and early twentieth centuries, found his life's mission through an accident and a journey. The twenty-nine-year-old Scottish immigrant had recently returned from Canada in early 1867 to pursue his career as a machinist in an Indianapolis shop.[1] While he was trying to loosen the knotted lacing of a drive belt for heavy machinery with the pointed end of a metal file, the file suddenly flipped up, tearing into his right eye, leaving ocular fluid flowing into his cupped hand. Stunned, alarmed, and increasingly frightened after the accident, Muir first lost sight in the injured eye; the other eye responded with sympathetic blindness.[2]

After a few weeks in a darkened room, Muir's punctured eye began to heal. About a month after the accident, he could dimly read.[3] Having been nearly blinded, the relieved Muir resumed a dream he had harbored earlier in his life. He decided to walk through the Southern states on a botanizing trip even as the region was recovering from the devastation of the Civil War. Immensely grateful to have his sight restored, the young Scot left his machinist career to plunge into the life of a naturalist and to see for himself "God's inventions."

During this walk through nature, Muir sought healing from other, deeper wounds. He and his father, Daniel, were locked in mental and theological combat. While his father thought the only book his son needed was the Bible, Muir saw things differently. He wrote to a friend a year before his departure:

> It may be a bad symptom, but I will confess that I take
> more intense delight from reading the power and goodness
> of God from "the things which are made" than from the

Bible. The two books, however, harmonize beautifully, and contain enough of divine truth for the study of all eternity.[4]

The young man sought a true home and vocation. He was formulating a new way to look at nature in contrast to his father's purely agrarian and utilitarian Christian perspective.

To pursue this dream, young Muir planned to walk south through Kentucky, Tennessee, a small part of North Carolina, Georgia, and across Northern Florida, from Fernandina to Cedar Key. This much he did.

Following the inspiration of Alexander von Humboldt, an intrepid eighteenth-century geographer of the Antilles and South America, and of Mungo Park, a young Scot who traveled the African interior in the eighteenth century, Muir dreamed of traveling up the Orinoco River to its headwaters, finding a tributary to the Amazon River and traveling down the Amazon to the Atlantic Ocean, then maybe onto Africa. This would be a taxing journey in terms of both physical strength and financial resources. Through his thousand-mile walk, Muir solidified an emerging bio-centric worldview informed by both his religious heritage and his new, ecological convictions. This experience and the resulting mental transformation fired his ambition to stay in the outdoors. The walk transformed Muir's thought to the point that he remained dedicated to the love of natural beauty for the rest of his life.

Muir's walk through the South thus became a prelude to the staggering accomplishments of his later life. It set the stage for his baptism into the new, "golden" light of California. The journal of this walk honed his skills in writing with such spiritual passion and engagement that, eventually, his words shaped national policy toward preservation of wilderness. The journey gave voice to Muir's profound theological and ecological conviction that "[a]ll is harmony divine."[5]

Three years before his death in 1914 at the age of seventy-six, John Muir made that journey to the Amazon—a dream he had held onto since he was just twenty-nine. Shortly before his departure, in 1911, he wrote to Elizabeth "Betty" Averell, a young relative of the E.H. Harriman family who traveled with Muir on the famous Harriman expedition to Alaska in 1899: "Have I forgotten the Amazon, Earth's greatest river? Never, never, never. It has been burning in me half a century, and will burn forever. For you must know, dear Betty, that even water and rocks, everything God possesses, burns like the stars in His Love."[6]

This book will recount the story of John Muir's thousand-mile walk through the South in 1867 and 1868. The story is an account of healing, re-formulation, and transformation. The journal of his journey records Muir's struggle with the received theology of his Scottish heritage and the ideas of his ardent and controlling father. Both the journal and his letters to family and friends report what Muir saw and experienced in both nature and the villages through which he passed. In the final analysis, the story sets forth the impact his walk and travel had in shaping Muir's environmental thought, ethics, and worldview. Muir's Southern walk profoundly shaped the spiritual, vocational, and philosophical direction of his life. The walk proved to be the crucible in which Muir's extraordinary capabilities were forged from a wide array of resources, life experiences, educational opportunities, mentors, and personal relationships.

How did John Muir's youthful walk through the South shape his thought, his ambitions, and his life goals? The resources in answering these questions are abundant; they reside in his journal of the walk, in his letters to friends and family, and in his reminiscences when he returned to the journal the year after the walk and in 1908, when he was working on materials for his autobiography. One can accompany him on this walk through a reconstruction of where he went, what he did, and how he thought about what he saw.[7]

Setting out on 1 September 1867, John Muir wrote a poignant inscription inside the cover of his journal that gave voice to an identity and direction in his life. Surrounding his inscription with an ornate circle, he wrote, "John Muir, Earth-planet, Universe."

Muir's excitement, anticipation, love of life, and dreams of seeing "splendid visions" are contagious. While he felt lonely, the live oaks bade him welcome.

On this journey Muir brought his heritage—powerful memories of Dunbar, Scotland, and Portage, Wisconsin. Muir traveled light, yet, he brought books, a plant press, toiletries, and a few articles of clothing in a rubberized bag. He brought his experience as the son of a merchant and his work as a farmer, inventor, and machinist. He brought his knowledge of botany and geology learned in his few years at the University of Wisconsin. Finally, he kept a journal where he recorded his thoughts and experiences. This journal shows how Muir transformed from a preacher's son, farmer and mechanical genius, to a wandering botanist fired by a new vision of how human beings should regard nature, death, and their role in the natural order.

What was the influence of travel in general, and this walk in particular, upon his formation as a young adult? What were the conditions of his boyhood and youth that impelled him to take a thousand-mile walk through the South just two years after the Civil War? What was he leaving behind and where was he going—and for what reasons? While the journey was an outward endeavor with a totally new environment for Muir, it was also an inward journey. The "restless fires" of curiosity, passion, and intellectual vitality propelled him forward in his decision to make the walk. One can follow Muir through Southern towns and villages devastated by war and can share in the experience of his love of welcoming oaks and heartening

4

*John Muir's inscription of an identity and direction in life.*

songs of birds. Through reading his work, one can delight in the wonder of beautiful plants and delicate flowers and share in Muir's sober reflection on the role of predatory reptiles. Who knows? In joining John Muir's journey we, too, may be changed.

# 1

# THE FORMATION OF JOHN MUIR

*"Gie me ae spark o' Nature's fire, that's a' the learning I desire."* —Robert Burns

As fog crept into the harbor town of Dunbar, Scotland, on the evening of 18 February 1849, eleven-year-old John Muir and his brother David sat studying their school lessons in front of their grandfather's warm fire. Suddenly their father, Daniel Muir, a tall and fervent merchant, burst through the door from across the street into their grandfather's home. "Bairns, you needna learn your lessons the nicht, for we're gan to America the morn!"[8]

For the boys, the news was "blindly glorious." In contrast, their retired grandfather, David Gilrye, was saddened and "looked very serious." He loved these boys, but was too old to make the rigorous journey. As a memento, he gave each boy a gold coin. Looking at their downcast grandfather, the boys promised to send back a "big box full of that tree sugar packed in gold from the glorious paradise over the sea...."[9]

John and David could barely contain their excitement. The trip promised an exciting adventure taking them away from the dreary school lessons and tedious Bible memorization. It would be John Muir's first sea voyage in a life full of future travel.

Taking John and David, as well as his daughter Sarah, Daniel formed a family advance party that sought out a new home in a new land with a new career: farming and preaching, leaving behind his life as a merchant. His wife, Ann, and another daughter would join him after a home was built. The

Muir party began their journey by walking down the foggy streets of Dunbar to take a train to Glasgow. In Glasgow they boarded an older-rigged, blunt-nosed sailing ship that was to be their home for six weeks and three days.

John and David loved their liberation from school lessons in classical languages, rote memorization and recitations. Their father and Sarah became seasick and spent their time confined to bed. John, however, later recalled the excitement and adventure of seeing sailors "at their rope-hauling and climbing work," getting sloshed about the decks during several storms, joining in the sailors' songs, learning names of ropes and knots, and hearing sailors' stories about whales, porpoises, seabirds, and dolphins.[10] Both boys impressed the captain with their education and their ability to speak English correctly despite the strong Scottish brogue in their informal conversation.[11]

Young Muir relished this travel; it provided some separation from his father due to Daniel's seasickness. The son's world opened up. He discovered he could make friends with an English captain and sailors despite cultural differences. Strangers welcomed him, and he excelled in sociability. Young Muir discovered the nautical world with its fascinating seamen, their work, their songs, and their compelling stories. He loved the roll and pitch of the ship with its waves washing over its blunt bow. Muir found sea travel exhilarating, sociable, and a stimulus to his restless curiosity.

After arriving in New York City around April 4, the Muir party, together with the father's four-hundred-pound iron box containing a beam scale and weights, iron tools, provisions, and a cast-iron stove, traveled up the Hudson River to Albany, New York. The family took a Mohawk packet boat up the Mohawk Valley along the Erie Canal to Buffalo; in Buffalo, Daniel decided to look for land in Wisconsin. Wisconsin had both productive soil and more open and clear land than Canada.[12] The Muir party crossed Lake Michigan by steamer to Milwaukee, Wisconsin, and met up with a farmer from Fort

Winnebago who was heading back to his home with an empty wagon after delivering his wheat. For a $30 fee, the farmer agreed to take the Muir party, their iron chest, and their cast-iron stove the one hundred miles to Kingston, Wisconsin, where Daniel sought land to farm and on which to build a home.[13]

It was a cruel overland passage, especially for the poor horses slogging through the Wisconsin mud. Recalling the difficulty of the wagon trail, John Muir wrote:

> [T]he roads over the prairies were heavy and miry, causing no end of lamentation, for we often got stuck in the mud, and the poor farmer sadly declared that never, never again would he be tempted to try to haul such a cruel, heart-breaking, wagon-breaking, horse-killing load, no, not for a hundred dollars.[14]

In Kingston, Daniel left the boys in a rooming house while he scouted out farmland. While he was gone, the boys discovered other boys in town and found they easily fit in after the usual challenges of foot races, wrestling, and tree climbing. "[I]n a day or two we felt at home, carefree and happy, notwithstanding our family was so widely divided."[15] Daniel found their home site "in a sunny open woods on the side of a lake" later known as the Fountain Lake farm. Steady, plodding oxen pulled the family ten miles to their farm near Portage, Wisconsin. They set up a small shanty as temporary shelter while building the main farmhouse.

Recalling the moment late in life, John Muir recorded his delight:

> This sudden plash into pure wildness-baptism in Nature's warm heart-how utterly happy it made us! Nature streaming into us, wooingly teaching her wonderful glowing lessons, so unlike the dismal grammar ashes and cinders so long thrashed into us. Here without knowing it we still were at school; every wild lesson a love lesson, not whipped but charmed into us.[16]

While the overland travel was challenging, Muir delighted in the prairies at springtime, despite mud and mire. Travel became not a threat to his security, but an introduction to a joyful and thrilling experience that he would repeat throughout his life.

Travel provided both escape from the slog of school and exposure to new worlds of delightful engagement. Travel also provided a means by which an eleven-year-old boy could begin to see a world larger than the constraints of his father's vision. Travel broadened John Muir's small-town Scottish world to the worlds of train and ocean travel and to a whole new way of life in North America; it became a liberating force in John Muir's life, one from which he would repeatedly seek knowledge and experience with the natural world and with understanding himself. This type of travel would provoke deep thoughts about his environment, his place in it, and his core beliefs.

As a child, John Muir was part of a larger social movement of some 55,132 migrants from the British Isles who left their homeland in 1849 for the United States.[17] The decision to migrate was largely Daniel Muir's, and the Muir family rode a great wave of humanity pouring out of Europe. Failed revolutions in France and Germany, famines in Ireland, restraints on nonconformist religious expression, legacies of privilege and encumbrances on land ownership, and incessant wars and burdensome taxes to finance those wars impelled Europeans towards North America.

Daniel Muir's decision to migrate was born out of difficult childhood experiences that persisted throughout his itinerant-preaching ministries. Orphaned at an early age, he ran away from his surrogate parents, his older sister, Mary, and her shepherd husband, Hamilton Blakely, when he was twenty-one. Heading towards Glasgow with a Bible and handmade fiddle, he found a new religious home with his conversion to a pietistic Campbellite Christianity in 1818.[18] "The ecstasy of the

Apostles" warmed his heart.[19] With the Campbellites, later known as Disciples of Christ, Daniel found inspiration in a creedless Christianity. The Campbellites sought to replicate the earliest form of the church presented in the Book of Acts and the work of the apostles who had direct contact with Jesus. This form of Christianity, an offshoot of established Presbyterianism, however, set aside creeds, scholarship, seminaries and church structures as vain human inventions. Increasingly, Daniel took a dim view of the established Presbyterian Church of Scotland, with its academic vestments and scholarly sermons, regarding it as a form of "devil worship."

Daniel's religious zeal found a militant tone when he joined the army as a penniless, homeless, and hungry recruit. At six feet tall, and confident in a new uniform, Daniel was ordered to Dunbar, Scotland, in 1829 to recruit soldiers. As an army officer, Muir practiced his heart religion with a military discipline. In attending the church on top of Kirkbrae Hill, he sang psalms with a booming enthusiasm. The ladies were entranced.[20]

Daniel Muir's marriage to Helen Kennerly ended quickly due to her poor health; she died after a union of "short duration." Upon her death Daniel became sole heir to a grain and food store.[21] The young widower was now comfortable with a good estate. Through integrity and hard work, he prospered. He had only to look across the street for an eligible second wife.

Before the Muirs' marriage, John's mother, Ann Gilrye, lived in a three-story building owned by a retired meat cutter who had done well and faced a secure retirement. Their family had ten children; only two, including Ann, lived to adulthood due to plagues that ravaged the Gilrye household.[22] Daniel courted Ann despite objections from friends and Ann's father, a member of the established Presbyterian Church. Daniel Muir held non-conformist ideas about religion, elections, and patronage. Despite her father's reservations, especially over

11

Daniel's religious zealotry, Daniel and Ann married in 1833 and moved into his shop and home.

The tall, grey-eyed, quiet bride loved nature and often took solitary walks through the country, gathering bouquets of flowers. John's interests in flowers and walking may have stemmed from his mother's influence. She also wrote poetry and had talent in painting and drawing.[23] Daniel's religious convictions were so strong that he prohibited any form of "idolatry" in his house and therefore banished all pictures from the walls. Even Ann's cross-stitching had to be sent back to her mother. Meals were lean and taken in silence. Ann's love of music, dance and humor silently slid from family life as years passed. Their one joy as a couple was the enclosed backyard garden of elms, hedges, fruit trees, and lilies, which Daniel attempted to make as perfect as Eden. Daniel especially loved the lilies because it was a flower to which Jesus made reference.

John Muir grew up in a large family. His oldest sister, Margaret, arrived a year after his parents' marriage; then, another sister, Sarah, was born in 1836. John, the Muirs' first son, arrived two years later, on 21 April 1838, followed by brothers David, in 1840, and Daniel, Jr., in 1843. Filling out the family in Scotland was a set of twin sisters, Mary and Annie, born in 1846. Muir's youngest sister, Joanna, would be the last child, and was born in Wisconsin. Altogether, the parents had seven children in twelve years. A healthy and sturdy brood, all the children lived into adulthood, in contrast to the fate of the Gilrye family and many other Scots of their time. The family was close. The children played together, worked together, and kept in touch with one another throughout their entire lives. This family of brothers and sisters provided a strong bond that drew John Muir inward toward the family as long as his siblings remained home, while his father ranged the countryside on itinerant preaching journeys.

There were strains in the family, however, particularly between John and his father. Much of the conflict focused on differences in religion, choices of reading materials, and the purpose for which one was to live.

Daniel had staunch religious expectations for his firstborn son. He hoped John would follow him into the Campbellite faith or at least become a pious, useful boy, wholly devoted to religion. For example, John wrote, "...father made me learn so many Bible verses every day that by the time I was eleven years of age I had about three fourths of the Old Testament and all of the New by heart and by sore flesh. I could recite the New Testament from the beginning of Matthew to the end of Revelation without a single stop."[24] Muir learned Scottish songs and ballads on his own, but was rewarded with a penny for memorizing hymns such as "Rock of Ages."[25] Daniel, worried about the bad influence of neighborhood boys who ran about the countryside, climbed the ruins of Dunbar castle, and raised eyebrows of the elderly locals, tried to confine his boys to the delights of his Eden—the locked and high-walled backyard.[26]

While John, too, loved the lilies, he acknowledged that he preferred boys' adventures: throwing stones at cats, gleefully watching dogfights, visiting slaughterhouses with the hope of a free pig's bladder for a football, and getting into schoolyard fights.[27] "To be a 'gude fechter' [good fighter] was our highest ambition, our dearest aim in life in or out of school. To be a good scholar was a secondary consideration, though we tried hard to hold high places in our classes ..."[28] Daniel made clear his desire to control his boys' Saturday adventures. Muir wrote, "Father sternly forbade David and me from playing truant in the fields with plundering wanderers like ourselves, fearing we might go on from bad to worse, get hurt in climbing over walls, caught by gamekeepers, or lost by falling over a cliff into the sea."[29]

In Muir's account, his father set the rules, with a "stern countenance," "looking very hard-hearted." Breaking rules was not just a matter of safety. The transgressions flirted with corporeal, if not eternal, punishment. "Play as much as you like in the back yard and garden … and mind what you'll get when you forget and disobey."[30] John saw through his father's dark looks that, as he wrote, "his heart was far from hard." Nevertheless, the boys found their way to the seashore or the open green fields, where they marveled at the singing birds and pillaged their nests. Even during the school week, John and David ran over to their grandfather's house, where they were sure to get a warm welcome and a cozy fire, to do their lessons. There seemed to be little warmth or affirmation coming from their father.[31]

Conflict between father and son persisted after their emigration to Wisconsin in 1849. The weight of clearing the fields, building the houses, splitting tough oak fence rails and harvesting crops fell upon the children. Grandfather Gilrye had been right when he warned, "'Ah, poor laddies, poor laddies, you'll find something else ower the sea forbye gold and sugar, birds' nests and freedom fra lesson and schools. You'll find plenty hard, hard work.'"[32]

As John grew into a strapping teenager, Daniel heaped on more farm labor. Daniel's ambitions led him to purchase a second farm, named Hickory Hill, and he expected John to help clear the land, build a house, and dig a well. When Daniel worked along with John, he frequently found opportunities to preach moral lessons to his son.

While clearing the fields of brush, Daniel used the bonfires "as warning lessons," comparing their heat with that of hell, and the branches with bad boys. "[N]ow, John, just think what an awful thing it would be to be thrown into that fire:—and then think of hellfire, that is so many times hotter." He told John, "Into that fire all bad boys, with sinners of every sort who disobey God, will be cast as we are casting branches into this brush fire, and although suffering so much, their sufferings will never, never end, because neither the fire nor the sinners can die."[33] As in Scotland, life in Wisconsin under his father's rule was a source of both delight and dissatisfaction: curiosity, adventure, and delight in the countryside melancholy, moral injunction, and dogmatism indoors. The conflict between father and son was especially pronounced with regard to John's reading preferences.

John Muir's personal dreams for travel grew during his years on the farm through reading poets and authors. But Daniel Muir preferred that his children read only the Bible and other religious books. While Daniel's library consisted largely of religious books, John struggled to add depth and dimension to his reading by borrowing books from his neighbors and developing his own library. He urged his father to purchase books in higher arithmetic and grammar and taught himself astronomy, algebra, geometry, and trigonometry; he also read in calculus, analytical geometry, and advanced grammar.[34] He read the novels of Walter Scott in secret since they had been forbidden by his father. A dispute broke out when John sought to read Josephus's *History of the Jews*, but Daniel opposed the book. John argued that "everybody, even religious people," read Plutarch's *Lives* and praised it as a grand book, but his father remained unconvinced.[35]

The unreasonable nature of the father's resistance to John's eclectic reading habits is no more clearly illustrated than in the story of William Duncan, a neighbor who lent the boy Thomas Dick's *The Christian Philosopher*. Daniel ordered his son to return the book to its owner because it had the word "philosopher" in it.[36] The son argued with his father, stating that books and science were even helpful in his father's reading of the Bible because his father used spectacles; thus, the science of optics proved useful in reading scripture. Muir recalled, "But he still objected to my reading that book, called me a contumacious quibbler too fond of disputation, and ordered me to return it to the accommodating owner. I managed, however, to read it later."[37]

John read his books in short slices of time at half-hour noonday meals and between dinner and bedtime, at eight o'clock, but it simply was not enough time. He tried to stretch out his reading beyond bedtime, but his father would have none of it. "*John, go to bed!* Must I give you a separate order every night to get you to go to bed? Now, I will have no irregularity in the family; you *must* go when the rest go, and without my having to tell you … If you *will* read, get up in the morning and read. You may get up in the morning as early as you like."[38] John seized the opportunity. He pushed his father's limits by getting up after only five hours sleep at one o'clock in the morning to read books or craft inventions, continuing this pattern for a few weeks. He spent much time in the basement working on handcrafted inventions, including a self-setting sawmill.

Soon there followed a flurry of whittled and hand-built inventions including water wheels, door locks and latches, thermometers, hygrometers, pyrometers, clocks, a barometer, an automatic horse feeder, a lamplighter, a fire lighter and, eventually, a self-rising bed operated by a clock, pulleys, gearing, and two Wisconsin boulders used for counterweights. He handcrafted the gears by whittling or fabricating mechanical parts from scraps of wood, leather, or metal. Even if his body needed more sleep, John forced himself up in the morning with the self-rising bed to read what he wanted to read, having extracted the concession from his father. The whirring of gears, the thump of the boulders landing on the floor accompanied by the rattle of the bedstead on the planking was a daily reminder to Daniel that John was reading and inventing, following his own agendas rather than those prescribed by his father.

Word of these marvels spread through the countryside, and visitors showed up to investigate reports of the wondrous machines. Muir's father offered scant welcome to this attention because his son became diverted from his farm work. The father thought these inventions an extravagant waste of time; attention to religion, in his view, was preferable. He asked his son, "Do you not think it is very wrong to waste your time on such nonsense?" He meekly replied, "No … I don't think I'm doing any wrong." "Well," Daniel replied, "I assure you I do; and if you were only half as zealous in the study of religion as you are in contriving and whittling these useless, nonsensical things, it would be infinitely better for you. I want you to be like Paul, who said that he desired to know nothing among men but Christ and Him crucified."[39] The son found it increasingly difficult to maintain his relationship with his father and a life constrained by his father's walls, rules, expectations, admonitions, harsh work regimes, silences, and confinement.

As his siblings married, moved away or took up occupations away from the home, the family slowly flowed away from Daniel Muir's orbit. The older sisters married and moved away, never to engage in farm work again. David left when John was twenty. John thus remained within a nine-mile radius of his two farm homes, at Fountain Lake and Hickory Hill near Portage, Wisconsin, until he was twenty-one. He was left with the heavy work.

As a consolation, he continued to work on his inventions. In the summer of 1860, William Duncan, a Scots neighbor who had loaned him Dick's *The Christian Philosopher*, brought John news about the Wisconsin State Agricultural Fair in Madison that September. Duncan, who was fond of Muir, believed in his prospects as an inventor. Duncan thought John would rise in the world if only his "genius" were recognized outside the small community of Portage.[40] On William Duncan's suggestion he show his inventions at the State Fair, John decided to go to Madison, a first step in leaving home.

17

Silence characterized the evening meal before John's departure. Muir's father refused financial support when John eventually asked for money to help with travel expenses. Daniel curtly replied, "No; depend entirely on yourself."[41] With no financial help from his father, John fingered the gold coin given to him by Grandfather Gilrye. That together with ten dollars he had saved by raising a little grain on his own plot of land gave him only fifteen dollars total.[42] Muir packed his clocks, thermometer, and gearing for the self-rising bed, ready for assembly. David drove him to Pardeeville, a town he had never seen, ten miles from the farms.

While waiting for the train, he drew curious bystanders, many complimenting his ingenuity. When the train arrived, Muir prevailed upon the conductor to allow him a ride on the front of the engine so the wind whistled through his long hair and beard. He wrote recalling the joyous event, "While seated on the cow-catcher platform, I seemed to be fairly flying, and the wonderful display of power and motion was enchanting."[43] Travel again, as in 1849, proved to be an enchanting path towards liberation.

Walking from the Madison train station to the State Fair grounds with his bulky pack, Muir made his way to the Temple of Art to set up his demonstrations of two clocks, a thermometer, and a self-rising bed. His demonstrations created a stir and sensation among the twenty thousand who surged through the fair's gates. Local papers gave him front-page coverage, "An Ingenious Whittler," one reported, "The wooden clocks of our Marquette Co. friends were among the objects most surrounded by crowds."[44] Two youngsters helped demonstrate the self-rising bed. One was the son of Mrs. Jeanne C. Carr, wife of Professor Ezra Carr at the University of Wisconsin. John received a special $15.00 honorarium from Mrs. Carr's committee. More importantly, this provided an initial meeting with a woman with whom he would establish an important and on-going correspondence and mentor relationship during the next two decades.

Eventually, as John found his way to the University in March 1861, his father surprisingly provided money and modest support, including clothing and a packing trunk. Almost all of Daniel's letters to John at the University of Wisconsin provided brief snippets of family news, short solicitations about John's well being, but were more often sermons urging his son to advance the glory of God and be cautious of thinking too highly of himself. For example, in one, Daniel wrote: "The love of the applause of man has been the ruin of many, if not coupled with that which cometh of [G]od ... Whatever way you can advance [G]od's glory the most should be your study. This is what will give you eternal satisfaction, and this is what the wise do ..."[45]

John distanced himself from these expectations. His journey to Madison was one way to escape his father's goal that he might become a pious and devoted Christian or a preacher. John's dream for another kind of life had been fueled by forbidden literature. His dream to travel was fired by his reading and self-study prior to, and including, his college years. Among the authors he read before his thousand-mile walk in 1867, the most important included Robert Burns, John Milton, and Alphonso Wood.

For educated and even less well-educated Scots, no works loomed larger in influence than the songs and poetry of Robert Burns. Burns's writings made a deep impression on young John Muir. As a collector and writer of Scottish songs and poetry, Burns, born in 1759, was a product of village schools, country life, and elements of the Scottish enlightenment. Both nationalistic and naturalistic, the poet reveled in natural imagery, with a strong preference for democratic equalitarianism. He crafted language using a Scottish twist of word, phrase, and rhythm. As a boy, John Muir prized Burns's love of nature. Yet, there was a deep spirituality in Burns that also resonated with Muir. Burns wrote:

"Gie me ae spark o' Nature's fire,
That's a' the learning I desire;
Then though I drudge through dub an' mire
At pleugh or cart,
My Muse, though hamely in attire,
May touch the heart."[46]

Burns's poetry exalted a personal relationship with nature together with a vision of the wandering life.

Pilgrimage and wandering was a deeply rooted Celtic tradition among both the religiously minded as well as those who saw profound metaphor and meaning in nature.[47] Burns tapped into that tradition. Beloved by schoolboy and scholar alike, he wrote in "To James Smith":

O Life! How pleasant in thy morning,
Young Fancy's rays the hills adorning!
Cold-pausing Cautions lesson scorning,
We frisk away,
Like school-boys, at th' expected warning,
To joy and play.
We wander there, we wander here,
We eye the rose upon the brier,
Unmindful that the thorn is near,
Among the leaves;
And though the puny wound appear,
Short while it grieves.[48]

The cadence of both song and poetry had a large influence on the formation of Muir's choice of words, phrasing, language, thinking, and beliefs. Immersed in this nationalistic and naturalistic poetry, Burns's language, thought forms, and worldview seeped into the young John Muir with inexorable force.

The English poet, John Milton, was also a favorite of Muir's as a teenager and young adult. Milton provided rich, religious language that depicted the natural world as God created it. His portrayal of paradise as an Edenic wilderness contrasted with the problematic human-created world of farms and cities. Thus, Milton delineated the natural world before the fall of humanity in verdant and glorious terms. Milton's description of a pure fountain flowing out of Eden's garden is such an example:

> How from that sapphire fount the crisped brooks,
> Rolling on orient pearl and sands of gold,
> With mazy error under pendent shades
> Ran nectar, visiting each plant, and fed
> Flowers worthy of Paradise, which not nice Art
> In beds and curious knots, but Nature boon
> Pour'd forth profuse on hill, and dale, and plain,
> Both where the morning sun first warmly smote
> The open field, and where the unpierced shaded
> Imbrown'd the noontide bowers: Thus was this place
> A happy rural seat of various view;
> Groves whose rich trees wept odorous gums and balm,
> [49]
> ...

Through his reading of Milton, Muir associated words like "glory," "glorious," "signs of worship," and the palms, fir, and cedar with the trees of Eden. Milton used the metaphor of wind-blown trees as making "signs of worship," shown in these lines:

> His praise, ye Winds, that from four quarters blow,
> Breathe soft or loud; and, wave your tops, ye Pines,
> With every plant, in sign of worship wave."[50]

In an Edenic paradise, trees worshipped God, according to Milton's view. Thus, the poet provided metaphors that led Muir to view the wilderness as a place of "glory" and verdure.

Muir particularly favored Book V of *Paradise Lost*, with its "hymn of praise" of the works of nature that begins with the lines, "These are thy glorious work, Parent of good, Almighty."[51] Forty-four years after he left Dunbar, Muir urged his daughter Wanda to "mind your lessons and get in a good store of the best words of the best people while your memory is retentive and then you will go through life rich." In particular, "commit to memory every day, mostly the sayings of Christ in the gospels, and selections from the poets. Find the hymn of praise in Paradise Lost ... and learn it well."[52] This view of wilderness as Edenic contrasted, in Muir's experience, with those things humans did to one another in schools, with thrashings and rote lessons; in farming, with the clearing of the forests; in cities, towns, and villages that were marked by noise, class distinctions, poverty, and filthiness; and, among states and nations, with their bloody, senseless warfare.

Muir included a copy of the New Testament on his walk through the South. The Campbellite faith of Muir's father privileged the Bible, and the New Testament in particular, as an authoritative guide for personal conduct and the structure of the church. Paying little heed to traditions, creeds, or structures, the Campbellites sought a pure, primitive faith that gave scant attention to denominational differences or academic theology learned in seminaries.[53]

Muir, too, appreciated the simplicity of the teachings of Jesus, uncluttered with traditions, ecclesiology, creeds, or commentaries as is evidenced in Muir's advice to his own daughter. This was a lesson driven home to him by his forced memorization as a child of the entire New Testament. Unlike the Old Testament with its stories of law, retribution, forced exiles, holy war, and prophecies, the New Testament seemed to emphasize hope, love, and healing, and urged the ethics of compassion and charity. These values were decidedly preferred in John Muir's spirituality.

Another key work in the formation of John Muir's fascination with nature was a textbook on botany that he discovered while at the University of Wisconsin. At first Muir pursued an irregular and personally appealing course of studies with Dr. Ezra S. Carr in chemistry and geology, and in classical languages under Dr. James Davie Butler, including the New Testament in Greek.

Then, in his second year, Muir discovered botany through conversation with a fellow student, Milton S. Griswold. Griswold came to his room one day to make his acquaintance and view the machines Muir had set up. He was immensely impressed with his thermometer, barometer, and large clock with its wooden wheels and gears decorated with a scythe and lettered with "The Scythe of Time."

Griswold was already well along in his study of botany using Alphonso Wood's *Class-Book of Botany*. In June 1861, Muir and Griswold studied together under a locust tree. Griswold noted the similarity between the seedpod of the locust flower and that of the pea, vetch, or bean. They took samples and followed up the tables in the text and found their likeness despite apparent differences. There appeared to be a hidden order in the apparent chaos of nature. Plants were not individual things, but related in all sorts of marvelous ways. Muir was astounded and delighted. "Why Griswold, that is perfectly wonderful. I am going to get me a Botany at once and then we can ramble the woods together."[54] Several days later he bought his own copy of Wood's text on botany.

Upon reading Wood's inclusion of one of Jesus' admonitions to "Consider the lilies of the Field ... even Solomon, in all his glory, was not arrayed like one of these,"[55] Muir's preference for the New Testament was reinforced. Wood affirmed that botany was neither a set of simple, ironclad laws "thus awakening no curiosity," nor so intricate as to become incomprehensible, but that the mind could comprehend nature in all its complexity, shaped by design. In Wood's view, botany yielded understanding about both the creation and the Creator. "It brings the operations of the Great Architect almost within the grasp of human intelligence, revealing the conceptions which occupied His mind before they were embodied in actual existence by His word."[56] The work entailed discipline that resulted in great rewards. Wood affirmed, "The works of His Hand are commensurate with the powers of the understanding. We study them not in vain. Step by step His plans are unfolded; and research, although never reaching the goal, yet never wearies, nor fails of its appropriate reward."[57]

Enthused and motivated, Muir and Griswold rambled through the Wisconsin countryside in June 1863 searching for new plants. Wood provided directions for constructing a plant press and a herbarium. Following Wood's recommendations, Muir took a plant press with him on the thousand-mile walk to the Gulf. He also kept a herbarium from his departure in Kentucky and sent a full one home from Kingston, Tennessee. Since he was unfamiliar with many of the Southern plants, Muir took the Wood text on his journey. Although he made little mention of the text in his journal, sketches of the plant press were prominent in the pages of his journal.[58]

While Burns, Milton, the New Testament, and even Wood's text on botany influenced Muir's religious view of nature, his reading of travel literature fired his dreams. The dream of traveling to South America persisted through his lifetime. His reading of the works of Mungo Park, a fellow Scot, and of Alexander von Humboldt, an intrepid German geographer, scientist, and naturalist, inspired Muir to make the thousand-mile walk through the South as a prelude to his travel to South America. Their travel writings made a deep impression upon John Muir, which even his mother acknowledged. Both Park's *Travels in the Interior Districts of*

*Africa* and Humboldt's *Personal Narrative of Travels* were compelling. In a recollection, Muir wrote that he was reading Park before he left home. His mother said, "Weel, John, maybe you will travel like Park and Humboldt some day." John's father, overhearing this comment "cried out in solemn deprecation, 'Oh, Anne! Dinna put sic notions in the laddie's heed.'"[59]

Mungo Park was a twenty-four year old Scot well educated in Edinburgh in medicine. Park, like Muir, loved botany and travel. Park's motive to travel included "a passionate desire to examine into the productions of a country so little known; and to become experimentally acquainted with the modes of life, and the character of the natives."[60] While the intrepid Scot had commercial and cultural curiosity not completely shared by Muir, Muir was intrigued by Park's travels through unknown territory with a lush plant life. Park gave Muir a sense that a single, intrepid traveler from northern Europe could successfully negotiate the tropics of central Africa.

Muir learned from Humboldt about the vast river systems of the Orinoco and the Amazon, whose tributaries met in the Andes Mountains. Muir appreciated Humboldt's scientific rigor and eloquence about geography, mineralogy, botany, and zoology. He shared with Humboldt a devotion to empirical methods in understanding environmental systems. Muir agreed with Humboldt's conviction that "The natural sciences are connected by the same ties which link together all the phenomena of nature"[61]—an idea that echoed Wood's *Class-Book in Botany*. Muir learned from Humboldt a unitary view of nature, a grand, unified system.

Both of these books shaped the direction of Muir's dreams and desire to travel. Park and Humboldt informed Muir about how one could travel to and through South America or Africa gathering, in a scientific way, new information about plants, geology, animals, and even human beings. This dream of traveling through South America on a botanizing adventure persisted with Muir into old age. His last journey was a fulfillment of this dream when, in 1911 and 1912, three years before his death, he made a journey to South America and Africa.[62] Thus Park and Humboldt inspired Muir who sought travel, not simply as an escape and liberation, but as a kind of quest and dream.

In 1860, eleven years after he left Scotland, Muir was still traveling, but this time it was to find a purpose, a vocation, and a home. In short, he was a wandering botanist and even a pilgrim. Unlike the time during his first twenty-one years, when travel was a set of punctuation points between long sentences of schooling and farming, John was now restless, staying put for less than two years in any one place. Despite forays into education and factory life that provided some semblance of being rooted in the communities of Madison, Meaford, and Indianapolis, Muir took month-long rambles into the woods and prairies studying plants and looking for rare flowers.

Not finding a home *at* home, despite his affection for his mother and siblings, Muir moved away from settled domesticity and commitments rather than toward them.

Shortly before his walk to the Gulf, twenty-nine year old John and his father had a rough parting of the ways. The son had returned home for a last visit. His father sat under a tree copying *Foxe's Book of Martyrs*, but he omitted copying Latin words as John peered over his shoulder. When John asked him why some words weren't being copied, Daniel replied, "Aboot a half of the book is in Layton (Latin), an' I dinna ken Layton, an' the words would be of sma' use to me."[63] Replaying old roles and passions, Daniel belittled his son's studies and plans. John's father considered geological studies "blasphemous" and botany almost as wicked; in Daniel's view, his wandering son was "walking in the paths of the Deevil." Exasperated, John struck out in anger: "I'll tell you this, Father, I've been spending my time a lot nearer the Almighty [referring to botany and his fieldwork] than you have!"[64]

The final insult came on their last day on Hickory Hill farm. John was saying his final goodbyes to his mother and sisters when his father reminded him, "My son, hae ye na forgotten something?"

"What have I forgotten, Father?"

"Hae ye no forgotten to pay for your board and lodging?"

Incredulous, John pulled out a coin, handed it to his father and said, "Father, you asked me to come home for a visit. I thought I was welcome. You may be sure it will be a long time before I come again."[65]

Clearly, Daniel was a force that repelled Muir away from life as a farmer and the orbit of his influence. As a son, John experienced a lifetime of his father belittling his choice of friends in Scotland, his reading preferences, his inventions, his study of science, geology, and botany, and his wandering lifestyle. This was the last meaningful interaction between father and son for almost twenty years until Daniel was on his deathbed, in 1885.

To find himself, John Muir chose to follow his dreams, to respect his abiding fascination with the created world, and to take his own extended journey. The journey, in turn, forged new ways of thinking and new understandings of nature. As in Burns's poem, "Gie me ae spark o' Nature's fire, That's a' the learning I desire"[66] the 1867 walk through the South became a quest, a pilgrimage, and a journey toward self-discovery; it also became a transformative experience in Muir's life.

John Muir chose to follow his dreams rather than the rules or expectations of his father. While invention was an avenue toward independence; it morphed into an opportunity to gain a university education that gave him tools for observation and networks of influence. Ultimately, it was the books he read that aroused his dreams. Thus, he took books with him on this journey that entailed a search for a life's direction. But, ironically, it was a factory accident in Indianapolis that

*Portrait of John Muir, c.1863 at age 25, about the time he was a student at the University of Wisconsin, Madison. Note the classical and romantic set as well as John's formality.*

propelled him to follow his dreams and enter into a life of exploration, study, and travel.

# 2

## "RESTLESS FIRES": FROM MECHANIC
## TO WALKING BOTANIST

Invention and travel were preludes to John Muir's independence. He left the University of Wisconsin in 1863 uncertain about his future, uncertain about his vocational path, and uncertain about marriage. Muir described his recent botanizing trip through Wisconsin as "pathless," a rich metaphor that contrasted starkly with life on the farm. Muir found a measure of liberation and employment in invention and machine work. While he was a genius with mechanisms, invention also became, for Muir, a way to gain distance from his father. While travel from home was initially directed toward the university and an education, he also traveled to study flowers, trees, geological formations, rocks, lakes, and rivers. Muir's double direction in life—first as a mechanic, and then as a wandering botanist—led in both ways away from home, but his definitive route at this point was not clear.

From 1863 to 1867, while in Wisconsin, Canada, and Indiana, Muir remained undecided about his vocational decisions, yet each locale influenced his future. Mechanics promised a livelihood; botany, personally satisfying, promised uncertainty. Between 1863 and 1867, while he balanced his life between these two pursuits, Muir made three critical decisions.

The first was a decision on marriage, which he began to consider while at Madison, and which came to a head in 1864; the second was to engage in correspondence with Mrs. Jeanne C. Carr while he lived and worked in Canada, beginning in 1865; and the third was to embark on the thousand-mile walk in September 1867 in the wake of his eye accident at a machine shop in Indianapolis. All three decisions proved fateful for John Muir's future, resulting in a transformation in his vocational direction and environmental thought and ethics.

John Muir enjoyed the company of women. Within the family, he worked the harvest side by side with his older sister, Maggie, and they formed a deep and meaningful relationship. He also kept in close, confiding correspondence with his sister Sarah. His friendship with Jeanne C. Carr was akin to that of a mentor, with Carr serving as sponsor, friend, and confidante. Although prim—even by the standards of the day—occasionally eccentric in behavior, and unkempt in appearance, John Muir was attractive to women.

He grew during his university days to a lean 5'11", had merry, twinkling, blue eyes, and was an engaging conversationalist, violin player, delightful singer, and humorous storyteller. Often flaunting social conventions, he had a sense of joy, wonder, and curiosity that was infectious. Once, while in attendance at a university social gathering where everyone was behaving in a most dignified manner, Muir became intrigued with the mechanism of a small grand piano. Rather than simply ask questions, he opened the top and crawled into the piano to see how the hammers were joined to the keys with such precision.[67]

While living at the Mondell House in Prairie du Chien, Wisconsin, Muir found warm company with the Pelton family who owned and operated the boarding house. The family included Edward Pelton, his wife, Frances, two young children, Fannie and Willie, and their eligible niece, Emily.[68] Muir and Emily took long walks together, enjoying each other's company. Mrs. Pelton became one of Muir's "closest confidantes" during his university years, as they shared news and ideas by letters, and little two-year-old, Fannie always greeted Muir's arrival at the house with gleeful smiles and upraised arms, asking to be picked up and enjoying Muir's rich Scottish songs.[69]

The friendship between Emily Pelton and Muir progressed to the point that by October 1861 David Galloway, who had visited Muir, reported back to the family at Fountain Lake that Emily had become "John's girl."[70] Muir's deep sympathies with both Mrs. Pelton and Emily were evident when he wrote of little Fannie's death.[71] Their loss was his loss. Distraught, Muir wrote,

> Fannie is dead. O God what can I say, or what can I do [?] Well[,] well do I know how little letterfuls of condolence can do here. Your little blessing is away but—Oh Mr. and Mrs. Pelton you know that Jesus loves the little dear, and all is well And, you'll go to her in just a little while though she cannot come to you.[72]

Mrs. Pelton's health was fragile as well. In March 1862, Muir wrote, "I feel your fevered brow, and wish my self near to bathe it, I still hear your difficult breathing and read the distresses you cannot speak...."[73] Mrs. Pelton's health did not improve, and she moved to Middlefield, Massachusetts, to stay with her brother. She acknowledged her poor health in October 1862 and asked Muir about his future. "It seems that you are going to continue on through [the university]—And what then [?] What are you going to make [?] Are you going to follow some business that will call out your mechanical genius [?] Are you going to take some profession [?]"[74] Muir had no answer to these questions.

In fall 1862, Muir acknowledged to his sister Sarah and his brother-in-law David, "We live in changing times, and our plans may easily be broken, but if not, I shall be seeking knowledge, for some years; here or elsewhere."[75] Medicine briefly captured Muir's interest. He witnessed wounded soldiers arriving at Camp Randall in Madison from Civil War battlefields. He knew that his aptitude in science could commend him to the University of Michigan for medical training, but he did not follow through, even though he acknowledged this interest to David Galloway in a letter dated 12 June 1863.[76] The University of Wisconsin was threatened with closure, occasioned by army enlistments of college-eligible young men.

Emily remained in Prairie du Chien to care for Mr. Pelton and Willie. In August, Muir learned of Mrs. Pelton's death. "She is now in the tomb," he wrote. "I shall not again receive her letters of cheer and encouragement, or hear her words of earnest kindness, but the marks of her goodness shall never be ef[f]aced, and her advice shall influence me all my life."[77] In 1863, as Muir contemplated his future on the hills above the university he decided to embark on a botanizing trip with classmates after he left school. Throughout this adventure he wrote lengthy, descriptive letters to Emily Pelton; perhaps to amuse or impress, perhaps to find a life partner.

Now 25, John Muir wrestled with Mrs. Pelton's questions. Would he seek the career of a mechanic or an inventor? Become a doctor? With more education, he could become a professor, like his mentors and teachers Ezra Carr, John Sterling, and James Davie Butler. What about marriage? He faced so many directions and choices, and then there was military conscription.

His brother Daniel went to Canada to get clear of the draft. John's parents had moved to Portage, Wisconsin; from here his mother wrote him, "As yet there seems to be no end to this unhappy *war*. It is rumoured there will be drafting in this state in the month of June. I hope it will not take place. The dreadful miseries occasioned by this awful war can never be known."[78] Having provided counsel to departing troops and having seen the wounded at Camp Randall, Muir had no interest either in enlisting or in being drafted into the army.

Rather than face decisions on marriage, career, and war, Muir decided not to decide. Instead, he went on a summer's botanizing trip with two classmates. "I need a rest. Perhaps my tour will do me good, though a three or four hundred mile walk with a load is not, at least in appearance, much of a rest."[79] The three companions, Muir, Rice, and Blake, saw this as a geological and botanical journey. These fields of scientific study had become strong interests of Muir's since his lessons in botany from a fellow student, Milton Griswold, and in geology from Professor Ezra Carr. In writing to Sarah and David, Muir told them, "You would like the study of botany. It is the most exciting thing in the form of even amusement much more of study that I ever knew very unlike the grave tangled Greek and Latin—..."[80] Muir's account of the trip is detailed in a series of retrospective letters written to Emily Pelton six months after the adventure but dated as if they were contemporary with his experience.[81]

Muir reported in these letters that after college commencement, in June 1863, the young men traveled up to Sauk City, crossed the Wisconsin River, and followed the gorge. He noted the "rock scriptures" along with the flora of the valley and the cliffs.[82] The trio walked westward for two weeks through the Wisconsin River gorge, which narrowed to a half-mile span at Bridgeport, just a few miles south of Prairie du Chien. Rice, the youngest in the party, sprained an ankle and gave up the trip. Muir called on the grieving Pelton household, his own heart heavy despite weeks of adventure. He and Emily took a walk, but there was no proposal. Emily's family was unsettled; Muir was unsettled. Muir and Blake changed their plans to go to St. Anthony's Falls, at Minneapolis, and struck south toward McGregor, Iowa, where the Wisconsin River joins the Mississippi. It was here that Muir began his account of their travels to Emily. Though the accounts were written in February 1864 after the adventure. However, he dated them beginning 7 July 1863, when he recalled being in the recesses of the bluffs near McGregor.[83]

Muir's letters provided Emily with insights about his easy manner, way with words, and jocular posture toward the world. Underscoring his innocence and virtue, Muir provided a depiction of an apparent brothel he and Blake saw near the riverbank, which had been cut out for a "ruinous old house." Muir wrote that when they first saw "four gaudily dressed females" lined up in the front with "two idle men" looking upon the women as "a successful merchant upon a stock of newly arrived goods," he did not know what to make of the scene. The women's clothes were "dipped many times in the most glaring dyes." It suddenly dawned on Muir that this was a brothel, and he moved behind his companion. Both took alarm and pushed ahead up the bluffs, made camp and "congratulated each other on our escape, recounting the 1st chapter of Proverbs, the risks to young men of temptation with loose women."[84]

Blake left Muir at Bridgeport and took a stage home. Alone, Muir headed overland through "wet places and fallen trees" to Wright's Ferry and thence back to Prairie du Chien, still thinking of Emily. When he knocked at the Pelton's door, Emily's uncle said that she was not at home—when, in fact, as Muir later learned, she was. Muir was taken aback.[85] The family members, who had shown so much consideration, now had closed their doors to his friendship. The letters Muir wrote to Emily in February may have been his attempt to reignite their relationship.

As letters passed back and forth, it became clear that there was too much uncertainty in Muir's life. His letters with Sarah and David revealed little of the schoolboy jocularity he had expressed in his February 1864 letters to Emily. He had written about his joy in finding plants with a kind of spiritual resonance that he knew they would understand. For example, he wrote about the Wisconsin Dells, "Those ravines are the most perfect, the most heavenly plant conservatories I ever saw. Thousands of happy flowers are there, but ferns and mosses are the favored ones. No human language will ever describe them."[86] Muir wrote in a different tone to his family than the one he took with Emily. He understood that Emily sought a domestic, settled life, whereas he loved the adventure of a walk through nature; neither appeared to be a good fit for the other. And the uncertainty of military conscription still hung over Muir's head.

Heading home to learn about the outcome of the draft, Muir chose not to live with his father and mother in Portage. Through fall and winter 1863 he worked and lived at the home of his sister and brother-in-law Sarah and David Galloway in Fountain Lake, waiting. Writing to his brother Daniel, who now resided in Canada, Muir recounted his summer adventures. He had learned that his other brother David was getting married to Katie Cairns, and about the impending marriage, Muir paraphrased David's view that "his life was the most perfect piece of mortality 'This side of the New Jerusalem'." Muir and Daniel, of course, wished David happiness.[87] In the wake of this news, Muir wrote to Daniel about his thoughts on marriage: "Dan, you & I must not on any account permit ourselves to think of marriage for five or six years yet, and I give this as a very grave limit, for if you permit yourself to fall in love, adieu to study."[88] Apparently Muir had made one decision; he was not going to get married, even though he witnessed his siblings' commitments. With this decision clear in his mind, Muir left home for Canada.

In Canada, Muir pursued both botany and mechanical work, beginning his venture with a long botanizing trip. Resuming his correspondence with Emily, he wrote just a half-hour before his train departure. Quoting Milton, he penned, "I really do not know where I shall halt. I feel like Milton's Adam and Eve—'The world was all before them where to choose their place of rest.'"[89] While Muir wrote to Emily his emotional, intellectual, and spiritual fires were fanned by Jeanne Carr, who understood Muir's unsettledness as well as his unique gifts and spiritual development. Two years in Canada reinforced Muir's skills as an inventor and business partner. It also gave him an experience that resulted in his first published article, although it was published without proper attribution.

In April, 1864, Muir wended his way through the wilderness of the Canadian swamps, lakes, and rivers in Simcoe and Grey counties, Ontario. He walked about three hundred miles through various townships such as Mono, "very uneven and somewhat sandy; many fields here are composed of abrupt gravel hillocks; inhabitants are nearly all Irish." He also ran into some Scots communities, including some Dunbar folk.[90] Apparently, few of those he encountered knew much about botany. In July, Muir was north of Toronto, in the Holland River swamps, and in August he was along the shores of Lake Ontario, near Niagara Falls. There he had a close encounter with a howling pack of wolves but kept them at bay by stoking his campfire and staying awake.[91] Muir was gaining confidence, like Mungo Park, in his ability to negotiate a wilderness. Late in life he wrote an autobiographical fragment on this Canadian botanizing trip:

> I set off on the first of my long lonely excursions, botanizing in glorious freedom around the Great Lakes and wander through innumerable tamarac and arbor-vitae swamps, and forests ... rejoicing in their boundless wealth and strength and beauty, climbing the trees, reveling in their flowers and fruit like bees in beds of goldenrods, glorying in the fresh cool beauty and charm of the bog and meadow heathworts, grasses, carices, ferns, mosses, liverworts displayed in boundless profusion.[92]

Muir was on the lookout for *Calypso borealis*, a rare white orchid known as "the Hider of the North."

After this botanical walk, he joined his brother Daniel, who had found work. Daniel was employed in a small mill at Meaford, only a mile from Georgian Bay on Lake Huron. The mill was run by a thirty-year-old bachelor, William Trout, and his partner Charles Jay. Discovering Daniel's whereabouts through family letters, Muir joined Daniel for winter work at

Trout's Hollow as his funds began to thin out. Trout lived with his two sisters, Mary and Harriet, who worked in Meaford— Mary as a housekeeper and Harriet as a teacher. The Trouts were Highland Scots rooted in the Campbellite religious tradition. As young, boisterous, and playful adults, Muir wrote, "We all live happily together."[93] On religious matters, though, there was tension between the more orthodox Trouts and Muir, with his more open-ended perspectives.

The Muir brothers worked for $10 a month, plus room and board, fabricating wooden broom handles and rakes. John's mechanical skills became immediately apparent. Rising at five a.m. with the help of his own invention, the self-rising bed, he improved the efficiency of the lathes and automatic sawing devices that allowed more productivity and leisure time. Eventually John was offered a partnership.

Daniel, in the meantime, returned to the United States in 1865 as the Civil War concluded. John stayed at the mill a year-and-a-half, until it accidentally caught fire and burned down. They lost its entire inventory—including thirty thousand broom handles, twelve thousand rakes, and some of Muir's possessions—in March 1866.[94]

As letters between Muir and Emily Pelton became less frequent, a new correspondent drew out reflections and commentary that Muir had shared only with close members of his family. Jeanne Carr initiated a correspondence with Muir in 1865. She told him that the faculty at the University of Wisconsin hoped Muir would continue his university education. Professor John W. Sterling had sent a letter inviting him to matriculate for free, but the letter never reached him.[95] Mrs. Carr wrote Muir to urge him to continue his education and to encourage an ongoing correspondence. In the midst of the loneliness caused by his brother's departure and his own desire to sort out his unsettledness, Muir responded with enthusiasm. Thus began a correspondence that continued for more than thirty years. Carr became a sounding board, an encourager, and a mentor for this young man's life.[96]

Carr saw in Muir a person who had both purity of heart and courage of convictions with enormous talents for literature, writing, and mechanics. Believing that these talents could be harnessed to form some greater purpose or destiny, Carr wrote words of encouragement that Muir longed to hear. The first lines of his initial letter of response to her were,

> Your precious letter with its burden of cheer and good wishes has come to our hollow, and has done for me that work of sympathy and encouragement which I know you kindly wished it to do. It came at a time when much needed, for I am subject to lonesomeness at times. Accept, then, my heartfelt gratitude would that I could make a better return.[97]

Who was Joanne C. Carr, and what did she and Muir find in each other? When they met, she was the 35-year-old wife of Professor Ezra S. Carr, Muir's professor in geology and chemistry at the University of Wisconsin. Muir was 22. Jeanne Carr was on the committee that gave Muir a reward for his "irregular" exhibit at the Wisconsin State Fair; one of her boys had helped to demonstrate Muir's self-rising bed. The Carr family employed Muir to help with chores around the house and with childcare for her sons and the son of Professor Butler on Saturdays. Delighting in his company and aware of his straitened financial circumstances, the Carrs invited Muir to stay with them. He refused, preferring the privacy of his own room. As friends, Muir and Jeanne Carr shared keen interest in flowers and plants; both were well-read and engaged in the world of ideas, and both shared a religious understanding of nature.

Born in Castleton, Vermont, on 12 May 1825, as Jane (Jeanne) Caroline Smith, Carr attended Castleton Seminary as a nine-year-old. Her interest in botany began at age seven, when she collected more than four hundred species of plants pressed into a herbarium. She loved to explore the cedar swamp looking for *Cypridedium arietinum*, the lady's slipper orchid, with Professor William Tully, who was at the Castleton Medical College.[98] In 1844, at age nineteen, she married Ezra Slocum Carr, professor of chemistry, who joined the faculty at Castleton Medical College. She became a reformer, publishing an anti-alcohol article in the *Temperance Herald* in 1846, "A Tale of Truth," but like many earnest and intelligent women of potential in the nineteenth century, she lived in the shadows of men. Her influence would be more indirect than direct. Endeavoring to write her autobiography later in life, she could only report in the third person:

> Mrs. Carr insists that she 'has yet no individual history to speak of;' having been until her eighteenth year simply the eldest daughter of Dr. Albert Smith of Castleton, Vermont, and of Caroline Carver, his wife; and since then the wife of Dr. Carr, well known as a college professor and educator for some forty years; that she is noted for nothing except for the fact that her eyes have always been open....[99]

This rueful self-assessment did not account for her spontaneity and love of life.

One who knew her well described her in her mid-thirties as "a young, pretty woman with tawny hair, a sweet expression and a charming voice. Plainly dressed, she was always going about botanizing, skipping like a girl."[100] Carr loved music and was skilled in sketching. While she had been raised in the staunch Calvinist ways of New England Puritanism, her religious convictions, like those of Muir, began to move beyond the orbit of orthodoxy. For her, flowers and trees became signs of God's creation every bit as important as the iconography of the cross. Like Muir, Carr was seeking a wide bridge between science and religion that could accommodate both through the twin arches of Scottish common-sense philosophy and transcendentalism. She believed that through nature one could fathom the divine.

Muir agreed with Carr in her first letter to him when she noted that few are called to "the pure and deep communion of the beautiful, all-loving Nature."[101] Finally, Carr was well connected with editors and publishers on the East Coast. Her access to these sources of influence would play a significant role in giving Muir access to publishers and notable intellectuals of the Northeast, such as Ralph Waldo Emerson.

Muir's passionate love of botany was beginning to be reflected in his writing. His first publication came as the result of a letter written to Jeanne Carr. Both appreciated rare flower specimens, such as the *Calypso borealis*. Muir embarked on one of his botanizing adventures to find a specimen of the flower.

In late fall 1866, after a day's plunging through the swamps of Canada by compass, Muir found the orchid shortly before nightfall. He wrote:

> I found beautiful Calypso on the mossy bank of a stream, growing not in the ground but on a bed of yellow mosses in which its small white bulb had found a soft nest and from which its one leaf and one flower sprung. The flower was white and made the impression of utmost simple purity like a snow flower. No other bloom was near it, for the bog a short distance below the surface was still frozen, and the water was ice cold. It seemed the most spiritual of all the flower people I had ever met. I sat down beside it and fairly cried for joy.[102]

Later, Muir put his ecstatic joy on paper in a letter to Jeanne Carr. The letter was discovered lying on Carr's desk by Dr. James Davie Butler. Reading it, he took it and had Muir's report published along with some of his own thoughts. Thus, by accident, Muir had his first article published, although Butler gave no reference or credit to Muir.[103] Muir took issue with Butler's tactics, and Carr reported that Butler would no longer have access to her papers or correspondence.

Jeanne Carr remained John Muir's source of support, offering him time, sympathy, and encouragement during this critical and formative period of his life. With her, he could unburden himself and discuss his indecisiveness about all the different opportunities that lay before him. He wrote about his difficulty in finding a direction in life:

> I would like to go to college, but then I have to say to myself, "You will die ere you can do anything else." I should like to invent useful machinery, but it comes, "You do not wish to spend your lifetime among machines and you will die ere you can do anything else." I should like to study medicine that I might do my part in lessening human misery, but again it comes, "You will die ere you are ready or able to do so." How intensely I desire to be a Humboldt! but again the chilling answer is reiterated.[104]

Muir was clearly feeling the press of time and a sense that he faced difficult life choices, few of which promised congruence with his deepest passions.

Muir's correspondence with Carr promised an avenue of reflection that might help with the decision-making process. Both Carr and Muir found their correspondence deeply satisfying—Muir had found a mentor, and Carr had found a young man who shared her passion for botany, religion, and risk-taking. Here was someone she could help sponsor and form.

Muir would now follow his own advice to Daniel and wait five or six years for marriage. The time in Canada had brought him a new source of support in his correspondence with Carr, who offered to help him with his vocational decisions. Muir looked forward to the correspondence as "a means of pleasure and improvement." But he also felt a distinct social distance. "I feel that I am altogether incapable of properly conducting a correspondence with one so much above me," he wrote. He hoped that Carr's letters would continue, offering the same quality as he had found in the first, and he wrote Carr of his wish that she might continue to write at least *"semi-occasionally."*[105]

Carr responded to Muir's letter on 24 September 1865: "I see from your letter that you suffer from that which is my most grievous burden—the pressure of Time upon Life." She then wrote that yes, eternity was the proper scale for weighing the studies of nature—the demands were larger than the span of a single life because there was so much to learn. Perhaps thinking Muir might return to the university, she encouraged him to build a structure of knowledge that would "outlast the fleeting years." In her private prayer book, she found a prayer that she commended to Muir: "Oh Lord, help me to feel in my heart the leisure in which Thou dost work thy works, and teach me the secret of that Labor which is not Toil."[106] What kind of labor would not be toil? Carr affirmed that mechanics could be a "wonderful gift." "A great mechanical genius is a wonderful gift," she wrote; "something one should hold in trust for mankind, a kind of seal and private mark which God has placed upon souls especially his own."[107]

Continuing the letter on Sunday in Madison, Carr wished that Muir were in the "kernel" of her house, the library, and that she could offer him the choice between talking and singing. They would look at Carr's collected mosses, ferns, and lichens in their cases, and Muir might contrive a little fountain for them. The letter ended with, "Believe in my cordial and constant interest in all that concerns you, and that I have a pleasant way of associating you with my highest and purest enjoyments."[108]

Muir followed Carr's letters with intense interest. She gave voice to ideas and interests that he did not find among his compatriots at Trout's Hollow. Although good-hearted laughter and teasing were abundant there, his fellows' religion was a little too similar to his father's orthodoxy, their interests in botany non-existent.

Writing to Carr in January 1866, Muir told her that he had read her Sabbath letter "a good many times." Her comments on the sermon she heard drew his special attention. She seemed to appreciate and relish the sermon, but he had a different take. Muir wondered, "But although the page of Nature is so replete with divine truth, it is silent concerning the fall of man and the wonders of Redeeming Love." While he believed that nature reveals much about the character and attributes of God, Muir understood that nature did not speak about the Fall or about redemption. "It may be a bad symptom, but I will confess that I take more intense delight from reading the power and *goodness* of God from 'the things which are made' than from the bible," he wrote.[109] He then acknowledged that it was easier to focus on "these beautiful tangible forms" than "to exercise 'a simple, humble living faith' such as you so well describe as enabling us to reach out joyfully into the future, to *expect* what is promised as a thing of tomorrow."[110]

Muir continued to acknowledge the fact that he liked practical machinery "exceedingly well, but would prefer inventions which would require some artistic as well as mechanical skill." He noted how his inventions at the factory had led to greater productivity. With this there was a social benefit. "Farmers will be able to produce grain at a lower rate, the poor get more bread to eat," he wrote.[111] Carr became Muir's confidante in some of the shifts he was making in religious thought, and his and Carr's views were so closely connected that they spurred one another to greater depths of insight. Still, the vocational issue remained unsettled. Then Muir had to confront another change in direction through an unexpected loss of his livelihood.

Muir's work at the Trout family mill had resulted in a new addition, improved cutting and lathe machinery, and the stockpile of six thousand rakes and thirty thousand brooms, filling every corner of the mill. On March 1, with a roaring blizzard howling outside, a spark from the cabin chimney flew onto the factory roof, setting the mill on fire. The mill was destroyed; so too were Muir's notebooks and herbarium. There was no insurance. Muir was out of work. Trout wanted Muir to rebuild the factory and share as a partner in the profits. This meant cutting down more of the forests to make lumber for the rebuild. "No, I love nature too well to spend my life in a work that involves the destruction of God's forests!" he told Trout.[112] The Trouts owed Muir $300, and gave him a note with a promise to pay. He cut the obligation to $200 and gathered what cash was available, said his goodbyes and took the train to Indianapolis. Though he declared his interest in nature to both Carr and the Trouts, he sought work as a machinist. His vocational direction seemed to be moving toward factory work.

Shortly after arriving in Indianapolis, Muir found work as a machinist at Osgood, Smith & Co., one of the largest manufacturers of wheels, spokes, hubs, and carriage parts in the region. He began work as a sawyer, earning about $10 a week. After one week, he received a raise to $18 a week and was put in charge of the machinery. He made improvements in design to the wheels, worked on the automatic milling of wheel parts and addressed the flow of the work to increase efficiency. Soon thereafter, he was supervising the installation of new machinery.

Muir boarded at the home of a fellow sawyer and Scot, Levi Sutherland, after having difficulty finding a suitable boarding house. His social network expanded when Professor Butler gave him a letter of introduction to a distinguished family in Indianapolis, the Merrill family, which included Catherine Merrill and the ten-year-old Merrill Moores, her nephew. Butler wrote to the Merrills, "If you walk the fields with him [Muir], you will find that Solomon could not speak more wisely about plants."[113] Muir had agreed to teach a class of boys at a mission Sunday school, and rather than repeat the activities of school, he took them out into the woods on Sunday mornings. Of course, they were delighted. Thus, in Indianapolis, Muir found good work, a congenial community, and affirmation. Still, he was restless.

In writing to his brother Daniel from Indianapolis in May 1866, Muir acknowledged that affirmation for his mechanical work was shaping his life course. He was in the process of making a model of his automatic wagon wheel milling machine in order to apply for a patent, and he was feeling good about its prospects. He wrote with a note of resignation, "I have about made up my mind that it is impossible for me to escape from mechanics. I begin to see and *feel* that I really have some talent for invention, and I just think that I will turn all my attention that way at once."[114] He was grateful for recent correspondence he had received from his friends at the university, as well as from Emily Pelton and her family. Muir quoted Emily's letter to him, which included this rather cryptic sentence, alluding to the prospects of marriage and invention: "'I wrote a letter to Mary & Anna full of advice about getting married, etc. I hope that like their brother Dan they will not have any *slavish fear* concerning it.' Emily sends me advice as follows: 'Stick to your inventions. God did not give you that inventive brain for naught,' etc."[115]

Muir's apparent decision to pursue machine work did not appear to be sitting well with him. Sometime in spring 1866, Muir read a description of Yosemite Valley that piqued his interest about the valley and the area in which it was located.[116] Despite a determination to follow the machinist path, he wrote to Sarah, his sister, and confessed, "I *feel* something within, some restless fires that urge me on in a way very different from my <u>real</u> wishes, and I suppose that I am doomed to live in some of these noisy commercial centres."[117] He keenly felt the loss of a home. "I never before felt so *utterly homeless* as now," he wrote.[118] He was also feeling powerless over his choices.

> Circumstances over which I have had no control almost compel me to abandon the profession of my choice, and to take up the business of an inventor, and now that I am among machines I begin to *feel* that I have some talent that

way, and so I almost think unless things change soon I shall turn my whole mind into that channel.[119]

This is a revealing letter. To his brother Daniel, Muir's chosen career path seemed fitting; to his sister, it seemed like a forced choice. The restlessness persisted despite Muir's apparent monetary and professional security. It seems apparent that John Muir had deeper longings than to be a machinist/inventor for the rest of his life. The "restless fires" alluded to his passion for botany and field work, but he felt trapped in factory and city with his prowess and success in invention and mechanical work. It would not be easy for him to resolve this vocational tension.

Jeanne Carr, with gentle sympathy, provided not just a sounding board for this tension and for Muir's emerging ideas, but provoked him to consider the importance of doing that which brought congruity between Muir's inner self and his outer life. Emily Pelton encouraged him only in his obvious talent, which seemed to promise security and well-being. Carr, on the other hand, seemed to understand more fully Muir's inner life. She affirmed Muir's love of living things and his changing religious views, and she was at ease with his unsettledness. Regretting the fire at the mill where Muir worked, Carr wrote to him, now in Indianapolis, "[D]id you not feel more at home with the nature there than in the human element now surrounding you?"[120] Carr then went on to recommend Alphonse de Lamartine's *The Stone-Mason of Saint Point* and urged Muir to read it. Carr noted Muir's unique love of nature in comparison with that of other students, and she knew that he would love nature even if it didn't provide useful energy and resources. She wrote, "Besides, I like you for your individualized acceptance of religious truth and feel a deep sympathy in it."[121] As Muir's friend, she encouraged him to leave behind his loneliness and visit her and her family in the fall. Muir did not make the trip to Madison, but he continued to rely upon Carr as someone with whom he could unburden his deepest thoughts and questions.

Muir wrote to Carr that he had not shared "these feelings and thoughts with anybody." He appreciated Carr's "long and deep communion with Nature," and was grateful for how she understood his feelings.[122] As to the picture of his perfect "fit" with the Canadian woods, he wrote, he was but "an insect, an animalcule," in comparison with "a majestic pine" waving its high branches "in signs of worship." His immersion in nature could be absolute. For example, Muir wrote that during storms he could forget "my very existence and thought myself unworthy to be made a leaf of such a tree."[123] Finally, he acknowledged he had not read Lamartine's book, but said that he looked for it.

At Osgood and Smith, Muir worked through the winter on efficiency charts for the firm. Using time and output charts, he concluded that workmen's productivity fell off after ten hours. "Lamp-lighted labor is not worth more than two-thirds day-light labor," he said.[124] He also observed and reported that temperature variations affected belt tension. Loose belts resulted in loss of energy and productivity. Through improving the arrangement of stock, machinery, and inventory, Muir increased efficiency. He even cut fuel costs by heating the factory with wood normally thrown away.[125]

Emerging as a successful manager and machinist, Muir had doubts about this vocational choice. In a letter to his brother Daniel, he reminded him that regardless of ambition, "Dan, remember that you must die." Muir brooded about the effects of being simply a workman among machines. He fretted that he would lose his creativity and originality, ceasing even to be an inventor—and that he certainly would lose his aesthetic tastes. Urging Dan not to become a factory workman, Muir wrote, "It is certainly a dreary thing to file in a great smoky shop among devilish men on two pieces of iron," to manufacture everyday items for "days and days and weeks

and weeks and months and months and years and years."
Even after fitting all the parts together, Muir told his brother,
"there would be but precious *little* more fun in the business or
romance either."[126] He wrote that he was studying geometry
and enjoying books more than machines; he encouraged
Daniel to take up geometry himself. Muir wondered if his own
machine work would allow him to read as much as he did on
the farm. He also acknowledged being "very thoroughly
homesick."[127]

In December 1866, Muir received another letter from Carr,
writing from Madison on a blustery and chilly Sunday. She
was delighted that Muir had found the Calypso: "[Y]ou
deserved to find it," she wrote; "you are such a true lover of
Nature." She urged him to develop a love for art, especially
sculpture and painting. Finally, she promised to send him her
copy of Lamartine's *Stone-Mason of Saint Point.*[128]

While working late one evening in early March 1867, Muir
had an accident that changed the course of his life. He needed
to tighten a new drive belt, and he decided to take up slack by
cutting a piece out of the belt, and he had to unlace it. The lace
was tightly woven around the rotor hub, and he forcefully
tried to pry the weave open with a file's sharpened end. The
file sprang up and punctured his right eye just above the
cornea with its pointed end. Both eyes shut. As he opened his
right eye, about a third of a teaspoon full of "aqueous humor"
dripped into his hand. His sight darkened immediately. "My
right eye is gone—I will never see with that eye again," he
wrote. He walked back to his boarding house. Shock—and
sympathetic blindness—set in. He lost sight in the uninjured
left eye, and feared he would become permanently blind.[129]
Despairing, Muir cried out, "My right eye is gone! Closed
forever on God's beauty." "I could gladly have died on the
spot," he wrote later, "because I did not feel that I could have
the heart to look at any flower again."[130] The accident appeared
to foreclose upon Muir's botanizing rambles through nature;

he feared he could no longer make close inspection of flowers, mosses and ferns.

The Merrill and Moores families heard about the injury, and, being well-connected, took Dr. Parvin, an eye specialist trained abroad, to see Muir shortly after the accident. Parvin was dubious that Muir would ever see clearly again from the right eye. Confined to a darkened room and to his bed for the first few days, Muir could see nothing. He received visitors such as eleven-year-old Merrill Moores and other children who were part of his Sunday school program. The boys brought handfuls of spring flowers and read to him. Letters flooded in from family members, the Trouts, the Butlers, and Jeanne Carr.[131]

News must have traveled quickly, because Carr's long letter, written March 15, arrived to encourage him. "Dear John," she wrote, "I have often in my heart wondered what God was training you for. He gave you the eye within the eye, to see in all natural objects the realized ideas of His mind." She referred to Muir as having been set aside for "a more individualized existence than is common," but encouraged him, "Do not be anxious about it. He will surely place you where your work is."[132] She asked if Muir had received Lamartine's *The Stone-Mason of Saint Point* around Christmas and worried that it was sent to another John Muir in Indianapolis since she didn't have his precise address. She wrote with deep sympathy: "May you feel the 'everlasting arms' beneath your pillow, may Infinite tenderness supply all the wants of your spirit and the needs of your life, may each of these days of trial be luminous with His Presence without whom the fairest scene is dark and sorrowful."[133]

By April 3, John felt lost. "The sunshine and the winds are working in all the gardens of God, but I—I am lost." He acknowledged having received Lamartine's *Stone-Mason*. It is likely that this was one of the books read to him by one of the children. On April 6, he acknowledged that some vision was returning, although it was murky and dim. He was healing well and was soon able to make out furniture in his room, but he couldn't yet read type.[134] In time, the right eye healed and the left eye compensated for the injury.[135]

It appears that Muir was giving serious thought to a trip to South America, because Jeanne Carr referred to this plan in her letter of April 15. She wrote, "Who knows but we shall see South America yet?" Yet, in the same letter, she wondered if Muir was considering becoming a minister. In the next sentence Carr asks if he knows Spanish and urges him to pick up the language, "if you mean to traverse the beautiful lands." She concluded the paragraph with this note of confidence, "I do believe you will yet carry out your plans."[136] It is evident that while Carr remained uncertain about Muir's life direction, Muir himself was preparing for the trip to South America, following the model of Alexander von Humboldt. This idea was one of several options that Muir weighed throughout his time as a student and while in Canada. As his eyesight improved, he set his life course with more focus and direction. The accident awakened him to the potential losses of continuing to pursue a machinist's career or any other career that entailed settling down.

Muir's "restless fires" inflamed his passion for botany, and his travel postponed the need for life-changing decision-making. During his botanizing trips through Wisconsin, Muir struggled with the prospect of marriage. To avoid the prospect of becoming a soldier, he made his journey to Canada and coupled it with botanical field work and study. His employment in Canada reinforced his success as a machinist. The discovery of the *Calypso Borealis* and his ecstatic description of its impact on him encouraged him in his work in botany.

The Trout factory fire and his eye injury in Indianapolis challenged his reluctant choice of the career of a machinist despite his evident capability. Having nearly lost his eyesight,

Muir was forced to reconsider the loss of seeing nature with the "eye within the eye" of which Carr had written. The recovery of his eyesight elevated the importance of botany so that Muir became passionate to see more of "God's inventions." Coupled with his desire to do field work and study botany at a deeper level was a desire to see plants of the tropics.

The return of his eyesight was "like a resurrection," Muir wrote. "Now, I have risen from the grave, the cup is removed, and I am alive."[137] After four weeks in bed, he began to take botanizing walks. By late April, Muir wrote, "sight is increasing. I have nearly an eye and a half left." He wrote to Carr that he had read a description of Yosemite "last year." "I feel, if possible, more anxious to travel than ever."[138] By May 2, Muir was imagining himself in Yosemite or in the "fields of the sunny South."[139] He was exuberant, revitalized, and now finding a direction in his life. He would travel. He would take a long walk.

Determined to be true to his dream, "I made haste with all my heart, bade *adieu* to all thoughts of inventing machinery, and determined to devote the rest of my life to studying the inventions of God."[140] John Muir had set his course.

Through an accident and sympathetic support, Muir resolved the final question confronting him as a young adult. He would take a walk to study plant life of the tropics. What would the walk mean for his future? What would he learn about plants, the environment, and his place in that environment? How would the walk affect him? The answers to these questions would be revealed in the walk. Presently, it would be enough to take a walk through the South to the Gulf of Mexico to study plants. After the upheavals of the fire and the eye accident, Muir was ready to heed the restless fires that drove him toward botany.

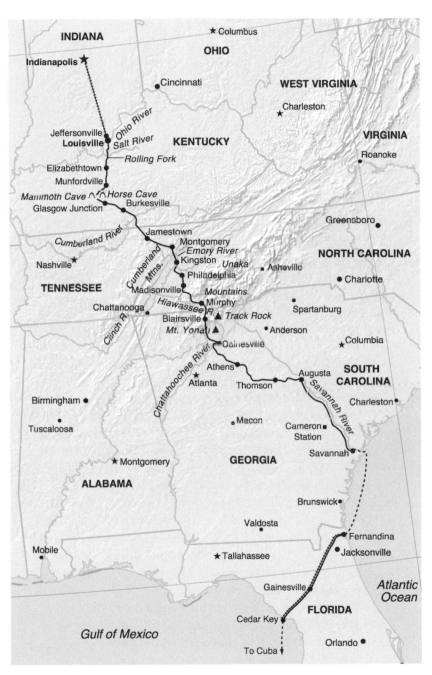

*Map of John Muir's Thousand Mile Walk to the Gulf, 1867–68.*

Scott Lockheed, Design Maps, Cary, North Carolina, 2011 info@designmaps.com

# 3

## SETTING OUT:
### "THE WILDEST, LEAFIEST AND LEAST
### TRODDEN WAY."—JOHN MUIR, 1867

The books of Mungo Park and Alexander von Humboldt inspired John Muir to travel, but as he made his plans to travel to the American South, he confided to Jeanne Carr that "this will be a journey I know very little about."[141] Drawn to the tropics, he was short on practical information about the South and the physical challenges of a long walk through lands devastated by the Civil War and rife with tropical heat, humidity, and disease. First, he knew little about the impact of the war, the consequences of Reconstruction policies, and the effects of both on the Southern population. Second, while he was confident that a single Scot could travel through the tropical world, as Park had done in Africa, he had never lived in or traveled through a tropical environment. With its swamps, prickly vines, briars, heat, humidity, predatory animals, poisonous snakes, and dangerous diseases, his Southern route promised a significant challenge, which was intensified by the South's postwar destruction, dislocation, and turmoil. Armed, unemployed, desperate men lurked through the countryside. Disease was pervasive, and no one knew how malaria, one of the most prevalent and debilitating of the tropical diseases, was transmitted. Theories of the day emphasized that "bad air" was responsible for illness; they eventually eclipsed the slowly dying "bodily humours" theory of contagion. Taking into account Muir's ignorance of the South and science's inability to track or cure the tropical diseases he might encounter there, it becomes obvious that Muir was ill-prepared for the rigors of the walk.

Jeanne Carr supported Muir's dreams to live life as a wandering botanist. Certainly, she would honor whatever Muir chose to do with his life—whether he chose the life of a machinist, a minister, a professor, a medical doctor, or a botanist. Carr, informed by "romantic" and Calvinist values, honored an individualistic approach to engagement with nature not unlike that of the American transcendentalist Ralph Waldo Emerson. Emerson affirmed a life of self-reliance, adhering to the lessons of nature, and urged a life of independent judgment. Carr appreciated Muir's "individualized" religious understanding of God and nature, and Muir deeply appreciated her support of his goals, which led him toward nature rather than in the direction of a confined machine shop or a noisy city.

Even before his factory accident, Muir was making plans for a walk; he had secured books and maps about South America, and he wrote that he was going over them "weeks" before the report of his eye injury.[142] In the midst of his convalescence, Muir wrote to Carr on April 3, "I have read your 'Stonemason' with a great deal of pleasure. I sent it with this and will write my thoughts upon it when I can."[143] Carr's selection of this book says a great deal about how she viewed Muir. Lamartine elevated the idea that one gains wisdom through personal engagement with nature. Subsequently, Muir wrote very little about the book, despite Carr's allusion to it in an April letter. While he appreciated elements of the book, Muir's decision to make the walk was shaped by his reading of Humboldt rather than of Lamartine.

*The Stone-Mason* was a product of Lamartine's romantic sensibility. The devoutly Catholic historian and poet wove a tale of an idealistic, uneducated Christian stonemason whose simple life in a remote valley of the Alps stood in stark contrast to the sophisticated, wealthy, and urbane ideals of the French

Enlightenment. The protagonist, Claude de Huttes, gained wisdom through sorrow and tragedy. He channeled his sorrow into a life of simplicity, love of nature and animals, and "pity" for the poor and destitute. As such, de Huttes became a role model for his wealthy employer. *The Stonemason* represented a story of sacrificial love and resignation to the will of God, whatever calamity one encountered. Without tutoring or a catechism, de Huttes learned about God. In one passage, his employer asked him where he got his images of God: "Sometimes I see him like a sky without end, sown with eyes in every direction, which envelops the world, and enlarges in proportion as more are thrown into it, seeming always empty though always full!"[144] De Huttes experienced mystic communion with God found in nature. "That which is felt, sir, is much more sure than that which is known. Man makes his own reasoning, but it is God who makes out feelings.... It is man who thinks ... but it is nature which feels."[145]

While Muir obviously derived pleasure from this book, Carr's message in recommending it implied that Muir needed to trust his feelings regarding his life choice and decision. Lamartine elevated his character as a person whose spirituality stemmed from his engagement with nature. Carr thought Muir fit this model, and she supported Muir's tentative plans to travel south and then on to South America. Carr's idealistic romanticism did not align well with Muir's empirical preferences, which could be found in his attachment to Humboldt's *Travels* and work.

Muir's determination to walk through the South was clear. Hampered by his dim eyesight, he received help and practice from the little community of friends and readers who led him outdoors in his first "groping among the flowers."[146] He wrote to Carr in April that "The poor eye is much better. I could read a letter with it. I believe that sight is increasing."[147] By April 27, Muir reported that he could see on a cloudy day.[148] In early June, his eyesight made rapid progress, but not enough to allow him to work. Too impatient to lie around, he set out on botanizing rambles through the Indiana countryside with one of his young readers, Merrill Moores. Increasingly, the two friends found mutual delight in looking for flowers in the Indianapolis fields. Before he embarked on his Southern walk, Muir decided to visit his friends and family in Wisconsin, walking and botanizing along the way.

The Moores family permitted Merrill to accompany Muir home. Leaving June 10, Muir and his young companion intended to go to Decatur, Illinois, then north through the prairies to Rockford, Janesville, and Pecatonica, "botanizing a few weeks," and then on to Madison.[149] Writing to Jeanne Carr, Muir made clear his plan to travel south. "I hope to go south towards the end of summer and as this will be a journey that I know very little about, I hope to profit by your counsel before setting out. I am happy with the thought of so soon seeing my Madison friends & Madison, and the plants of Madison and yours."[150] By now Muir was determined to embark on his thousand-mile walk to the Gulf of Mexico and then on to South America.

Muir and Merrill visited Muir's sister Sarah and her husband, David Galloway, at Mound Hill north of Portage, Wisconsin.[151] Using their new home as a stopping place, the two travelers botanized throughout the region. They had picnics with family members and discovered a beautiful small lake surrounded by ferns. This lake, together with the Fountain Lake farm, now owned by Sam Ennis, provided strong inspiration for Muir to seek its preservation from further development.[152] After their visit to Fountain Lake, Muir and Merrill set out for the Hickory Hill farm where his mother and father lived.

Taking the train to Kilbourn, a small town on the Wisconsin River near La Crosse, Muir and Merrill "rambled all day among the glorious tangled valleys and lofty perpendicular rocks of the dells."[153] Muir noted carefully the plants they found in the Dells. Weaving the description of the plants into his theology, Muir wrote,

> Thousands of happy flowers are there, but ferns and mosses are the favored ones... The light is measured and mellow... The walls are fringed and painted most divinely with the bright green *polypodium* and *asplenium* and mosses and liverworts and gray lichens, and here and there a clump of flowers and little bushes... Over all and above all in all the glorious ferns, tall, perfect, godlike, here and there amid their fronds a long cylindrical spike of the grand fringed purple orchi[d]s. But who can describe a greenhouse planned and made and planted and tended by the Great Creator himself.[154]

The fellow travelers made a log raft and floated thirty miles down to Portage with the thought of seeing Muir's brother, David, now a prominent Portage merchant, and his wife, Katie. Much to David's consternation and embarrassment, a barefoot brother strode into his store needing to replace shoes lost on the river when a steamboat washed them off the logs.[155] Not finding a pair large enough at the store, Muir, his brother, and Merrill walked up the street to David's house, with John in a jocular mood and David brooding about appearances.[156]

Muir stayed in Portage about four weeks, and Merrill Moores remained there with David and Sarah Galloway while Muir visited David's mother, who had often expressed confidence in his future. She followed his education and career choices with interest and enthusiasm, and she affirmed him in the continuation of his academic work. "There is no end to the kind of studies you are engaged in," she wrote, "and you are sure to go on and on... "[157] On August 30, John Muir and Merrill Moores returned to Indianapolis by train from Chicago. Writing to Jeanne Carr on that day, he complained of finding only a few flowers during his five-hour visit to Chicago. "I did not find many flowers in her tumultuous streets; only a few grassy plants of wheat and two or three species of weeds ... some green algae, but no mosses."[158] Confessing both a determination to begin the journey and uncertainty about its direction, Muir wrote, quoting Milton, "I wish I knew where I was going. Doomed to be 'carried of the spirit into the wilderness,' I suppose. I wish I could be more moderate in my desires, but I cannot, and so there is no rest."[159]

Muir understood his walk south as a prelude to seeing South America. He recorded his daily discoveries, experiences, and reflections in a journal. He preserved plant specimens with a plant press, providing a biological record of his journey and discoveries. In it he noted the flora and specimens that were new to him. Having traveled and botanized through Northern Canada and the Midwest, he felt that now was the time to discover and see flowers of the tropical South. Questioning his vocation as a machinist and inventor and nearly losing his eyesight, his passion was to see "God's inventions." In this context sight and light carried important spiritual, psychological and emotional freight with Muir.

For Muir, the Southern walk was a preparatory journey whose delights, challenges, and influence he little understood at the time. Had he fully known the practical obstacles to his health, his personal safety, and his physical well-being, one wonders whether he would have made the journey at all. He could have simply taken the train to the nearest port and shipped directly to South America. But he wanted to see the plants, and the walk was the best way to accomplish this goal.

On September 1, Muir took the Jeffersonville, Madison, and Indianapolis Railroad to Jeffersonville, a railroad terminus with a modest population of around seven thousand on the Indiana side of the Ohio River.[160] Writing to his brother Dan, Muir set his affairs in order. The letter reads like a last will and testament. Dan was to take Muir's personal effects, which were stored at the home of John's friends, the Sutherlands, in Indianapolis. Money owed John by the Trouts, Jonathan Reid, and David Muir, about \$180 Canadian, should be distributed among the Muir sisters. Sarah would get the clock, "if she wishes it," and the rest of the machinery and tools would go to Dan. Personal property, such as books, pictures and plants, would be divided up among Sarah Galloway, Jonathan Reid, David Muir, and their children; and, finally, he wrote, "[L]et Mother have choice of everything."[161] Muir made no mention of his father in his will. He clearly looked forward to the upcoming walk, writing, "I anticipate a great deal of pleasure from this walk and also a good deal of fatigue," but he ended with an encouraging note to Dan: "I hope you will not infer from all this that I am going into great danger."[162] Thus began John Muir's Southern thousand-mile walk to the Gulf.

Muir crossed the Ohio River the next morning. He began his journey on September 2, 1867 by walking through Louisville, using a compass, "without speaking a word to anyone."[163] Dressed in simple, tough wool clothing and a cap, he carried with him a plant press and a little rubberized bag containing underclothing, a brush, a towel and books. Robert Burns's poems, John Milton's *Paradise Lost*, a New Testament, and Woods's 1862 edition of *Class-Book on Botany* filled out the bag.[164] Muir seldom carried more than \$30 dollars with him, and David and Dan had agreed to send him money at selected destinations.

Congruent with Emerson's advice to young men, Muir kept a commonplace journal. It was a small, leather-bound volume with lined paper, in which he wrote his daily notes and reflections. He kept a calendar by noting the number of the days since his departure from Indianapolis. It includes some engaging and revealing prefatory comments made either on the eve of his departure or at a later time of reflection. The journal has 28 small and full-page sketches in pencil, some combined with ink. A number of these sketches come from another sketchbook and were later cut and glued into the journal. On the inside of the journal Muir inscribed, within an ornate circle, "John Muir, Earth-planet, Universe" with an underline. The same inscription is found in one of his first journals from the Sierra Nevada Mountains, in California.[165]

With this short inscription, Muir established his identity, not as a Scot, not as an American, but as one linked to the planet and to the scope and breadth of the universe. His place was within the human stream, not defined by social class or by ethnic, nationalistic, or urban identities. His identity was with nature and the cosmos. His prefatory notes underscored his sense that he was following strong internal forces like those of rivers, tides, wind and earthquakes to embark on this journey.

> For many a year I have been impelled toward the Lords tropic gardens of the south. Many influences well calculated to blunt or bury this tendency—this constant longing, have been at work, but it has out-lived and overpowered them all & on the first day of September of eighteen sixty seven soul and body began to move to the magnificent attractions of the flowery South ...[166]

After crossing the Ohio at "the big social establishment of Louisville," he walked through the city.[167] No doubt it reminded Muir of his time in Chicago. His original notation stated, "the plan for my journey which was simply this, anywhere, on any lines of direction wheresoever the Spirit attracts which evidently is southward through Georgia & Florida to some point on the Gulf."[168] His revised statement became, "My plan was simply to push on in a general southward direction by the wildest, leafiest, and least trodden way I could find, promising the greatest extent of virgin forest."[169] The original note focuses on Muir being led by "the Spirit," with an imprecise sense of direction evidenced in the line "to some point in the Gulf." The way was not the "least trodden," because he followed well-used roads leading through villages, towns and county seats to make good time.

Louisville was a bustling city of about one hundred thousand people occupied by Union troops under a recently enacted Congressional and military Reconstruction plan. Walking up Second Street, Muir headed directly south across Broadway through the beautiful tree-lined street of grand homes and mansions. After passing the Union barracks, he reached the southern outskirts of the city. He passed ice houses, the Hebrew and Catholic cemeteries, and a set of homes adjacent to a schoolhouse along the Shepherdsville Turnpike, a plank road through the marshes to Spring Garden.[170] He wrote and revised in his original journal, "(Beyond) the city I found a road running southward, ~~which I of course followed~~ and after passing ~~the compressing~~ (a) scatterment of suburban cabins and cottages I reached the green woods and spread out my (pocket) map to rough-hew a ~~road or rather~~ plan for my journey." [171] (The original journal reveals Muir's strike-overs and added words which are retained here.)

His plan entailed passing through some twenty-two villages, small towns, county seats, and even sizeable cities. Still, he had extensive engagement with nature, finding the noise, bustle, and confusion of most communities obnoxious. Writing on September 9 to Jeanne Carr, Muir was specific: "I was a few miles south of Louisville when I planned my journey. I put my map under a tree and made up my mind to go through Kentucky, Tennessee, and Georgia to Florida, thence to Cuba, thence to some part of South America, but it will be only a hasty walk. I am thankful, however, for so much."[172] Muir later sketched the moment in his first pencil-and-ink drawing in the journal.

It shows a young, bearded man with a hat and a suit-like coat, kneeling at the base of a large oak tree in a forest surrounded by grasses and shrubs, surveying his foldout map on the ground.

well calculated to blunt or bury
up this tendency—this constant
longing, have been at work but
it has out-lived & over powered them
all, & on the first day of September
of eighteen sixty seven soul & body began
to move to the magnificent attractions
of the flowery south — — —

Planning my journey outside of Louisville, KY,

"The world was all before them where to choose"

*"Planning my journey outside of Louisville, KY"*
*"The world was all before them where to choose"*

> Folding my map, I shouldered my little bag and plant press and strode away among the old Kentucky oaks, rejoicing in the splendid vision of pines and palms and tropic flowers in glorious array, not, however, without a few cold shadows of loneliness, although the great oaks seem to spread their arms in welcome.[173]

His route through Kentucky led him to the Salt River and the Kentucky Knobs, across Rolling Fork, Elizabethtown, Munfordville, Horse Cave, Mammoth Cave, Glasgow Junction, Burkesville, and then on to Tennessee.

Enchanted with the scenery and oaks of Kentucky, Muir must have heard Stephen Foster's "My Old Kentucky Home" running through his mind for he made frequent reference to the song. He walked twenty miles the first day to a "rickety tavern" near the Salt River.[174] Muir averaged eighteen to twenty miles a day in the initial days of the walk.[175] He mentioned in his journal that the Kentucky oaks he saw during these long walks "excel in grandeur all I had ever before beheld." Writing to Jeanne Carr on September 9, Muir wondered,

> How shall I ever tell of the miles and miles of beauty that has been flowing into me in such measure? These lofty curving ranks of bobbing, swelling hills, these concealed valleys of fathomless verdure, and these lordly trees with the nursing sunlight glancing in their leaves among their wide branches, —these are cut into my memory to go with me forever.[176]

It was not just the oaks that attracted his attention.

Leaving "the dust and squalor of my garret bedroom," on September 3, Muir found that many of the streams entering the Ohio from this region had a salty taste. He passed over "naked limestone" and level ground for twenty-five or thirty miles and came to the Kentucky Knobs. Intrigued with the geology of this terrain, Muir placed a small sketch of the knobs at the bottom of a page in his journal.[177] He not only wrote about his sleeping quarters, the taste of the water, and the geology of the region; he also commented on the people he encountered along the way.

The walk through Kentucky brought Muir into contact with the impact of the Civil War and the strained race relations that had both preceded and followed it. He had avoided direct participation in the war by going to Canada to join his brother, who was already there. He also lacked previous contact with African-Americans and shared some of the commonly held racial views of the nineteenth century. Yet there is an under-current of a common humanity and democratic egalitarianism that softens stereotypical terms sprinkled across the pages of his private writings. The published journal edited by Badé uses the words of the early twentieth century, such as "Negro," "little, sable negro boy," and "little Nig." Muir, in the original narrative, encounters African Americans trying to cross a river; he portrays their behavior toward him as caring, sensible and a source of self-deprecating fun. His language is not clichéd, but it does carry the freight of a stereotype.

While waiting at the shore of the Rolling Fork River, "a tumbling rocky stream," a black woman on the opposite side, who was concerned for his safety, "earnestly" called on him to hold up and she would get some "men-folks" to help out.[178] She warned that the river was deep, swift, and treacherous, and he would "sartin be drown'd." Muir, confident in his swimming ability, was reluctant to accept the offer. He trusted the ballast of his bag and plant press and was willing to dry out in the sun afterward. The "cautious old soul" cheerily replied, "it was no trouble at all." Soon, a lanky, thin, ungainly white horse ambled into view with a "little sable [negro boy]" (Muir's revision in brackets) on its back. He "looked like a bug." Muir mounted behind the "little Nig." The two tottered and haltingly worked their way across the river. Muir wrote of the boy, "He was a queer specimen, puffy & jet as an India rubber doll. His hair was matted & laid off in sections like the wool of a merino sheep." The ride was so unsteady that Muir was sure both would be thrown into the river. "I wished all the way over that we would be wrecked for the fun of it ... I could swim & little Afric looked as if he might float like a bladder."[179]

In this first encounter with African Americans, reported in the original narrative, a number of themes are evident. Muir characterized African Americans as good-hearted people. He was willing to let people help him even though he was confident of his self-sufficiency. Muir wrote this episode in a humorous vein. There is no evidence of racist fear in the episode. Some of the humor is directed at the situation, some at the woman, boy and horse, and some at himself.

While Muir falls back on colloquial language like "nig" and "sable Negro boy," underneath all this is the recognition of African-American compassion toward a white man. The complexity of the relationship in this episode is not easily understood in terms of either virulent racism or an unthinking observer enslaved to stereotypes.

Like most human contacts, the relationships Muir struck with African Americans were complex, partly informed by his culture and partly by his egalitarian temperament. His outlook and his congeniality generally proved helpful in his interactions with all kinds of people among all different classes. He was put off by white people too easily persuaded by prejudice and political bitterness, as well as by African Americans who paid too little attention to ordering their lives or keeping themselves or their children clean. His racial language was various and descriptive, carrying cultural bias, but generally the journal seems to step away from racist thinking. And, indeed, when Muir encounters racism from some Southerners, he notes his impatience with this kind of thinking.

Departing from the "rickety tavern," Muir spent a portion of September 3 in a Southern plantation house he identified as an "old Kentucky home." He described it as "airy, large, & with a huge transverse central hall that looked like a railway tunnel." He viewed the workmanship on the chimneys as "heavy" and "inelegant." He noted the rows of former slave quarters. Then, leaving Elizabethtown, he passed logging crews cutting down oaks for market. The evening of that day, Muir groped around in the dark and lay down amidst a laurel thicket, the site of his first full night outdoors.[180]

Rising the next morning to the song and scolding of birds in their thicket, Muir found new plants of gold and hazel flowers near his head and the sun glinting off the hilltops. In contrast to his quarters at the Salt River, he described his natural campsite as "beyond comparison the most delightful sleeping apartments I ever occupied." He lingered in the spot a long time "enjoying its shades & soft lights & music & sweet flowers."[181]

After walking about ten miles, Muir entered an area known as "Barrens," consisting of sixty- to seventy-foot-high black oak trees in an area denuded by fire twenty years earlier. There he encountered Kentucky farmers, "tall, stout happy fellows fond of guns & horses." As night was coming on, Muir entered a declining village he described as "drawing its last breath." There he met a "negro who was extremely accommodating," and who said that it would be "no trouble at all" to guide him to a tavern for a night's rest.[182] Their destination proved to be another garret—squalid, dusty, and full of rubbish. Muir "escaped to the woods" yet again the following morning, September 5, and walked toward the region of the great caves carved out of layers of limestone rock.

Along the road to Munfordville, Muir found a cave with a difficult entrance—a slippery tree descending into its mouth. The cool air issuing from the cave's mouth provided an entirely different ecosystem than did the surrounding forests. It was also an air-conditioning system for Southerners seeking to escape the late-summer heat and humidity. Ferns at the mouth of the cave appeared similar to those that grew in Wisconsin. White wood asters, arrowhead, ladies' tresses, and nodding pogonia were in bloom. In openings and fields, Muir saw yellow woodland coneflowers, goldenrod, partridge pea, and evening primrose. The stunningly brilliant flowers also included the scarlet cardinal flower, the pink false dragonhead, and the violet-blue silky aster.[183] He pressed these and other flowers, noting their location and providing identification from the *Class-Book on Botany*.

Arriving at Munfordville around noon, Muir ran into the town's founding father, Mr. Munford, a self-proclaimed expert and collector of plants and fossils, who was also knowledgeable about caves. Not realizing that Muir had been to the university, Mr. Munford provided "long lessons concerning roots and herbs for every mortal ill." Muir "escaped" to the fields once more, following a railroad track toward Horse Cave and Mammoth Cave. He lodged the evening of September 5 in a log schoolhouse upon "the softest looking of the benches."[184]

Early the next morning he set out for Horse and Mammoth Caves and got a ride from "an old negro driving an ox team." Riding a few miles, Muir and the man chatted about the war. They passed a skirmish site where Confederate troops had made a hasty retreat, and the driver exclaimed, "Lo'd, how dey run." Muir asked about the man's thoughts on the war. "Oh, Lo'd, want no mo wa, Lo'd no," he said. The opinion fit well with Muir's own thoughts and feelings on the subject. He concluded, "Many of these Kentucky negroes are shrewd and intelligent, and when warmed upon a subject that interests them, are eloquent in no mean degree."[185]

After arriving at Horse Cave, Muir walked another ten miles out of his way to Mammoth Cave. Townspeople from nearby villages often gathered to cool off at Horse Cave during the hot summer months, and Muir discovered that locals considered travel to other caves not worth the time; he found the residents' provinciality and practicality evidence of a lack of initiative and curiosity. For example, he wrote about one of the local men at Horse Cave, "He was one of the useful, practical men—too wise to waste precious time with weeds, caves, fossils or anything else that he could not eat."[186] In Muir's view, humans with power never quite got things right; they either had over-inflated views that led to a narrowed curiosity or they bent nature too strongly to their interests. Or, worse, they visited violence upon one another.

The contrived beauty of the hotel grounds at Mammoth Cave, with its "parlor taste," geometrically shaped trees and gardens with "many a beautiful plant cultivated to deformity," paled in comparison with plants around the Mammoth Cave mouth. Muir noted that plants at the cave's mouth were unlike plants in the surrounding area because the cave's ecosystem was evenly cool and humid [187]

Starting out for Glasgow Junction the morning after his visit to the caves, Muir was urged by one "old Kentuckian" to remain at Mammoth Cave. The man said that Muir could teach school in a nearby community. Resisting one more person's agenda for his life, Muir pushed on, pursuing his own plans.

Muir's last days in Kentucky impressed him with the friendliness of the people and the grandeur of the region's oaks. Most travelers he met, both white and black, rode horses. They greeted each other "with familiar kindly greetings, addressing them always as 'Uncles' and 'Aunts.'"[188] On Sunday, September 8, Muir noted "a great many negroes going to meeting, dressed in their Sunday best. Fat, happy looking, and contented."[189] Muir also found the scenery along the Cumberland River striking. He said in his journal, "I think I could enjoy traveling with it in the midst of such beauty all my life." Of the oaks, he wrote, "Far grandest of all Kentucky plants are her noble oaks. They are the master existences of her exuberant forest. Here is the Eden, the paradise of oaks."[190]

Muir passed through Burkesville on September 9. About seven miles southeast of the town he wrote a letter to Jeanne Carr. Sitting on a ridge top with his back against a moss-clad log, he reflected on his journey to date. "I often thought as I went along how dearly Mrs. Carr would appreciate all this," he wrote to his friend. He described eloquently the trees and scenery of Kentucky and asked to know more about the geology of caves from Carr's husband. He laid out his intended route through Tennessee: by the towns of Kingston on the junction of the Tennessee and Clinch rivers and Madisonville, and then up the Unaka Mountains to North Carolina. Knowing about mail delays, he suggested that Carr send her letters to Gainesville, Georgia. His plant press was filling up, and he needed to send it home in the care of David. He would do so in Kingston. He also knew that Kingston provided the best express route, using river steamboats for mail and money deliveries from Wisconsin.[191]

Muir's report of his experience in Kentucky underscored his fundamental contentment with its people and the grandeur of its fields, hills, caves and oaks. The ten-day walk through Kentucky was like the welcoming embrace he saw in the oak tree outside of Louisville. There was more than just a song in Muir's heart; there was a sense of well-being and contentment as he strode through the state. Muir found friendly, helpful people along the way among both whites and blacks, including former slaves, local farmers, and well-to-do planters. He found settled communities problematic, as in Mammoth Caves' trimmed, artificial gardens, and the squalid, dusty, and rubbish-filled taverns in many towns; and he also encountered humans who were too practical about the "uses" of nature to serve narrow ends and who lacked curiosity about what lay beyond their towns. Muir found he preferred the wild to the tamed, the natural flowers and trees to the shaped, pruned, and arranged plants of domestic, conventional taste. Walking up to twenty miles a day, he was making good time. It was not quite a "hasty" walk, but his preferences for wilderness were being shaped. In this largely pleasant walk through Kentucky, Muir found a sense of contentment, and given the eloquence of his expression regarding nature, he found an inner poetry and song coming out in the writing of his journal and letters. His plans had become a song of the road.

# 4

## CHALLENGES IN TENNESSEE

*"Picking up blossoms doesn't seem to be a man's work at all in any kind of times."* — *Tennessee blacksmith challenge to John Muir, 1867.*

The warm welcome John Muir experienced in Kentucky, with the wide open arms of the oaks and the generous hearts of its people, was challenged in Tennessee and in the mountains of North Carolina, "the first real mountains that my foot ever touched or eyes beheld."[192] While he discovered exquisite beauty in both the river valleys and mountain ridges, Muir also experienced first-hand how the ravages of the Civil War had forged a culture of desperation and potential violence. Muir had to defend his botanizing and vocational choice, as well as his personal safety, with his wits and courage. He learned that the "bossy, verdant woods" had its perils of dense, thorny vines. Prickly plants tore at his clothes and left drops of his blood on thorns and leaves.

The Civil War had reinforced this region's cultural suspicion of strangers. The region was notable for its blood feuds and revenge without reconciliation. Whole counties became depopulated, towns disappeared, and houses and fields were abandoned, with the remaining population at the mercy of marauding bands of bushwhackers, thieves, and murderers. Needless to say, a Northerner with a Scottish accent invited close questioning and suspicion. Locals wondered if he was a government agent or a carpetbagger. Did he work, and if so, where, and at what? One pointedly challenged Muir, "Picking up blossoms doesn't seem to be a man's work at all in any kind of times."[193]

Tennessee was a notably split state during the Civil War. Its population of 1.2 million people was divided culturally, geographically, and socially. The western half of the state, with its alluvial lands, access to river transportation, and large plantations dependent on slavery, supported secession. Eastern Tennessee, closer to the mountains with its independent farmers, sympathized with free labor and lived with a fierce independence and hostility toward the aristocratic pretenses of large landowners. People in the region sympathized with their gun-loving parsons and militant preachers.[194] An 1868 handbook and immigrant's guide described the Tennessee mountains as "but a few years ago ... cut off from the world..."[195] To the middle and south of the state, steamboat traffic moved up and down the Tennessee River, connecting Kingston in Roane County and Tennessee with the Mississippi—and, northward, to the Wisconsin River and Portage.

Middle Tennessee had both broad alluvial plains, such as the Cumberland Plateau and Tellico Plains, and, further southeast, the first large mountain ranges John Muir ever saw. These included the Cumberland Mountains, in east central Tennessee, and the Unaka, or Great Smoky, range near the North Carolina border. The deep forests, clear sparkling streams, and isolated coves meant subsistence living and a powerful folklore. Storytelling, song, and survival coupled with fierce independence iced the region's gun culture. Resentment, hatred, confusion, pessimism, and a tragic sense of life marked the plight of many people of Tennessee, well-represented in its militant parsons, mountain guerrillas, and wary folk tucked away in its many mountain coves.[196] It was into this context of embitterment, combined with a tumultuous election year, that John Muir ventured in 1867.

As elections neared, a Republican-controlled "radical" militia was ordered to take posts at the polls. The election proceeded, and the Loyal League and black voters returned Governor William G. Brownlow to the statehouse for a second term; the white aristocracy resented this "occupation" of their government and land by "foreigners." In reaction, white leadership sympathetic to the Old South formed the Ku Klux Klan in Pulaski, Tennessee, in 1867. An underground militia rose up to intimidate Radical Loyal League Republicans and black voters. Governor Brownlow declared martial law and ordered $500 fines or a five-year prison term assessed to those conspiring against the Republican administration or the freedmen. A private detective seeking to infiltrate the Ku Klux Klan was shot and murdered. Robed horsemen and vigilantes swept the countryside, and nightriders intimidated Loyal League Republicans and freedmen, especially those seeking access to the ballot box.[197] Muir, largely unaware of this political and social turmoil, nevertheless encountered thieves and other desperate groups of men who were by-products of this turmoil.

If Muir thought he was in Eden in Kentucky, his first encounter with a suspicious Tennessee farmer was a harbinger of thorny things to come. Suspicion pervaded Tennessee. After crossing the state line toward evening, he "obtained food & shelter from [a] thrifty Tennessee farmer after he had made use of all the ordinary inhospitable arguments of cautious comfortable families."[198] On the morning of September 10, Muir left the "uncordial kindnesses" and "escaped" to "the generous bosom of green woods" to begin his ascent up the Cumberland Mountains. Following switchbacks through the tunnel-like arches of oaks, he noted that, unlike the "hillocky regions" of the Wisconsin Dells, Tennessee offered a stiff climb, unrelentingly upward. With fewer clearings in the woods, tall forests deeply shaded his path. Along his route, a man on a horse caught up to Muir, inveigled Muir's bag from him, and then spurred and gaited his horse quickly ahead. Muir ran to catch up and did so, finding the man peering into his bag. The lad found nothing of value to him — only toiletries, a towel, and books. Returning the bag to Muir, the young man said he had forgotten something and went off down the road.[199]

Warned that the region was desolate for the next forty or fifty miles, Muir began to look for a night's lodging. Along the way he fell into conversation with an elderly bearded man who was sure that England, Ireland, and Russia had declared war on the United States. "But are you sure this news is true?" Muir asked. "Yes," the old man said. He was quite sure after talking to some neighbors at the store the previous night, "and Jim somebody could read, and he found out all about it in a poor paper." The man affirmed his patriotism and his concerns. "These kingdoms have declared war agin' the United States. All I have to say is America forever but I'd heap rather they wouldn't fight."[200]

The sketch showed a bearded man with a dog in the midst of a dense forest, arms outstretched to emphasize his opinion. Muir holds a bouquet of wildflowers. Given the man's heated views, it is unlikely that he noticed the flowers, but Muir emphasizes that he did.

Following a public road from Burkesville, Kentucky, across the state line to Jamestown, in Fentress County, Tennessee, Muir saw a state in distress. As a rural town and county seat, Jamestown had opened its first one-room, wooden schoolhouse, the Jamestown Academy, in 1860. When Muir passed through, Jamestown's populace of around three hundred was hard at work reconstructing its public buildings. Its courthouse had burned down in 1860 and had been recently rebuilt, in 1865. Its first two log churches were not built until the 1870s. Muir, unimpressed with the town, noted, "Passed the rickety, filthy thrice-dead village of Jamestown. [N]o clump

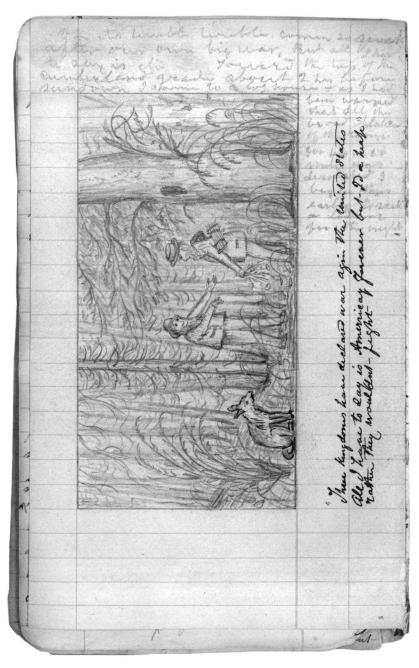

*Muir encounters rumors of war.*

of huts in the darkest wild could be so repulsive."[201] The Civil War had hit this region hard. Money was scarce, and people told long stories "of the terrible times of war." One poor old woman would not house Muir because she did not have change for his $5 bill; however, seeing Muir's exhaustion, "taking pity after climbing m[oun]t[ain], offered drink of milk."[202]

Eventually, Muir made his way to the home of a farmer/blacksmith and his wife, one of the last homes before the crest of the Cumberland Mountains. The elderly smith, an eminently practical and devout man, would challenge Muir's manhood and his life's purpose.

Muir came upon the blacksmith working at his anvil, bare-chested, "sweaty, begrimed, and covered with shaggy black hair."[203] Though he needed food and lodging, Muir had nothing smaller than a five-dollar bill, and locals had barely any cash to break that bill for him. Initially walking away from Muir's request, the blacksmith changed his mind. He said to his wife, "Tell him to go into the house. A man that comes right out like that beforehand is welcomed to eat my bread."[204] The simple dinner of cornbread and bacon began with a blessing. At dinner the couple described the "terrible times of war," and followed this with hunting stories. Looking at Muir's plant press, the blacksmith "was puzzled with the real character of my journey." He challenged Muir: "Young man, what are you doing down here?" Muir recorded the exchange in his journal:

> "I replied that I was looking at plants."
> "Plants? What kind of plants?"
> "Oh, all kinds; grass, weeds, flowers, trees, mosses, ferns,—almost everything that grows is interesting to me."
> "Well, young man...you mean to say that you are not employed by the Government on some private business?"

"No, I am not employed by anyone except just myself. I love all kinds of plants, and I came down here to these Southern States to get acquainted with as many of them as possible."[205]

More questions followed underscoring the blacksmith's skepticism regarding Muir's work. "It seems very strange, sir, that you should come so far into these rough mountains just for *weeds & blossoms*."[206]

Fond of debate, the blacksmith challenged Muir's purposes and plans. Muir reported that the blacksmith "marshaled a long ugly regiment of musty orthodox arguments against wasting useful time." The blacksmith said, pointedly, "You look like a strong-minded man, and surely you are able to do something better than wander over the country and look at weeds and blossoms. These are hard times, and real work is required of every man that is able. Picking up blossoms doesn't seem to be a man's work at all in any kind of times." Remembering the blacksmith's blessing, Muir asked, "You are a believer in the Bible[,] are you not?"

"Oh, yes."[207]

Using memorized texts from the Bible, Muir pointed out that Solomon had studied and collected plants, including the cedars of Lebanon and the hyssop that grew in the cracks of walls. He said that Solomon walked the mountains of Judea to see every plant. Even Jesus referred to flowers, urging his disciples "to consider the lilies, how they grow," and comparing their beauty with Solomon in all his glory.[208] Driving his point home, Muir asked, "Now, whose advice am I to take, yours or Christ's? Christ says, 'Consider the lilies.' You say, 'Don't consider them. It is n't worth while for any strong-minded man.'"[209] The man's position fell away in the face of Muir's arguments. "[H]e had never thought of blossoms in that way before," Muir wrote. Repeating how strong-minded Muir was, he relented and said that Muir was justified in picking up blossoms.[210]

After earning the blacksmith's respect, Muir received from him warnings about small bands of guerrillas who lurked along the roads. They were known to kill a man for five dollars. He urged Muir not to walk to the Gulf, but instead to settle down, to live in the country and wait for the times to become "quiet and orderly once more."[211] Muir rejected his warnings and solicitude. He said he had no fear, little to lose and "anyhow, I always had good luck."[212]

These queries and challenges were a very different type of exchange than the attempted robbery. The blacksmith challenged Muir's purpose and goal for the walk and his identity as a wandering botanist. The religious, elderly, hard-working, and ultimately charitable host posed a more significant threat than did the young would-be robber. Muir defended, in religious terms, an attack on his newly formed identity as a collector of biological specimens. He also maintained a seemingly indifferent attitude toward the risks and desperate times those in Tennessee now confronted. The smith had challenged Muir's work as mere self-indulgence in the face of the hard work of reconstruction that was required. To this challenge, Muir offered his best defense to justify his work to the pious blacksmith: the authority of scripture and the teachings of Jesus. In the mind of the blacksmith, his argument trumped all the arguments criticizing Muir's vocation in the face of tough times. Muir had made his point.

Having been on the road for ten days, Muir entered the Cumberland Plateau, a furrowed and dimpled land of sandstone and "shallow groove-like valleys and hills," on September 11.[213] Along with finding milkworts, asters, and goldenrods, he discovered cinnamon and royal ferns along river and stream banks. The oaks were similar to those in Wisconsin, but they were "defended by a network of impenetrable, formidable prickly greenbriars & brambles armed with hooked claws," he wrote.[214]

The "sad marks of war" fell upon the plateau. Houses were uninhabited. Orchards and fences were "in ruins." The tone of Muir's journal entries becomes increasingly anxious and fearful during this time. He wrote about how the road became "dim" and vanished into "desolate fields." At a point when he was hungry and lost, the "terrible southern brambles" obstructed his way. He noted in his journal that while there were lovely flowers, there were also brambles and spiky vines "as thorny, alas, as mortal ever trod," causing plenty of cuts and punctures. Fording a stream vexed him. With the "cat plants" on the shores of the river, one was not simply pricked, but was "caught held fast." He wrote, "The toothed arching branches come down over and about your victim like cruel living arms in hundreds, & the more you struggle the more terribly you are entangled & the more are your wounds deepened & multiplied."[215] Like a cat, the brambles sank their nails and teeth into Muir's shoulder blade. "The south has plant flycatchers," he wrote; "it also has plant man-catchers."[216]

While there was delight in the flowers, Muir now found nature itself setting up challenges and obstacles; it was hardly Eden. The walk through Tennessee challenged Muir's sense of safety, his physical ease; even the state's people challenged his purpose with threats of robbery and challenges to his purpose and goals.

Toward sundown, Muir strode along a straight stretch of road. Ten mounted men, hair hanging down to their shoulders, rode into view on their "scrawny" horses. Here was one of the guerilla bands about which the blacksmith had warned Muir. The bushwhackers did not know what to make of this solitary, bearded young man with a plant press on his back. Since the ground was open, there was nothing Muir could do but face the interlopers. He dared not run, so he swiftly walked toward the men. Striding past them, he looked them straight in the eye, smiled, bade them "Howdy" and kept on going. He quickly glanced back after walking about one hundred yards. All ten had turned their horses toward him in a tight group. They chatted in low murmurs. "Who is this strange-looking man?" "Does he carry money?" "No, look at the plants hanging out of the contraption on his back." "He is an herb collector, an herbalist." "Let him be—he is poor."[217] The bushwhackers let Muir walk on unmolested.

That evening he had a dinner of string beans, buttermilk, and cornbread at the home of hospitable African Americans not far from Montgomery, Tennessee. His appetite was constrained because he sat in a bottomless chair with his chin nearly resting against his knees. He decided to spend the night outside the home among the trees as mountain fog swept in.

Muir awoke the morning of the twelfth "drenched with mountain mist which showed grandly as it moves the way before the hot sun." He passed through "shabby," dying Montgomery.[218] Populated by only thirty people in 1870, Montgomery was currently the county seat in sparsely populated and impoverished Morgan County. Voters of Morgan County would decide to move the county seat from Montgomery to Wartburg in 1870. In just a few years, the only remnant of the village was its cemetery. Muir took breakfast in a "clean" house and crossed the Emory River. Through his twelfth day on the road, Muir faced some significant challenges both to his decision to become a botanist and in the experience of hard travel through prickly vines and mountainous terrain. The journey was not proving as easy as his time in Kentucky.

In the face of the challenges, nature provided elements of consolation. Muir described the Emory River as "luxuriantly peopled with rare & lovely flowers." Every plant and movement of the stream "seemed solemnly to feel the presence of the great Creator." Muir wrote that he "[l]ingered in this sanctuary a long time thanking the Lord with all my heart for his goodness in allowing me to enter & enjoy it."[219]

It was the beauty of the mountains and its streams and plant life that drew Muir toward gratitude and confidence as his trip continued. Though the thorns were a nuisance, the major problems, he noted, were among humans and their shabby towns, their lawless behavior, and their narrow ideas. Nature, in Muir's mind, despite its briars, possessed elements of innocent beauty. His experiences of this beauty could become a source of reverence and worship despite the thorns and "cat plants."

The theme of gratitude is frequently evidenced in Muir's journal. He was not just a reborn person with renewed eyesight; he frequently included, in his journal, entries of gratitude for the wonders of creation, even when he had recently felt the sting of opposition from nature's thorns and vines.[220] This trait of gratitude provided Muir with a measure of resilience in dealing with the challenges of travel through Tennessee. In this portion of his walk, Muir was beginning to demonstrate his mettle and to provide anecdotes that unintentionally portray his wit and courage. The synthesis of these character traits provides evidence of Muir's growth and development and his deepening engagement with nature, which would come to influence his environmental thought and ethics.

In his grateful response to what he was experiencing, Muir cataloged plants along the Emory River: a Dicksonia and a polypod fern that grew on trees; large-leafed Magnolias with their scarlet, conical fruit; mosses; flowers; oaks; laurels; azaleas; asters; and towering clumps of beautiful hemlocks. As he worked his way south on September 12, Muir came into pine forests along the Tennessee and Clinch River valleys. He forded the Clinch and made his way before dark to the busy and well-populated river port of Kingston, Tennessee.

At the confluence of the Clinch and Tennessee rivers, Kingston, the county seat for Roane County, was a prosperous town of 1,429; its flourishing economy relied in large part on steamboat traffic connecting mid-Tennessee with the Mississippi River and the upper Midwest. From Kingston, Muir shipped plant specimens he had collected to David and Sarah Galloway in Wisconsin for safekeeping.[221]

On September 13, Muir walked along the flint-ridged valleys on the outskirts of Kingston, toward the Unaka Mountains, but he became disoriented trying to reach Philadelphia, Tennessee. One woman said he could get to North Carolina by following the old Unicoe Turnpike, which she had followed to get over the Unaka Mountains looming in the distance.

Muir gave up using a map and compass to work his way through the region.[222] He spent the evening with a "gruff" North Carolina African-American teamster. The next morning he arrived at Philadelphia, characterizing it as a "very filthy village in a beautiful situation." While it was a town of only 563 people in 1870, Philadelphia's prospects turned even bleaker for a time; its population would drop one hundred in the next decade. Muir noted the abundance of pines and the variety of ferns in the region, but despite the abundance of land and resources, the region was war-torn in 1867. Muir described the county seat of Madisonville as "a brisk village." Monroe County, through which he passed, grew from 10,998 in 1860 to 11,574 in 1870 with Madisonville's population numbering 563 in 1870, growing to 667 in 1880.[223] With the possible exceptions of Kingston and Madisonville, statistics show that rural Tennessee and its communities remained under stress five years post-bellum.

Despite signs of the war's devastation, Muir was entranced with the distant mountains, calling them "a magnificent sight." On September 14, he stayed the night with a "pleasant young farmer."[224] As Muir trekked towards the Unaka Mountains, he saw that they were far higher than the Cumberland Mountains. He wrote that he "[m]ade many a halt at open places to take a breath and to admire."[225]

Working his way southeast to the Tellico Plains and, eventually, to the Hiawassee River, he stayed with an elderly man who underscored the poverty of his circumstances with his greeting, "Well, you're welcome to stop, if you think you can live till morning on what I have to live on all the time."[226] Muir's host was talkative and generous. Regaling his guest with hunting stories, he urged Muir to stay with him a day or two, offering to be his guide to the top of the mountains. Finally, he encouraged Muir to see the local copper and gold mines. Muir decided to visit the gold mines making notes on miner's wages of 50 cents to two dollars a day or $10 a month. Muir had entered a region of subsistence mountain farming, placer mining, small-scale milling, homespun weaving, barter, story-telling, and mountain folklore. This was a unique world unto itself, rich in its language, culture, stories, and sense of independence.

Things had not changed much in this region in comparison to the invention and technology in the North. Muir saw, for example, that the grist mills of Kentucky and Tennessee were much less sophisticated than those in the North. He described them as small, hand-held affairs with "boyish-looking, back-action water wheels," driven by small trenches dug into the hillsides rather than dams." All the machines of Kentucky and Tennessee are far behind the age,"[227] Muir concluded. Muir characterized mountain life as it appeared to him in 1867: "Wild unshorn uncombed men" came out of the woods on Sundays with a bag of corn on their backs. They threw their peck or bushel of grain into the hopper, set the mill to grind and went to the house to smoke and chat. The men cared little if the stones kept on grinding despite lack of grain: "No harm," they would say. Before they emerged into more-populated areas, the men's long Sunday walks led over many hills and valleys and through rhododendron groves where the shiny leaves knocked off their coonskin caps. Compared with Muir's experience of the restless drive for efficient innovation in the North, this region seemed backward and primitive. Muir wrote, for example, "There is not the faintest sign of that restless spirit of speculation & invention so conspicuous in the north." Muir concluded this comment with the speculation that some law must have been passed to make improvement a crime in this region.[228] "This," wrote Muir, "is the most primitive country I have seen, primitive in everything."[229]

Muir then walked into Tennessee mining country. One of his hosts provided an explanation for increased mining in the region, saying that when people first came to the valleys, they farmed. After a few years, soil became exhausted. Quoting his host, Muir wrote, "The worn-out ground won't yield no roastin' ears now. But the Lord foresaw this state of affairs, and prepared something else for us." Muir asked, "And what is it?" The man replied, "Why, He meant us to bust open these copper mines and gold mines, so that we may have money to buy the corn that we cannot raise." Muir observed with slight sarcasm, "A most profound observation."[230] The trenchant comment suggests that Muir questioned the man's presumption in purporting to know the purposes of Providence in moving portions of the American South from an agricultural economy to one built on mining.

On September 18, Muir approached the Tennessee/North Carolina line on the western slope of the Unaka Mountains. He entered a remote and beautiful area where "The scenery is far grander than any I ever before beheld," he wrote. It was an "ocean of wood" and "swelling mountain beauty."[231] Again, Muir was ecstatic.

> All were united by curves and slopes of inimitable softness and beauty. Oh, these forest gardens of our Father! What perfection, what divinity in their architecture! What simplicity and mysterious complexity of detail! Who shall

read the teaching of these sylvan pages, the glad brotherhood of rills that sing in the valleys, and all the happy creatures that dwell in them under the tender keeping of a Father's care?[232]

In his journal, Muir continued to address the paradox of nature as both Eden and the lair of challenges and dangers. On September 19, he heard warnings about bushwhackers and guerillas in the mountains. His host urged him to see the petroglyphs at Track Rock, on the Georgia side of the Unaka Mountains. Despite wondrous mountain views and the curiosities of Track Rock, feuds characterized the region and even the life of his host. This good-hearted man provided a haven for a neighbor who had to move nightly since he was caught up in a feud. Muir noted that his host's neighbor was well armed with a rifle, pistol, and long knife; could not work; and, lived in fear. This was yet another example that the volatile interactions of humans could be a greater source of danger to people's well-being and stability than could nature, with its thorns and briars.

Heading toward North Carolina, Muir came to the Hiawassee River, which he described as "a most impressive mountain river." The large pinkish-red Joe Pye flower bloomed there, along with a wide variety of goldenrods and purple asters. The upturned flint rock in the riverbed gave the water an unusually glittery character. Muir wrote in his journal that the river surface "gemmed and burnished with the brightness of the sky." The river created a bond with Muir's "inner life" and his powerful feelings—feelings "that we did not know ourselves possessed of"—with the "overwhelming eloquence of its cataracts." The Hiawassee's surface was "broken into a thousand gems," "bright as the sky with a pathway for the angels of heaven." The forest wall was "vine draped & flowery as Eden." Muir found the totality of the experience to be "overlaid & wrapt in the multitude of its everchanging notes of song." [233] Surely, this was a glory.

It is uncertain which track Muir took to Murphy, North Carolina. He could have followed the Hiawassee all the way into Murphy along its bare shoreline, since its water level is low in September. It is also possible that he took an Indian trail and wagon road up through the mountains from Coker Creek, along the Unicoe Turnpike to Murphy.

After Muir strode into Murphy, he met close questioning by the local lawman, Sheriff Beale. The war had instilled worry and suspicion among law enforcers since many "vagrant" men—runaways, bushwhackers, guerrillas, thieves, and murderers—were known to be in the area. Satisfied with Muir's answers to his questions about the traveler's origins and intentions, Beale invited Muir into his home and welcomed him to the small village of fewer than two hundred people.

Originally occupied solely by Cherokee Native Americans before whites made their initial incursion during Hernando de Soto's reconnaissance of the region in the 1540s, the city was hemmed in by the mountains that lay alongside the Hia-wassee.[234] A.R.S. Hunter established an early white settlement with the founding of his store in 1828. When gold was discovered in Georgia in 1828, pressures mounted to remove the Cherokees despite their longstanding diplomatic relationship with the US government, going back to the 1790 Holston Treaty. The Cherokee became US allies against the Creeks in the Indian Wars of the early 1800s. They invited Christian missionaries to join their ranks; many Cherokees converted, became independent landholders, learned English, and wore Western clothing. In short, the Cherokee had begun the process of assimilating into "American" culture by owning plantations, building large southern mansions, and even owning slaves.

Increasing conflict between miners and Cherokees led the state of Georgia to seek the removal of the Native Americans after gold was discovered on their land. President Andrew Jackson, fearing a bloodbath and generally sympathetic to his power base of white settlers and miners, had supported the claims of Georgians against the Cherokee Nation and ordered the Cherokees forcibly removed in 1833. Nearby Fort Butler, situated on a bluff outside of Murphy, was used by General Winfield Scott as a detention camp until sufficient numbers of the Cherokee could be sent out on the "Trail of Tears" to Oklahoma, known primarily as Indian Territory.

When Muir came through Murphy, on 19 September 1867, he visited the ruins of Fort Butler with his escort, Sheriff Beale. Muir wrote, "[I] was shown site of Camp Butler where General Scott had his headquarters when removing the Cherokee Indians."[235] Muir's silence on the plight of the Cherokee is noteworthy.

While Muir had frequent opportunities to interact with African Americans on the walk, he apparently had less contact with Native Americans. In his journal, Muir contrasted Sheriff Beale's home, "decked with flowers & vines, clean without & within & stamped with the comforts of culture & refinement in all its arrangements," with "the uncouth transition establishments from the savage wigwam to the clumsy but clean log castles of the thrifty pioneers."[236] Muir preferred the clean, tidy, and orderly homes of the townsfolk to the "transitional" dwellings of Native American and mountain people. In his comparisons he showed his marked preference for well-ordered communities over those informed by different priorities and values.

Muir met challenges on his walk through Tennessee that he had not faced in Kentucky. In Tennessee, he dealt with the threat of robbery, the pain of prickly, unfriendly flora, and with questions regarding his botanical work. Muir met these challenges with wit and courage, constantly demonstrating his adaptability and flexibility. The journal also gives insight into one of the sources of his resilience: his sense of gratitude for nature's lovely mountains, scenery, glinting rivers, and flowery plants (though not for those that threatened to engulf him or tore at his clothing). The journey through Tennessee was not an easy ramble, but it had its rewards. Muir kept his focus on nature's beauty rather than on the problems he encountered. His journal evidences that he was growing in his ability to confront difficulties and overcome them. Muir responded to the challenges of his trip with resilience, flexibility, gratitude, and focus. These are certainly traits that would continue to draw others toward him and reward him with influence in the future.

It is also evident that as Muir traveled, his engagement with the world around him resulted in a heightened poetic and lyrical quality to his writing. His prose is certainly more energetic and, indeed, spiritual, in his journal entries in Tennessee than in the record of his Kentucky walk. Facing Tennessee's trials, he deepens as a person more mindful of the beauties of nature than of its spiky thorns, briars, and "cat plants." This portion of the journal bears witness to the beginnings of Muir's transformation.

# 5

# GEORGIA AND "THE NATURAL BEAUTY OF DEATH"—JOHN MUIR, 1867

The welcome that Muir experienced in Kentucky and the challenges of Tennessee gave way to the unexpected "strangeness" of Muir's experiences in Georgia, which provoked even deeper and more profound journal reflections on life and death. Muir's journey led from the mountains of Blairsville to Savannah, on the coast, where he lived in a cemetery for five days.

Following Sheriff Beale's recommendation to seek out Track Rock, John Muir left Murphy, North Carolina, on 20 September 1867.[237] In the afternoon, he reached "a commanding ridge," where he saw holly for the first time and encountered "a most glorious view of blue, softly curved, forested mountain scenery."[238] Passing through Unicoi Gap and the Georgia mountains, fording small, cool brooks, walking by the Ivy Log Baptist Church, Muir strode into Blairsville, the Union County seat, which had a population of 616 in 1870.[239] In Muir's words, the village was "shapeless & insignificant but grandly encircled with banded hills."[240] He spent the night with a farmer and his wife who smoked and chewed tobacco. Muir wrote that the wife "could spit farther & faster than any male I ever saw," incorporating a sudden jerk of her head, during which the tobacco flew out of the side of her mouth with no "disorder of the lips."[241] As with other populations of mountain people in Tennessee and North Carolina, most people in Union County had been opposed to secession; however, when Union troops came into the region, local men joined the Confederate Army to protect their property and possessions, thus reluctantly siding with the Confederacy.

The following day, Muir crossed through "knob land." Farmers and slaves scratched out their subsistence there, living on the tops of the knobs, using one-toothed cultivators to gouge its thin soil. Muir followed "three poor but merry mountaineers" whose "shackly" wagon, "held together by spiritualism," tumbled and lurched up and down the knobs. Its four occupants—two women, one old, and a young man, along with Muir—hurtled back and forth from front end to back end of the wagon in "unmannerly and impolite disorder."[242] Conversation lurched from topic to topic, including love, marriage, and camp meeting revivals, while the wagon's occupants slipped and slid into heaps inside the wagon. Throughout, the old woman grasped in her hand a bouquet of French marigolds.

From the last overlook of the Blue Ridge Mountains, Muir could see "a prospect very different from what I had passed, namely a vast uniform expanse of dark pine woods, extending to the sea."[243] In the evening, he came to a large granite monolith, Mount Yonah, on the road between Cleveland and Helen. A Methodist slave owner and miner provided an evening's lodging, giving Muir some cider. They talked into the evening about slavery, mines, politics, and Northern and Southern folkways.[244]

Muir noted that mountain altitudes and climates allowed for the interpenetration of Northern and Southern plants. He found fewer Wisconsin and Northern flowers and encountered new species of plants. The southeastern slopes of the Blue Ridge Mountains had "the greatest number of hardy, enterprising representatives of the two climates."[245] There were more than 85 species of goldenrod; the dramatic Jack in the Pulpit; partridge pea, from which the leaves made good tea; St. John's Wort, an effective anti-depressant; and the rare, fringed Gentian, found near Track Rock.[246]

Following the road into Gainesville, Georgia, Muir described it as a "comfortable townlet," and called it "finely shaded & ornamented." The town had around a thousand inhabitants and lay along the slow-moving, opaque, and sleek Chattahoochee River, which Muir described as "richly embanked with massive, bossy, dark green water oaks, and wreathed with a dense growth of muscadine grapevines."[247] He spent the evening at the home of the son of Aaron Prater, whom he had met in Osgood and Smith's factory in Indianapolis. Prater was the owner of 103 acres and the head of "a plain backwoods family among the knobby timbered hillocks, not far from the river."[248] Muir lingered a couple of days with the Praters, collecting boatloads of muscadine grapes that dropped from the vines into the river and swirled together into back eddies. These inch-wide purple or pale-white grapes made fine jellies and wine and were good eating, as well. Muir and Prater took long rambles along the river so that Muir could gather more plants and flowers.

The Civil War had left its mark on the Gainesville area. Slave owners had lost 40 percent of their worth with the war's destruction and the ensuing emancipation. From a total value of $2.1 million in 1866, property values plummeted to $946,000 the following year.[249] The leadership of the region called for practical, hard work. Attorney John Gray wrote in July 1865, "As the war is ended, and we survive, let us up and be doing."[250] Much of the work of the South at this time entailed Reconstruction, and not all Georgians appreciated Republican efforts to rebuild their state.

Mail service had been recently restored by a postmaster. While Muir was anxious to get a letter from his friend Jeanne Carr, he was likely unaware that the postmaster had been appointed by the fragile Republican Party and forced to take a loyalty oath. In other Reconstruction policies, the Freedman's Bureau had been set up to establish work contracts; thus, former slaves began to earn about $7 to $10 a month as salaried and contracted laborers. Out of a population of 1,000 to 1,200, only about 152 freedmen were on the tax rolls in 1867.[251]

The region was also politically contentious. A handful of African Americans owned property, including Aleck Deavours, who had a twenty-five-acre farm. While violence against freedmen was restrained in the Gainesville area during Reconstruction, racist thinking prevailed among some of the distressed, educated aristocracy of northern Georgia. Dr. Matthew F. Stephenson, a noted scientist and assayer at the Dahlonega Mint, writing in September 1867, argued that "The Chinese, Indians and Negroes, with all other inferior races, were evidently created before Adam and Eve." He also wrote that it was "a great crime to practice miscegenation or have intercourse with Negroes and Indians."[252] Muir encountered Southerners who held these views, coming across more and more people with racist beliefs as he walked southward to Athens and Savannah. The Ku Klux Klan ranged about the countryside in nearby White County, and some citizens of Hall County cooperated with the White County Klan.[253] Muir's note of a pertinent conversation between his Georgia host Aaron Prater and himself was vague and general; he simply wrote, "The social & mixed conversation [centered] [u]pon southern & northern generalities."[254] As a polite guest, he avoided specific mention of race and politics even in his journal. His detailed notes focused on the plants.

Leaving the Prater family on September 25, Muir walked toward Athens, trying to find a ford across the Chattahoochee; and as Muir headed south, he got lost. Forcing his way through vines and high grasses trying to ford the river, he was swept off his feet; he swam to a rock and pulled himself out. Given Aaron Prater's warnings about rattlesnakes in the area, along with the treacherous fords and struggles against the thickets of the bottomland, Muir considered making a boat to use "for a sail instead of a march through Georgia."[255] He set aside the idea eventually and found housing at a farmhouse with unfamiliar tropical plants in the garden.

Muir began to see more cotton fields similar to those south of Burkesville, Kentucky. He had imagined cotton to be a magnificent flowering plant. Instead, he wrote, "cotton is a ~~very shabby~~, (coarse, rough) straggling unhappy plant...not half as good-looking as a field of Irish potatoes."[256] Cotton-picking had begun in the region with the harvesting of the fully ripened bolls on the lower levels of the plants. Muir wrote on the easy-going joking and calling out among the African-American laborers now being paid cash for their labor, but he was not impressed with their work ethic. Muir, like many Northerners, believed free labor could outwork slave labor. He never went into the fields himself to prove it, although he did consider gleaning corn or rice fields when he was short of money.[257]

On the afternoon of September 26, Muir reached the size-able, growing university town of Athens, Georgia. In 1860, its population was 3,848 people; in 1867 it was over 4,200, with 150 students; by 1870 it grew to 4,251; and, it was a well-order-ed town featuring wealthy mansions along the Milledgeville Road.[258] Muir described Athens as "a remarkably beautiful and aristocratic town, containing many classic and magnificent mansions of wealthy planters, who formerly owned large negro-stocked plantations in the best cotton and sugar regions farther south." Continuing his assessment of the refined, cultured, and wealthy Athens, Muir noted, "This is the most beautiful town I have seen on the journey, so far, and the only one in the South that I would like to visit."[259] The African Americans he encountered in Athens were, in his words, "well trained and are extremely polite." Most he met were likely house servants and had some form of employment. Muir underscored, but did not question, the deference of blacks to authority; blacks removed their hats upon the approach of a white man and left their heads uncovered until they were well beyond sight.

Muir fretted about drifting, unemployed freedmen in the countryside, many of who were seeking to rejoin family members. Often he referred to them as "robber negroes," thus presuming their lawlessness when, in fact, many were just trying to survive or to reconnect their families in desperate times. Throughout Georgia, Muir saw the marks of war in broken fences and abandoned houses, but when he walked through tidy, growing, orderly Athens, he found the town praiseworthy. He did not understand the undercurrents of authoritarianism, fear, and anxiety that produced this order until later in his journey. For now, he felt secure in a university town where thriving citizens evinced courtly civility. Not all citizens agreed with Muir's assessment. A school teacher, Fannie Atkinson, out of work in 1866, wrote, "Blessed is he who is a cotton holder or a factory stockholder. Want does not seem to tarry at their thresholds "[260] Yes, Athens was a courtly, well ordered town of good manners; yet underneath its propriety there were serious political, economic, and social tensions and problems. It appears that Muir was largely unaware of these tensions.

Unlike the mountain regions of Georgia, the town of Athens had been enthusiastic for secession. More than two thousand men joined the Confederate Army, urged on by the oration of one of the state's luminaries, T.R.R. Cobb. Federal troops had occupied Athens since the end of the war in 1865, and the university had reopened in 1866. The Ku Klux Klan sought to control African-American freedmen and their Loyal League and radical Republican allies. Augustus Longstreet Hull wrote that he knew many Athens citizens who joined the Clarke County Klan. Klan members "were aided and abetted by older men of character and means, members of the various churches and esteemed for their worth."[261]

Opposition to Republican reconstruction policy was voiced at the June 1867 university commencement. Albert H. Cox, a commencement speaker, "arraigned the Republican

Party and scolded the scalawag without mercy." In response to this rhetoric, Union General John Pope threatened to close down the university and to withhold $8,000 of state support. The American Missionary Association brought in two New England school teachers, but no free black or white schools were funded until 1872.

Klan meetings, held at night, with oath-taking and the donning of the "frightful paraphernalia of skulls and cross-bones," were frequent. Klansmen intimidated black legislators and burned down the home of Alf Richardson, a black leader from nearby Oconee County, who was going to testify in a Congressional hearing against the Ku Klux Klan.[262] Many African Americans still lived in their old slave quarters, but they now received low pay for their work—a payment system that would morph into one of debt peonage. Clearly, not all was pleasant in Athens in the month of September 1867 when Muir passed through. Yet this was the only Southern town that reminded him of the civility and order of Madison, Wisconsin.

On September 27, after a hot, tiring walk along "sandy, lightly shaded, lowland levels," Muir became thirsty. "[D]irected by Providence," in his words, Muir found a lovely spring that reminded him of one in Wisconsin that he visited shortly before he left home. It was "in a sandstone basin overhung with shady bushes and vines where I enjoyed to the utmost the blessing of pure cold water. Discovered here a fine southern fern, some new grasses."[263]

At sundown, Muir wrote, "[I] witnessed the most gorgeous sunset I ever enjoyed in this bright world of light. The sunny South is indeed sunny."

As Muir walked his way to Savannah, a metaphor began to take on religious significance and meaning. Milton's metaphor for God, and Muir's temporary blindness, gave "light" special meaning for Muir. Light became for Muir, as it was for Milton, one of the signs of God in nature. Like trees "waving in signs of worship," light stood as a metaphor for the

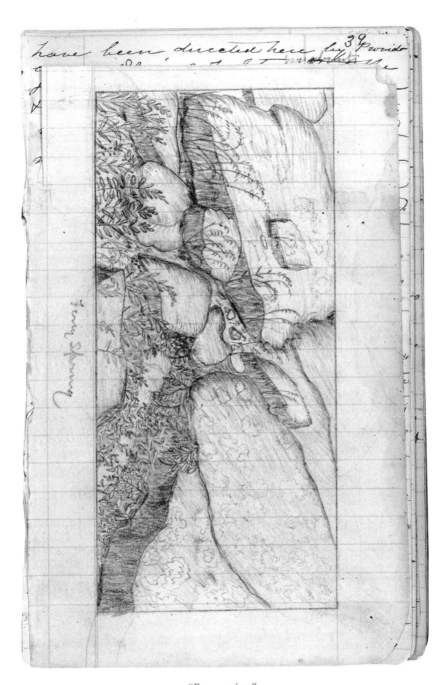

*"Fern spring"*

presence of God. With both his discovery of the spring and his joy in the sunset, Muir felt a religious kinship to a region and a flora that became increasingly unfamiliar as he traveled further south—especially the tropical plants, the heat, the soft winds, and the humidity.

Through the help of "a very civil negro," Muir found lodging for the night, and on September 28, moving ever closer to the Savannah River, Muir found that "Strange plants are crowding about me now. Scarce a familiar face appears among all the flowers of the day's walk."[264] Tall grasses with heads of "glossy purple flowers" along the watery open fields and the slow streams and swamps were particularly notable. Their waving in the winds was like that of the "worshipping" trees. "[S]urely every panicle would wave & bow in joyous allegiance and acknowledge their King."[265] Between Thomson and Augusta, Muir found a sixty-foot tall, remarkable, long-leafed pine, whose needles were about a foot long. He drew a sketch of its seedling, surrounded by tall, waving grasses. Long-leafed pine seedlings looked like smooth-stalked palm trees; children used their tops as brooms for their playhouses.[266]

In Georgia, Muir picked up the pace of his walk, since he was running low on funds. He pushed forty miles without a meal to get to Augusta and awoke the next day "with a sore stomach—sore, I suppose, from its walls rubbing on each other without anything to grind." That night he stayed at the Planter's Hotel in Augusta; his lodging cost him $1.[267]

Augusta was a city of more than fifteen thousand, with 40 percent of its population African American and more than 16 percent were foreign-born. Seven of the nine free schools were run by the American Missionary Society and generally supported by sympathetic Northern Republicans and their Union League allies.[268] Like Athens, Augusta confronted the realities of Congressional Radical Reconstruction and military

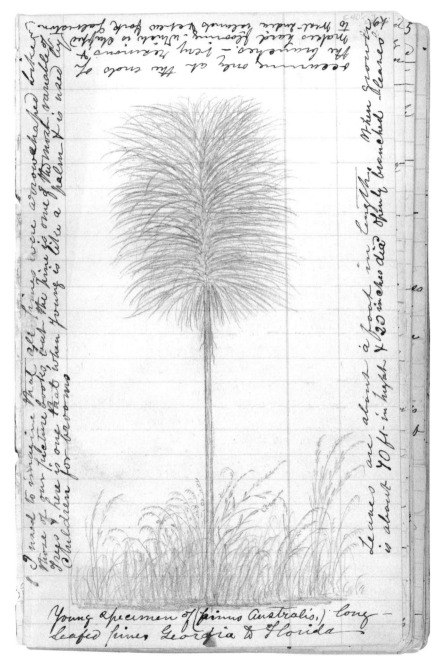

*"Young specimen of (pinus Australis.) long-leafed pine Georgia to Florida"*

occupation. Labor shortages brought wages up to $10 to $12 per month, which many planters could not afford in the wake of their sustained losses as a result of the war; therefore, significant unemployment troubled the city. Idle, roving men in the city made Muir nervous. He quickly left Augusta.[269] On the first of October he set out from the center of town to buy an inexpensive breakfast at the local market and then followed the Savannah River toward the town for which it was named.

Like the Chattahoochee, the Savannah River's bottom land featured tall grasses, "rich, dense, vine-clad forests," muscadine grapes, asters, and goldenrod. The sedges of the northern latitudes became rarer, but legumes grew prolifically in the thin, sandy soil. Two tropical plants drew Muir's attention: the "apricot vine," a kind of passion flower with delicious fruit, and the pomegranate, which he had never seen before. He described it in delightful detail as "a many chambered box full of translucent purple candies."[270] Muir found the lacey, green/grey drapery of Spanish moss hanging from long-armed oak trees fascinating. Much to his surprise, he discovered that the moss was a flowering plant related to the pineapple. The swamp cypress was another tree new to Muir. He noted especially its uniform flat top, as if it had grown against a ceiling. It was the first level-topped tree Muir had ever seen.[271] Increasingly, Muir felt that he was in a strange and unfamiliar world—a theme he repeated several times in his journal in southern Georgia and Florida. In his original journal he wrote the following, for example:

> [I] am in a strange land[.] I know hardly any of the ~~flowers~~ (plants) & cannot see ~~any place~~ (the country) for the solemn dark mysterious (cypress) forest, I ~~do not~~ know (but few) ~~any~~ of the birds, & the winds (are) full of strange sounds—feel far from the people & plants & ~~lighted~~ fields of home[.] [N]ight is coming on & I am beset with indescribable loneliness. Felt feverish[.] [B]athed in a black silent stream, nervously watchful for al[l]igators.[272]

His tense, uncertain tone in this account is different than the sense of welcome he felt in Kentucky or the appreciation he expressed for the beauty and dangers of Tennessee and the mountains. In Georgia, Muir felt an undefined threat from the tropical character of nature. The alligator was a potent emblem of that threat, as were the strange plants and the strange winds. This is also the first note that mentions Muir feeling feverish.

How was his experience in the tropics anything like an Eden experience or even like the sense of welcome he had received in Kentucky? What would he make of this environment? To what extent could he feel comfortable and at home in this environment? If this was Eden, what would he make of the poisonous snakes or the reptilian predator, the alligator? Fear underscored his first-felt response. In this environment, humans could well be food for the alligators. How did human beings fit into this "strange" environment? For Muir, these were troubling questions, and they began to provoke his thought. He spent the evening of October 1 in a comfortable farmhouse lit only by pitchy wood. Gloom seemed to pervade people's homes during the night.[273]

Recovering from his fever the next day, Muir decided to catalog the strangeness of his surroundings, and he dove into his botany. As he collected many specimens of new plants, including rough-hair grass, he again felt a welcome, like that of Kentucky, from the vast forests along his route. His temperament improved. As a talkative and lonely man, Muir easily fell into conversations with people from all ranks of society. He was "amused" by the hunting and ghost stories of an African American with whom he shared a long talk at the site of a train wreck. One young man who was part of this conversation insisted that the ghosts of the dead passengers could be seen there "every dark night."[274]

Muir made his way through twilight to the house of Dr. Edward Alonzo Perkins, a widower whose wife had died in 1864. He, too, was lonely. Perkins, who had followed his father into the medical profession, had a scientific bent due to his medical training.[275] Perkins and Muir shared this interest, but their conversation soon turned to Southern politics. Muir later noted in his journal that he had found Perkins's chatter to be an echo of what he had heard from other white Southerners. He simply wrote, "Long recitals of war havoc, the slave question, Northern politics etc."[276] Muir characterized the Perkins family as "a thoroughly southern family polished & prejudiced."[277] It is clear that Muir did not share in his host's prejudices, but it is also clear that he was behaving as a good guest; it was best not to rile up the one offering the graciousness of his hospitality. Muir did appreciate the Perkins's Lazy Susan, which spun breakfast around to those seated at the table. When he left the Perkins's home and walked through the welcoming barrens of pine trees on October 3, Muir enjoyed the sunny open spaces between the pines with grasses, waving heads of goldenrod and short saw palmettos. No "cat plants" clawed at his clothes; he "sauntered in delightful freedom."[278]

Muir found his way to a wealthy planter's house at Mile Station No. 55 of the Central Georgia Railroad, known as "Cameron Station." Railroad maps show a long private road leading to a residence with a dam and a mill pond on the Indian Branch Creek, which fed the Ogeechee River.[279] Muir's host, Mr. Cameron, cultivated large fields of cotton, and "his" freedmen still referred to him as "Massa." General William Tecumseh Sherman and the Union Army had marched through this region in 1865, destroying railroad track, farm machinery, crops, livestock, and houses. Fearful of Sherman's march, Cameron had thrown his cotton gin and other equipment into the mill pond. As Cameron was cleaning rust from this equipment, Muir noted the planter's hostility: "If Bill Sherman should come down now without his army, he would never go back," said the disgruntled cotton farmer.

Resentments such as Cameron's festered for years among southern property holders.[280]

Seeking food and lodging from Cameron, Muir found the planter to be suspicious of him. Sizing up his potential guest after a few questions, Cameron gradually relented after he got his wife's opinion on the stranger. The Cameron's caution was understandable because the couple had previously been robbed of their silverware by a neatly dressed gentleman. But Muir, enthusiastic about the flora he had seen, shared with them his passion for the plants of the South, and his easy manner won them over. While he excitedly talked about botany, Cameron extolled the merits of "e-lec-tricity." Muir's host was prescient on the subject. Muir reported Cameron as saying, "I believe that the time is coming, though we may not live to see it, when that mysterious power or force, used now only for telegraphy, will eventually supply the power for running railroad trains and steamships, for lighting, and in a word, electricity will do all the work of the world."[281] After his night spent in the Cameron's home, Muir left the household to resume his walk toward Savannah along relatively flat, sandy ground; his traveling funds continued to dwindle.

Over the next five days, Muir walked toward Savannah through watery open spaces; he saw his first banana plant in a garden on October 5; he strode past immense swamps on the 6th and 7th; and he marveled at the great magnolia trees draped in Spanish moss upon his arrival to Savannah on the 8th. Along the way, he found housing among farm families, many of whom admitted him after some very close questioning.[282] Housing had become more difficult as Muir approached Savannah. He found no housing on the 8th and decided to push on to Savannah, arriving there at 11 p.m. The river and port city of more than 28,000 people was largely asleep.[283] Only hotel lights blazed through the night. The rest of the town was dark. Muir walked directly to the Adams Express office to see if there was "word" (and money) from home. He wrote poignantly in his journal, "no word from home. *Alone.*"[284] Given the suspicious questioning he had undergone on several occasions and his continuing difficulty in finding shelter, Muir keenly missed letters from his brothers and sisters.

Arriving in Savannah, he had only $3—no letters and no certificate of credit. Forced to stay in Savannah to wait for money, Muir asked a kindly African American if he knew the direction to a good hotel. "Yes, sah, this way sah," said the man, who pointed to a blazingly lit hotel. The clerk declared the hotel full; even so, Muir did not have enough money for its expensive rooms. He wandered around town and, eventually, "went to [a] poor lodging house," for which he paid 50 cents.[285]

The next morning, October 9, Muir went directly to Adams Express company office and the post office to see if letters had arrived for him. "No, Mr. Muir, nothing yet," said the clerk.[286] So he wandered about Savannah's streets admiring the city's lovely historic squares and its palms. Muir looked for work without success; there was too little cash available, and too few jobs. Moreover, Muir encountered much noise and bustle, too many idle and unemployed people, and rumors of the dangers of plagues and malaria. Wandering southeast of the city, along the white-shelled Thunderbolt Road, Muir passed several African-American communities. He described this impoverished sector of Savannah as home to "Rickety long huts, broken fences & with every trace of agricultural devastation."[287] He sought an open, secure place where he could bed down for the night undisturbed. Walking four to five miles along the road, he came to the lovely moss-draped, live oak-lined entrance into St. Bonaventure Cemetery.

St. Bonaventure seemed to be an Eden of the dead, and, for Muir, a sanctuary of safety. He wrote that the cemetery was "just the place for safety from superstitious prowlers, black or white."[288] Clearly, it provided him with even more.

You hear the song of birds—cross a small stream & you are with nature in the grand old forest graveyard, so beautiful that almost any sensible person would choose to dwell here with the dead rather than with the lazy, disorderly living.... The place is half surrounded by the salt marshes & islets of the river, their reeds & sedges make a delightful fringe. Many bald eagles roost on trees along the side of the marsh, their screams are constantly heard joined with the noise of crows & the sweet songs of countless warblers hidden deep in their dwellings of leaf & flowers. Myriads of the most gorgeous butterflies too, all kinds of happy insects seem to be in a perfect fever of joy & sportive gladness. The whole place seems like a center of life. The dead do not 'reign there alone.'[289]

Muir had found a place where he could stay in relative comfort, given his limited funds, and still check his mail.

The delay in getting his money gave Muir time for reflection. The cemetery stimulated his thoughts on the problems of death, nature and humanity's relationship to nature.

St. Bonaventure's was formerly the plantation of Colonel John Mulryne. The mansion remained a hollowed-out ruin, having been accidentally burned down during a festive dinner party before the war. A few years after that the ruined plantation became a cemetery.[290] Its entrance was lined with a long avenue of enormous live oaks draped with lengthy skeins of Spanish moss that waved gently in the soft, warm winds. Moss covered brick walls and chimneys in the shell of a home.[291] By 1867, citizens of Savannah had been charmed by the cemetery, but its upkeep had become difficult during the war years. Typical of townspeople's sentiment, I.M. Marsh wrote in 1860 a poem of consolation for his cousin Susie on the loss of her fiancé, buried at St. Bonaventure:

could present. So I relying on my
knowledge of machinery I spent the
3° day visiting every mill in Savannah
looking for work but could find
none, then I thought if worst came
to worst I would strike out into
the surrounding country + steal corn
or rice enough for a bawny while
waiting for that money, In the mean
time I cut down my expenses to 3 or 4
cents a day. But I began to grow

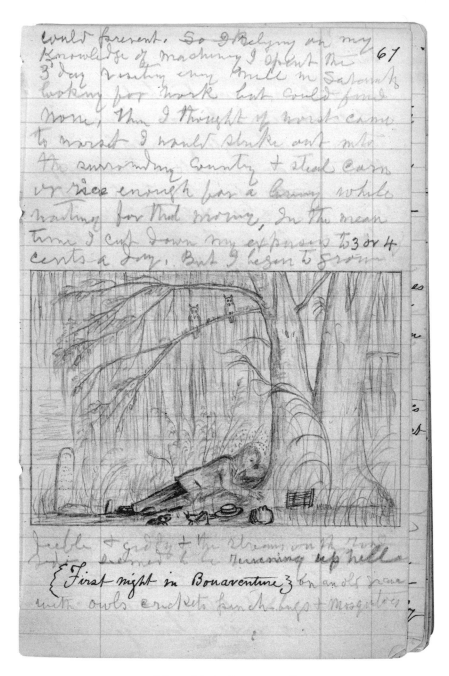

feeble + giddy + the streams on the road
seemed to be running up hill

{First night in Bonaventure} on an old grave
with owls crickets finch bugs + mosquitoes

*"First night in Bonaventure"*

Roam tho' the world, there's not a spot
The consecrated cave, or hallowed grot,
Or flashing isle, set 'mid the restless sea
Wakes a loftier thought, or deeper love than thee;
The stranger wandering from his distant home
Gazes upon these, solemnly, sublime
Thy vista'd corridors thy far reaching dome,
Slumbering beneath the touch of time,
As he onward passes measuredly by and slow,
Heart-spelled by thy moss-drapery of woe.[292]

Like Marsh, Muir was "heart-spelled" by this place during his five- to six-day stay at the cemetery.

Muir's journal provides full entries, revisions, and added commentary on life, death, and nature. He criticized conventional society's lessons on these subjects, and through his writing and his time at St. Bonaventure, Muir began to come to terms with his own mortality. The cemetery took on even greater importance in the walk because in Florida Muir had to contend with malaria—a disease he had likely contracted at St. Bonaventure.[293] Muir extensively revised the St. Bonaventure experience in his journal. While principally desperate for money and news from home, he realized much later the significance of the Bonaventure experience in the wake of his struggle with malaria. The journal entries are thus written with extensive revisions, cross-outs, and re-writes that were likely written after leaving Savannah. As such, Muir's reflections on death are likely made in the wake of his experience with malaria and after considerable reflection.

As one steeped in the New Testament, Muir used the language of new eyes and rebirth as a way to explain his experience in the St. Bonaventure Cemetery. While he was there, he listed all the new, wonderful plants he had seen in the South, such as the live oaks of Bonaventure, the level-topped cypress, expanses of black pine, massive heaps of vines, muscadine grapes, the magnolias, and the palmettos. Muir then wrote,

"[A]ll that I hoped to see in the gorgeous fields of topic light, all were forgotten. I gazed in this peerless avenue of inverted forest awestruck as one new born new arrived from another world without past or future, alive only to the presence of the most adorned and most loving of all the tree companies I have ever beheld."[294]

The graveyard was alive! With life! "This Bonaventure," Muir wrote, is "one of the Lords elect most favored abodes of clearest light of life."[295]

With nearly identical wording Muir wrote to Jeanne Carr exploring the implications of his graveyard experience, "I gazed at this peerless avenue as one newly arrived from another planet, without a past or a future, alive only to the presence of the most adorned and living of the tree companies I have ever beheld."[296]

While society called this a graveyard, even gravestones were powerless against the forces of life. Despite the stone memorials to death that surrounded him, Muir saw "depth of life" in the cemetery. "The rippling of living waters, the songs of birds, the cordial rejoicing of busy insects, the calm grandeur of the forest, make it rather one of the Lord's elect and favored field of clearest light and life," he wrote. Muir noted that "Few people have considered the natural beauty of death." Recalling his romps through the countryside with his Sunday school students in Indianapolis and his trek home with Merrill Moores, Muir wrote that a child who grew up in nature would "behold her beautiful and harmonious blends of death and life; their joyous, inseparable unity, and Death will be stingless indeed to him."[297] Here was life evident in the midst of a place devoted to death. Muir began to conclude that civilized people had been misled.

Muir thought that conventional ideas on death were "warped & pitiable." Conventional Christianity, in Muir's view, taught that "death is an Eve made accident, a deplorable punishment for the oldest sin, the Arch enemy of life, etc." He characterized these ideas as "never to be questioned principles, dogmas, ... time honored bones of doctrine, ... cemented, tissue after tissue in hideous development until they form the grimmest body to be found in the whole catalogue of civilized Christian manufactures."[298] Children, he wrote, who are taught these dogmas understand none of the "natural beauties of death." Devoid of contact with wild places and nature, they do not see the "mingling," "the <u>union</u> of life & death so apparent in nature's house." Children see, instead, only death, slaughter, murder among families: Conventional thinking affirms "<u>proper</u> slaughter of flies" for domestic comfort and slaughter of birds "for economy." Society pays little heed to the drowning gurgles of a sack full of kittens, or the dying groans of cattle and squeals of pigs for meat amidst the filth and blood of a slaughterhouse, and even less outrage against murder and war among the human species.[299]

Even the "happy deaths" are surrounded by "groans & tears," with "morbid exultations, burial companies black in cloth & last of all a black burial box smothering tight & a deep hole in a deserted, illumined place haunted by glooms & ghosts of every degree & thus death becomes fearful, abhorrent & the most notable & incredible thing that a wild fanatic hears on death beds is 'I fear not to die.'"[300] Thinking back to his walks with children, Muir wrote:

> But let a child walk with nature, let him behold the beautiful blending & communions of death & life, their joyous inseparable unity as taught in woods & meadows, & plains & mountains, & streams & seas of our blessed lovely star & he will learn that death is stingless indeed & as beautiful as purest life & that the grave has no victory for it never fights, all is in harmony divine.[301]

Religious dogma, in Muir's view, taught that life and death were oppositional forces. In nature, life and death were part of the natural processes. Muir saw life and death linked in a divine harmony in nature. This was Muir's revelation—his new birth, as he had written in his journal: "new born as new arrived from another world."[302] Though he had been temporarily blinded by an accident, Muir found that his walking journey through the South had led to new insights. Through this walk, Muir's worldview deepened and matured. In Kentucky, Muir had experienced nature and its people as welcoming; in Tennessee and North Carolina he had found them challenging; now, in Georgia, Muir began to grapple with the profound relationship between life and death in the context of nature's lessons.

Muir deemed it unnatural to fear death, even in a strange new land. Gravestones were simply a transient human memorial that futilely contended against the forces of nature. "It is interesting to observe how assiduously Nature seeks to remedy these labored art blunders. She corrodes the iron & levels the hillock."[303] Before Muir's own eyes was the evidence of how natural life overwhelms manmade monuments to death. He found it egocentric of the makers and "installers" of these stones to think that human manufactures could hold the inexorable forces of nature at bay. Life, organic life, trumps death. There is no reason for fear. Eden has the final word despite natural obstacles of thorns and fevers.

Muir noted how townspeople gave tacit assent to these notions when they planted brilliant flowers and magnolias at the foot of the headstones. While rain and sun gradually wore away the inscriptions and, indeed, even the stones, mosses grew out of the decaying inscriptions, vines crawled and covered the grave, and birds perched on the stones and sang their songs. This was life overwhelming "Lord Man's" efforts to contend with death.[304]

Spending his first night in the cemetery asleep on a grave underneath a live oak, Muir awoke to the scolding chirps of birds, the screams of nearby eagles, and the "halloas" of African Americans walking out to distant fields. "The deep weariness of excitement made my sleep but little less profound than that of the buried ones around & beneath me," he wrote.[305] Muir watched the "beautiful life" of birds, squirrels, and insects that "inhabit this tropic paradise," and then he walked five miles back to Savannah to check for the arrival of letters and money and to get something to eat. There was no word from home, and he returned to the tombs, where he made a little square shelter under a bed of sparkleberry bushes and out of sight of the cemetery's main roadway with branches, palm fronds, and Spanish moss for a bed. One evening as he lay in his shelter, a reptile crawled across his face; he quickly grasped it and threw it over his head into the sparkleberry bushes.[306] This was the only fright he got while at St. Bonaventure.

Muir returned his third day in Savannah to Adams Express Company. He was becoming suspicious that his $75 packet was being withheld from him, since he knew that his brother had sent it.[307] With money now getting desperately low, he cut his expenses by buying just a few crackers to eat and visiting every mill in Savannah to look for work. No luck. "If worse came to worst I would strike out into the surrounding country & steal corn or rice enough for a living while waiting for that money, in the meantime I cut down my expenses to 3 or 4 cents a day," he wrote.[308] Muir grew faint with hunger.

By the fourth day of his Savannah stay, Muir had learned the calls of many local birds and had noted that domesticated plants return to a primitive and wild state if they are not cultivated or trimmed. Plants, he had observed, accommodated themselves to their environment. This observation occasioned a reflection: "Well perhaps I may yet become a proper cultivator," he wrote; "cease my wild wandering & form a so

64

I had ere this sought for work in all
the mills. & thought of setting out for the fields,
to pick cotton, or shell corn.

On the sixth day I bade a last
farewell to Bonaventure & to all its
glories, held a jubilee of bread
& took passage in the steamer Sylvan
Shore for Fernandina, & thus hand-
somely terminated my "marching
through Georgia." The agent
at last said Yes, the moneys
come, but how am I
to know. You
are John Muir, I said I know
nobody here to testify me, but
look at this letter telling how
much is sent by whom and
to whom. He said Yes. N

My Bonaventure home

called pillar or something in society & repent of my outlawry to society, but if so[,] I must[,] like a revived Methodist[,] learn to love what I hate & to hate what I most intensely & devoutly love."[309] Despite the dilemma, Muir cemented his commitment to the study of natural areas and wild places. He had no intention of settling down as a farmer; he would remain an "outlaw to society."

By his sixth day in Savannah, Muir was down to just 25 cents. He became light headed with hunger: The road seemed to rise before him, the streams appeared to run uphill, and he staggered into town.[310] Still worried that the express office was withholding his letters, he prepared himself to argue for his right to the money.

A package addressed to John Muir had arrived. The clerk asked Muir for identification, and Muir handed him his brother's letter, which stated the amount of money in the package, where it came from, and the day it was put into the mail at Portage.

Muir wryly declared, "I should think that would be enough."[311]

Unimpressed, the clerk said, "No, that is not enough. How do I know that this letter is yours? You may have stolen it. How do I know that you are John Muir?" Muir shot back: "Well, don't you see that this letter indicates that I am a botanist? For in it my brother says, 'I hope you are having a good time and finding many new plants.'" He defended his right to the letter and the money, arguing that even if he had stolen it, he could not have stolen John Muir's knowledge of botany. Muir challenged the clerk to examine his knowledge of botany.[312]

The clerk laughed "good naturedly," impressed with Muir's logic, and maybe feeling a little pity, given Muir's gaunt and pale face.

Turning around, the clerk knocked on a supervisor's door. He told his boss that on each day since Muir's arrival in

Savannah, the visitor had asked about a package from Portage, Wisconsin. He said that Muir knew the amount of money in the packet and that he also knew the name of the sender. The letter said Muir was a botanist, and to prove his identity, Muir wanted to be examined in botany.[313]

Smiling, the supervisor looked into Muir's face, waved his hand, and said, "Let him have it."[314]

Relieved, Muir pocketed his money, left the office, walked about fifty feet and bought some gingerbread from a large African-American woman. Gleefully, Muir ate his gingerbread while striding down the street.[315] The following day he bought a steamship ticket for the regularly scheduled departure of the *Sylvan Shore*, to Fernandina, Florida. Muir's difficult time in Georgia had come to an end.

In Georgia, John Muir had become more than a collector of plants; he had become an observer of the human condition and one who thought deeply about nature. The challenge of Georgia was not just Muir's encounter with strange plants, strange winds and a strange climate. The walk, and Muir's reflections on his experience in St. Bonaventure Cemetery, had begun to transform the young man's worldview. Along the way, he contended with the consequences of war and the problems of the freedmen in the context of Reconstruction. While engaged in conversations with white Southerners, Muir steered a course around politics when that topic intruded upon the purpose of his journey. He had been critically low on funds, had not been able to find work, and had been hungry. Feeling marginalized in the city of Savannah, Muir had retreated to a cemetery and discovered it was full of life—surely an ironic observation. Although Muir had already contended with human challenges, in Georgia he confronted the problem of death within the context of nature. His positive view of nature as Eden was squarely challenged by the strangeness of Georgia's flora and fauna, with the state's "cat plants" and reptiles. His experiences in Georgia challenged a naïve view of nature as predominantly benevolent. Death had its natural beauty. Children could learn from this beauty. What could adult humans learn from it? In St. Bonaventure, Muir learned that nature trumped society's false and dogmatic notions of death, which emphasized a false dichotomy. Instead, death was part of a divine harmony, not something to be feared.

As meaningful as his interactions with Georgians and with the state's "new" plants were; Muir's thoughts on life and death deepened as a result of his experiences in Georgia. He concluded that nature was characterized by balance and harmony, not a simplistic dichotomy between the life and death. From Muir's perspective, civilization—villages, towns, and cities with their disorderly and filthy conditions—was problematic. One became more awakened to life in nature. Thus, one's spiritual reverence for life and sense of the presence of God was found in nature more easily than in communities. Nature provided "signs of worship," such as its waving grasses. In his view, civilization had promoted morbid views of death, with mourners erecting temporary monuments, the gravestones, in vainly trying to contend with its power. Nature was all about an even more powerful source: life itself. Muir, therefore, found himself radically at odds with conventional thinking; he became, in his words, "an outlaw to society."

The educational implications of his thoughts suggested that children go to nature to observe, to learn and to emerge from childhood confident and unafraid of death. War, slaughterhouses, robbery, murder, and the attempted dominance of nature by slashing, cutting, trimming, and domesticating were paths to death. As Muir further awakened to nature, his perspective on death changed. Life and death were part of nature where, following Humboldt, Muir concluded that "all is harmony divine." This was a transformational moment in Muir's thousand-mile Southern walk.

The implications of his insights would be worked out during Muir's walk through Florida and his personal near-death experience. In Florida, death became not an objective topic of reflection as it had been in Savannah, but a subjective, existential experience. Muir's learning and growth continued to deepen.

More than adaptability, John Muir gained a vision of a life in an environment he found "strange" and unfamiliar. This vision matured, developed, and became more radical during his walk through Florida, but his transformational moment began with his experience at St. Bonaventure. The transformation became more deeply engaged by his personal encounter with disease and with death itself in the forms of the dreaded malaria and a hungry alligator.

# 6

# FLORIDA: A "STRANGE" LAND AND SHARPENED THOUGHT

The *Sylvan Shore* steamed into "rickety" Fernandina, Florida, on the morning of 15 October 1867, John Muir's forty-fifth day of travel. The regularly scheduled half-day trip along the inland coast avoided extensive swamps that were impassable for a walker. Instead of being on foot, Muir gazed out over a smooth, watery passage adjacent to low islands, estuaries, and mangrove swamps. For some time Muir had looked forward to passing through Florida, this "land of flowers." He described his journey on the steamer as "a flat, watery, reedy coast, with clumps of mangrove and forests of moss-dressed, strange trees appearing low in the distance."[316] Florida was unlike any land he had previously experienced.

The "strangeness" that Muir encountered with the plant life and winds in Georgia only deepened in Florida. He delighted in the lovely magnolia and tulip trees and was fascinated with the palmetto. Moreover, Florida was a land not only of tropical flowers but of the alligator, too. How did this predatory "evil," which could snap up an unwary walker, fit into an Edenic nature? Moreover, poverty, disease, muddy and dirty people were abundantly apparent; how did they fit into this watery tropic of flowers? The journey was not just an observational tour. Muir's experience seemed at odds with the cultural presuppositions he had heard his entire life from his preacher father, from farmers of the Wisconsin prairies, and from urbanites who viewed nature as a warehouse of resources rather than as an existing presence with its own reasons for being. The walk through Florida forced Muir to sharpen his thoughts about how humans should view nature. This process generated new lines of thinking that shaped his engagement with the environment for the rest of his life.

After disembarking from the *Sylvan Shore*, Muir walked quickly through the town of Fernandina into the swamps and pine forests of Florida, following a railroad track.

> Everything in earth and sky had an impression of strangeness; not a mark of friendly recognition, not a breath, not a spirit whisper of sympathy came from anything about me, and of course I was lonely. I lay on my elbow eating my bread, gazing, and listening to the profound strangeness.[317]

Muir felt lonely, anxious, and hungry.

Fernandina, adjacent to the Florida-Georgia state line on the Atlantic Ocean at the mouth of the St. John's River, had become the site of a newly established cross-state railroad that had been built in 1861 by David Levy Yulee and slave labor.[318] Muir needed the railroad bed to make the walk across the state. The track cut across north Florida through Gainesville to Cedar Key on the Gulf of Mexico. The railroad cut shipping costs and time in comparison with the slower sail around the Florida peninsula.

As one of the best harbors in Eastern Florida, Fernandina became a target by the US Navy for blockade and supply of Confederate forces during the Civil War. The blockade became increasingly effective from 1862 to the war's end. While Fernandina was occupied, a union-organized tax commission auctioned properties of Confederate sympathizers who were delinquent in paying property taxes. As a result, southern Unionists and freedmen bought lots and properties including David Yulee's Florida Central Railroad.[319] At the end of the war, Southerners sought to retrieve their properties through "redemption." Yulee had been imprisoned as a Confederate sympathizer, but he was released in spring 1866. Shortly thereafter, he sought to reorganize his railroad by making it a functioning enterprise.[320] Yulee's efforts at "redemption" created turmoil at the railheads over land titles. Delay in the settlement of his claims was complicated by the sale of his assets to New York investors during the war years—and by the year he spent in jail in Pulaski, Georgia, for his lukewarm support for the Confederacy.

Fernandina's population of about 1,600 whites and 959 "colored" people (a term used in the census) was in turmoil over the legitimacy of these auctions and unclear titles in 1867.[321] With a Republican administration approving the Congressional Reconstruction Act, in early 1867, President Johnson's sympathy for the Southerners' redemption of their properties was stalemated by military occupation.[322]

Fernandina's sheriff, working on behalf of white redemptioners, attempted to serve "writs of ejectment" on African American freedmen and squatters living on railroad and town land in January 1867. According to Jerrell H. Shofner, a historian of the episode, "He was resisted by tax sale purchasers who claimed that only the United States courts and the tax commission had jurisdiction."[323] Using ex-Confederates, the sheriff formed a *posse comitatus* to enforce evictions. This posse met forceful resistance from a group that included, as one observer wrote, "nearly all the colored men in Town ... armed with pistols, guns, rifles, axes, etc: greatly out-numbering the sheriff's posse. The greatest excitement prevailed."[324]

Similar incidents broke out in September 1867, and again in January and October 1868, after Muir passed through Fernandina. Rancor rose in the town as sizeable numbers of unemployed men and angry freedmen agitated about their land titles. Muir likely felt this tension because he hurriedly left the area. Muir followed the existing railroad bed, occasionally lunging through the brackish water to examine a plant. On the whole, he found the swamps and thorny vines would have

119

made for a difficult walk had it not for the relief of a railroad embankment and right of way.

As Muir approached a "close forest of trees" near the outskirts of Fernandina, he heard a "rustling sound in the rushes behind me." Fearing an alligator, Muir later wrote, "I fancied I could feel the stroke of his long notched tail, and could see his big jaws and rows of teeth, closing with a springy snap on me, as I had seen in pictures." The rustling turned out to be simply "a tall white crane, handsome as a minister from spirit land—'only that.' I was ashamed and tried to excuse myself on account of Bonaventure anxiety and hunger."[325] The combination of Muir's serious thoughts about his mortality, the strangeness of the terrain, and the predatory reptiles unnerved Muir.

In his first hours on the road, Muir stayed close to the track, "gazing into the mysterious forest, Nature's own." As he walked along it, he found "new, canelike grass," big lilies, and gorgeous flowers on both trees and vines. Splashing into the "coffee-brown" water, he lunged for new specimens, wading in deeper and deeper until he was compelled to turn back. He wrote, "I was overwhelmed with the vastness and un-approachableness of the great guarded sea of sunny places."[326]

Muir acknowledged that he had explored only within a few hundred yards of the track's right of way. Water was everywhere, and, if there was no water, "Oftentimes I was tangled in a labyrinth of armed vines like a fly in a spider-web."[327] Muir discovered pine trees, purple liatris and cinnamon fern. While he was impressed with magnolia trees, his "grandest discovery of this great, wild day was the palmetto."[328] The sight of a palmetto moved him to draw its picture in his journal, together with a portrait of himself, wearing beard and hat, carrying his plant-press and a large palm leaf in his left hand, with his right hand raised in salutation.[329] The palmetto Muir had found was about twenty-five-feet tall, with fifteen to twenty leaves, each ten feet in length with a blade four feet in diameter and a stalk about six feet long. The leaves, closely gathered at the top, formed "an oval crown over which tropic light is poured and reflected from its slanting mirrors in sparks and splinters and long-rayed stars."[330] The light, the crown, the soft sounds of wind blowing through its leaves impressed Muir. He wrote, "They tell us that plants are perishable, soulless creatures, that only man is immortal, etc; but this, I think, is something that we know very nearly nothing about." Muir found the palm "indescribably impressive" and wrote that it "told me grander things than I ever got from human priest."[331]

Muir's delight in this new, strange world was palpable in his end-of-the-day prayer of gratitude:

> Well, I am now in the hot gardens of the sun, where grows the palm longed & prayed for & often visited in dreams, &, though lonely to-night in this multitude of strangers, plants of a strange kingdom, strange winds blowing (gently, whispering, cooing,) in a language I never learned, & strange birds also, everything solid or spiritual are full of influences that I never felt before, but I thank the Lord my Maker with all my heart for his goodness in granting me admission to this magnificent realm of sunshiney plant peoples.[332]

It is clear that Muir's encounter with this strange, new world provoked powerful reflections that elevated the Book of Nature while, at the same time, dethroning traditional sources of religious authority and humans who valued nature only as a resource. In this regard, Muir was moving deliberately away from the priorities of his father's utilitarian and conventional religious perspective on nature. Muir saw nature with "new eyes" and experienced it with new feelings. His uncomfortable journey through Florida provoked insights into humanity's relationship to the natural world; it also challenged his presuppositions about the extent to which this hostile, tropical

*"{Cabbage Palmetto} my first specimen near Fernandina"*

Picture of Muir and a palmetto, JMP 23:73 [, John Muir Papers, Holt-Atherton Special Collections,
University of the Pacific Library. Copyright 1984 Muir-Hanna Trust

world conformed to the depiction of Eden in Milton's *Paradise Lost*. Nature could be glorious, but it drew blood. What was Muir to make of the paradox, and how did this apparent contradiction fit into the image of Nature as Eden?

Around 10 p.m., Muir sought out a dry place to lie down and found a small, "precious" hillock. His meal was dry bread and coffee-brown water. He fell asleep amidst the hoots of owls and the strange rustles and splashes of nearby waters.

Muir arose the next morning, "cold and wet with dew," but now without bread or breakfast; he struck out to look for both a house and "the grand assemblies of novel plants." He came upon a rough group of loggers who shared their meal of yellow pork and hominy. Walking along the track, he ran into a group of three men and their hostile dogs. The dogs viciously attacked Muir, who later wrote that they were undertaking "to undress me with their teeth." Once the men had the dogs under control, Muir shared their meal of liver pie, sweet potatoes and "fat duff."[333] Florida was proving to be a difficult walk despite the ease of the route.

Throughout the day Muir encountered alligator tracks and evidence of their wallows. At one site, a man declared, "See, what a track that is! He must have been a mighty big fellow. Alligators wallow like hogs and like to lie in the sun. I'd like a shot at that fellow." Another man reported a battle between a four-foot alligator and the man's dog and told how, in rescuing his dog, he had sustained a bite from the alligator.[334] While Muir reported seeing only one alligator during his entire trip, the reptiles were clearly a source of anxiety.

The 'gators were not only strange and mysterious animals; Muir heard about a natural antipathy between them and men. Sometimes 'gators attacked boats, and Muir was worried that he might accidentally step on the back of one of these thinking it was a log. This anxiety led to a remarkable observation by Muir in which he inverted the great chain of being, in which humans claimed "dominion" over nature. Instead, in Muir's judgment, humans became an equal part of nature, thus laying an ethical foundation for respecting the rights of all of nature for its continued existence including that of the alligator. For example, he wrote:

> Many good people believe that alligators were created by the Devil, thus accounting for their all-consuming appetite and ugliness. But doubtless these creatures are happy and fill the place assigned them by the great Creator of us all. Fierce and cruel they appear to us, but beautiful in the eyes of God. They, also, are his children, for He hears their cries, cares for them tenderly, and provides their daily bread.[335]

Muir leveled the playing field between the human and the animal world. Nature provided equality of condition and access to the Creator. Muir believed that even alligators issued silent prayers to God for food.

How then to explain the "natural antipathies" between man and 'gator? Muir drew an analogy from the magnetic properties of the "mineral kingdom." Antipathies among animals "must be wisely planned," he wrote. Humans had "narrow," "selfish," and "conceitful" sympathies and were "blind to the rights of all the rest of creation." They spoke with "dismal irreverence" of "our fellow mortals." Like positive and negative forces in minerals, alligators and snakes "naturally repel us." Yet "they are not mysterious evils." Alligators "dwell happily in these flower wilds, are part of God's family, unfallen, undepraved, and cared for with the same species of tenderness and love as is bestowed on angels in heaven or saints on earth."[336] In this keen and generous observation, Muir moved toward a worldview that affirmed the "rights of creation." For Muir, pure, unspoiled Nature remained a garden of innocence.

Muir wrote in his conclusion, "I think that most of the antipathies which haunt and terrify us are morbid productions of ignorance and weakness. I have better thoughts of those alligators now that I have seen them at home." He ended his thoughts with a benediction: "Honorable representatives of the great saurians of an older creation, may you long enjoy your lilies and rushes, and be blessed now and then with a mouthful of terror-stricken man by way of dainty!"[337]

Following this passage is a startling sketch of two alligators. One 'gator is looking upon the other from a sunny bank. The other in the water has a man between its teeth; both alligators are surrounded by rushes and water.

Despite his fears and anxieties about alligators, Muir wished them well. His picture does not reveal a bearded man; hence, it is likely that John Muir did not imagine himself to be food for the alligators—though he felt fear along with his curiosity. Whatever ill will existed between humans and alligators was a production not of God (or the Devil), but one of human ignorance and witless fear.

Florida's thick canopy of leaves and vines created a strange, dark forest floor. While light pierced the woods and forests of the north, scarcely a plant could grow in the shade of Florida forests. "All the flowers, all the verdure, all the glory is up in the light," Muir wrote.[338] Rivers and streams also seemed strange. Unlike those in the north, the streams of Florida "are not yet possessed of banks and braes and definite channels." Florida swamps were black as ink; "glossy...as if varnished"; no one could be certain of the direction of their flow "or [their] creeping."[339] "The flowers here are strangers to me, but not more so than the rivers and lakes," Muir wrote. Most rivers in the north channeled their way to the sea, but Florida's rivers "do not appear to be traveling at all, and seem to know nothing of the sea."[340] For Muir, Florida opened up a new way of thinking about nature, with its strange flowers, rivers, trees and animals. This encounter led to new thoughts about how limited and vulnerable he felt in the midst of so much unfamiliarity. Exotic Florida challenged much that he had previously experienced in nature.

seen them at home - honored representatives of the great saurians of an
older creation, May you long enjoy always be
happy among your lilies & rushes
& be blessed with now & then with a mouth
ful of terror-stricken men by way of
dainty.

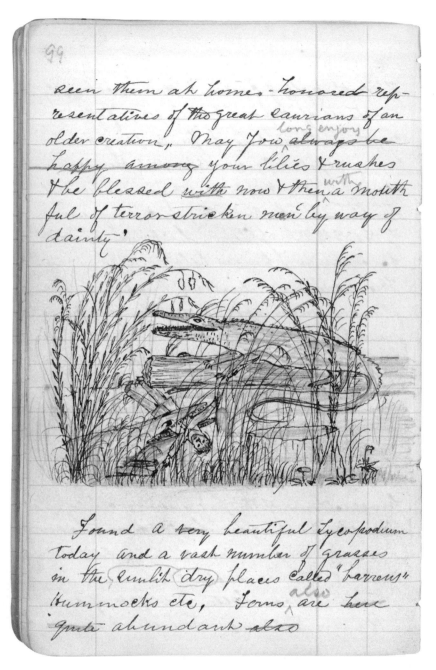

Found a very beautiful Lycopodium
today and a vast number of grasses
in the sunlit dry places called "barrens"
Hummocks etc, Ferns are here also
quite abundant also

*Two alligators and "a mouthful of terror stricken man"*

Through this journey in Florida, Muir began to construct a new vision and worldview regarding his and, possibly, humanity's relationship with nature. He pondered the idea of life and death "in divine harmony." These were the beliefs that all of nature had its own purposes for being, the concept that human ignorance and arrogance were the reasons for humans deciding what was "useful" and what was not. At the root of the problem was ignorance of God's "divine harmony and human arrogance." These were a set of profound insights gained from a difficult journey.

Muir was taking his first steps toward enhancing the power of his writing, deepening his own understanding, and crafting original and new insights. Muir gave direction to his life by sharpening his thought and his vision and honing the tools of his literary craft through the daily discipline of journal-writing. Through his experiences and reflections, Muir was transforming his own thoughts about humanity's relationship to the environment from a utilitarian to an ecological perspective and from an anthropocentric view to a bio-centric view.[341]

Muir's travel the next day, October 18, was almost entirely on dry land. He noted both the magnificent magnolias and the dirt-poor people living in huts along the railroad right-of-way. Many were squatters that Yulee, the railroad builder, wanted to evict from land that he considered his. As time went by, Yulee was able to exact rent with the help of the state and county court system.[342] Some people Muir encountered appeared to him to be covered with layers of dirt on both their persons and their clothing—with these "regularly stratified layers" "indicating different periods of life." In his view, "Man and other civilized animals are the only creatures that ever become dirty."[343] The houses of the poorer Floridians lacked the tidy gardens of thyme and honeysuckle common in the north. The owners' Southern hospitality was genuine, however, and people offered to share what little they had with Muir.

While traveling late at night, about three or four miles east of Gainesville, Muir saw a bright light in the forest. Thirsty after a long trek, he thought water might be available at this site. Not knowing if it might be an encampment of "robber negroes," he crept up to the bonfire in the pinewoods and saw a black man and woman. "I could see their ivory gleaming from the great lips, and their smooth cheeks flashing off light as if made of glass."[344] The couple stared at him and then offered a gourd of water. The three exchanged pleasantries, and Muir asked about the road to Gainesville. Then he noticed a black lump near the fire. The woman bent over the mound and "with motherly kindness" called to her little boy, "Come, honey, eat yo' hominy."[345] A naked boy rose from the earth. "Had he emerged from the black muck of a marsh, we might easily have believed that the Lord had manufactured him like Adam direct from the earth," Muir wrote.[346] He took this occasion to comment on the disparity between nature and humans. Aware that Milton had called clothing "troublesome disguises," he noted that the climate in Florida was one in which clothing was not needed; nonetheless, birds made nests for their young as did almost all beasts of the forest, "but these negroes allow their younglings to lie nestless and naked in the dirt dust."[347] Touched by his experience with this black family, Muir drew a picture of the couple with the young boy in his journal.[348]

Muir pressed on, eventually arriving in Gainesville at 9 o'clock that night, finding food and lodging in a tavern. He thought Gainesville "rather good looking—an oasis in the desert, compared with other villages."[349] Noting the "several thrifty cotton plantations," the abundant use of limestone, flint, and coral, and the area's comfortable residences, Muir observed that these homes stood in stark contrast with the impoverished housing he had seen from Fernandina to Gainesville.

Things that we know are connected
with things that we do not know
There is that in the glance of
a flower *may at times* *the greatest*
which controls *frequently*
the whole mind of Creations braggart
Lord

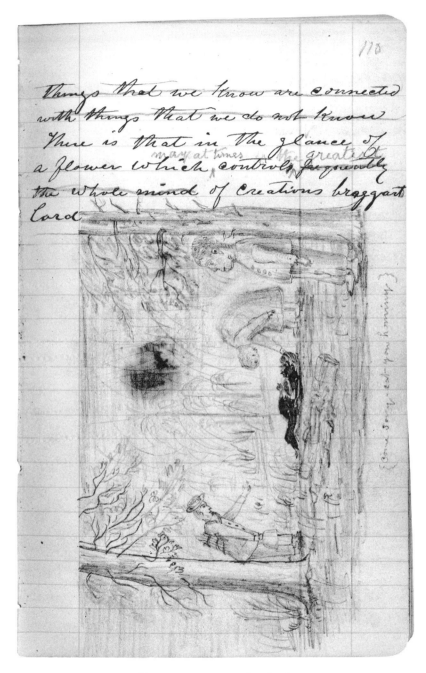

{Come sonny eat your hominy}

*"Come sonny eat your hominy"*
Picture of Muir and Black couple with boy, JMP 23:84, John Muir Papers, Holt-Atherton
Special Collections, University of the Pacific Library. Copyright 1984 Muir-Hanna Trust

The county seat was founded in 1853 and named after a Seminole Indian War general, Edmund P. Gaines, Gainesville had a population of 269 in 1860. Laid out in an eight-block grid around a two-story wooden courthouse situated in the central square, the town had a general store and three hotels. Town growth was due to expansion of cotton processing plants. While having fewer people than Fernandina in 1867, Gainesville grew rapidly, to 1,444 people, in 1870.[350] The railway provided transportation for cotton and citrus harvests. The first schools opened in 1866, with the Gainesville Academy and the African-American Union Academy being dedicated in 1867, shortly before Muir's arrival. While on the cusp of growth, Gainesville was a relatively small county seat when Muir passed through. Preferring not to spend too much time in the village, Muir walked on toward the west and Cedar Key, still following the track.[351]

Along the way, Muir found a "handsome little plant" that brought to him a strong recollection of "a young friend" [Merrill Moores], with whom he had botanized before he began his walk. The memory provoked by a plant took his breath away. "How wonderfully our thoughts and impressions are stored," he wrote. "There is that in the glance of a flower which (may at times) control frequently (the greatest) of creation's braggart Lord."[352] The rest of the day Muir continued to note groves of magnolia, polygonums, petalostelmons, yellow vines, long leaf and Cuban pines, grasses, goldenrods, and lime trees. About noon he stopped at a hut for a meal. The couple within appeared to be suffering from malaria, and he depicted them as "very dirty." The dirt, Muir noted, "appeared to stand out a little on contact like a hazy, misty, half-aerial mud envelope, the most diseased and incurable dirt that I ever saw, evidently desperately chronic and hereditary."[353] He wondered, as he'd mused earlier, if he could tell the age of each person by the layers of dirt on his or her skin. That same evening Muir found his bed in the dirt beside a log. He dared not start a fire for fear of robbers. He wrote that he was lonely. There was no companion who could provide comfort or conversation. Scrambling around the edges of slimy pools to quench his thirst, he drank swamp water, moving away from each pool quickly for fear of alligators. Awakening the next morning, October 20, Muir found himself dripping wet with the night's dew.[354]

On this day Muir passed through some "very dense" and extensive swamps. Streams meandered in every direction. Muir saw "an alligator splash in the sedgy brown water by the roadside from an old log."[355] Apparently this was his first and only such sighting.

He found housing at the home of the recently married Captain H.C. Simmons, whom Muir described as "one of the few scholarly, intelligent men that I have met in Florida."[356] A former Confederate officer, Simmons was "prejudiced against the North," especially in matters of race and politics, but Muir switched topics to birds, animals, the climate, and what the seasons were like in Florida. Simmons took a liking to Muir, as frequently happened with Muir in his encounters with strangers. Being an enthusiastic hunter, Simmons urged Muir to stay a while and join him in a deer hunt. Muir wanted to see alligators. His host reported that there were large alligators nearby and that some could be spotted as they went out to sea. Local lore said they attacked fishing boats. Of more interest to Muir, Simmons said there was a magnificent grove of palmetto trees, but the way to them led through difficult briars, thickets, deep pools, and swamps. In the end Muir decided to stay a day to see the palm grove rather than hunt.[357]

Simmons walked with Muir through his cornfield to point out the general direction of the palm grove. He warned Muir about the region's tangled thickets of briars; that the paths through them were angular and hidden; and that he should avoid swamps and deep water. With some difficulty, Muir made his way to the extensive palm grove. He reveled in its beauty. Muir quoted Linnaeus in calling palms, "the princes of the vegetable world." He enthused about this "sun-drenched palm garden," writing, "I walked enchanted in their midst. What landscape! Only palms as far as the eye could reach!" He wrote about the "smooth pillars rising from the grass," with "each capped with a sphere of leaves, shining in the sun as bright as a star." Comparing this Florida experience with his experience in Canada, he wrote, "the silence and calm were as deep as ever I found in the dark, solemn pine woods of Canada." He noted that his "contentment" was as "impressively felt in this alligator wilderness as in the homes of the happy, healthy people of the North."[358]

The strangeness of Florida's environment forcefully struck Muir. While the tops of the palms shined like crowns, alligators lurked in inky waters. Both were symbols not always far from Muir's observations and reflections. He found noteworthy beauty in both, but for different reasons.

In his judgment, alligators were not essentially evil; conventional thinking simply misunderstood the role of predatory animals in the balance of nature. The palm represented stately nobility that symbolizes an elegant and divine beauty and exudes a spirituality of God's presence. Having been steeped in biblical literature, Muir was aware of the palm's use as a symbol of adoration for Jesus' triumphal entry into Jerusalem in the New Testament. It was his memory of certain biblical passages that may have driven him to seek out a plant that was unknown to him except in Bible stories or Milton's *Paradise Lost*.

Muir was more critical of the human conditions he encountered along the railroad tracks than he was of nature. In his view, many of the Floridians he encountered tended to be untidy, even dirty, and, for the most part, uneducated. If this were not the case, he wrote, they harbored fixed prejudices. If they enjoyed some measure of education and wealth, such as

about from six to twelve inches dia
This stem is of equal thickness at
top & bottom, & when young is
covered with the broken petioles but
as they become old the petiole stumps
disappear & the trunk becomes smooth
as if turned in the Lathe

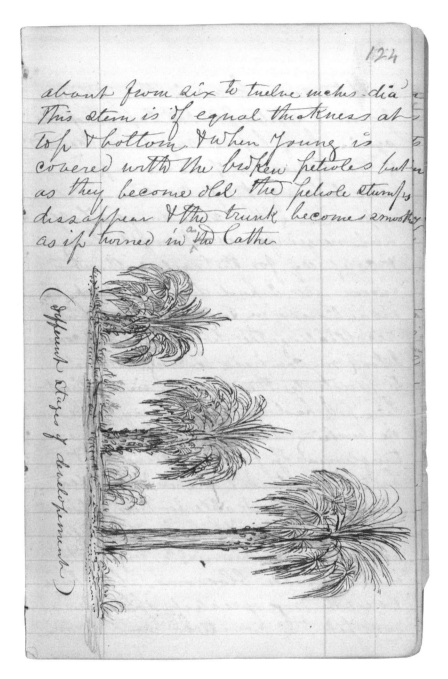

(Different stages of development)

*"(Different stages of development)"*

Capt. Simmons, they often were prejudiced, and they killed animals for sport. As for poor blacks, it seemed, based on his experience with the African-American couple outside Gainesville, that they lived in squalor, dirt, and rags. Clearly, Muir did not fully understand the desperate poverty of African Americans in post-Civil War Florida.

Thus, he contrasted the "innocence" of the wild nature with the "civilized" people who lived in homes, huts and the woods along the way suffering through postwar turmoil and poverty. In some measure, Muir saw what he wanted to see, but the encounter with this strangeness focused and sharpened his reflections on both the value of wilderness and the problems associated with human habitations and civilization.

Having little understanding of the legacies of slavery, race relations, postwar dislocation, and personal loss, Muir gave cursory attention to the human plights to which he bore passing witness. How do African-American parents learn to take care of their children when their masters had borne this responsibility for generations? How does a young black man earn money if he doesn't have a paying job? How does he *get* a job when his former master is bankrupt? When there was work, even the worst jobs, such as logging, went to white laborers. One cannot fault Muir for his lack of attention to these realities, for he was focused on other matters. But he did note in Tennessee the legacy of the marks of war on people's faces. In Florida he thought more about his fears than he did of the desperation that he confronted in the faces of the people he met during his walk from Fernandina to Gainesville.

While not entirely aware of the desperation of both the poor and well-to-do he encountered in Florida, Muir faced significant personal trials in his slog to the palmetto grove. Worried that he might have to spend an evening in the swamps, Muir made the decision to leave the palm grove early in the afternoon of October 21 because he knew that the return journey would be difficult. Deciding to follow a compass line directly through the swamps, he soon found himself tangled in knotted vines with "interlocking and lancing prickers." He wrote, "I had a sore weary time in pushing through the tanglements of fallen & standing & half-fallen trees."[359] Not wanting to spend the night in the swamp with mosquitoes and the alligators he feared, Muir sought out the return path through the "cat briers."[360] He kept straight to his bearing, only occasionally diverted by an unusual plant. Wading through opaque water, Muir fretted about stepping on alligators, and he cautiously placed each footstep, ready to spring away should he need to. Some lagoons were so deep that he took several different directions to work his way through them. Eventually, "after miles of wading and wallowing," Muir came upon the dreaded briar "encampment." He could not find the return trail as the sun dropped to the horizon. For a while, he thought of spending the night in a tree platform, but he decided to push on. After another mile of reconnoitering the briars, "perspiring and bleeding," he found "the blessed trail" and "escaped to dry land and the light" just as the sun was setting. Captain Simmons congratulated Muir on his successful return and his "woodcraft" skills. After a meal of milk, johnny cake, and fresh venison, the weary traveler fell into a deep sleep.[361]

On the next morning, October 22, Simmons invited Muir to hunt deer. Muir enjoyed the walk through tall grasses, but not the hunt. He startled one deer, but "did not draw a single shot." "To me it appeared as 'd—dest' work to slaughter God's cattle for sport."[362] "While," he wrote, "some 'preachers' might argue that deer were made 'for us,' 'our food, our recreation, or other uses not yet discovered,' what of bears who end up dispatching 'the unfortunate hunter?'" Turning the prevailing viewpoint about hunting on its head, Muir wrote that "Men and other bipeds were made for bears [to eat], and thanks be to God for claws and teeth so long."[363] Like alligators, bears, in Muir's mind, fulfilled a divine purpose. Muir went on to engage in a remarkable reflection that inverted the order of dominion as prescribed by conventional religious reasoning and authority (this too bears his hand at revision):

> Let a Christian hunter go to the Lord's groves & kill his well kept beasts, or wild Indians, and it is well; but let an enterprising specimen of these proper, predestined victims go among rectangular houses & fields and kill the most worthless person of the vertical godlike killers—O[!] that is horridly unorthodox & on the part of the Indians atrocious murder. Well I have precious little sympathy for the ~~myriad~~ bat eyed proprieties of civilized man, & if a war of races should occur between the wild beasts and Lord Man, I would be tempted to ~~side~~ sympathize with the bears.[364]

Thus, for Muir, predatory animals balanced predatory human beings. Given some of his encounters with the inhabitants of Florida, whether the impoverished dwellers of huts, careless farmers, or prejudiced hunters and soldiers who had participated in the Civil War, he had little sympathy with "Lord Man" who, in this environment, was anything but lordly.

John Muir's walk along Yulee and the slaves' railroad brought him into contact with a nature he found "strange." Nature bore fangs and drew blood. Its poisonous and predatory reptiles silently sought out victims, including the unwary Lord Man. Nature was an active force that could thwart Lord Man's attempts to tame it. Muir's Edenic view of nature as benevolent was challenged by the obstacles of swamps, cat briars, and randomly flowing and opaque streams. Muir's Florida encounter focused on two images. The palmetto became a sign of "worship," with the sun glinting off its fronds, waving in the soft Florida breezes. The alligator was another matter, but Muir sharpened his thought to include the alligator as a creature of divine creation. But the ultimate problem was with Lord Man, who dimly understood the importance of the alligator in nature's balance between its negative and positive charges. There, indeed, was an order; but, self-interest, pride, arrogance, and ignorance distorted Lord Man's understanding of creation as in the example of the alligator. Despite Muir's obvious fear of alligators, he thought more highly of alligators and bears than he did of the some of the people and villages through which he passed.

In contrast to Lord Man's presumptive separation of plants, minerals, and animals useful to his interest, John Muir viewed nature as a system, "a divine harmony" that humans would do well to understand. Thus, the alligator was not a Satanic predator, though it was deemed as such by Lord Man; instead, it was a creature of God's creation, living for its own reasons apart from the interests of Lord Man. The alligator's cries and prayers for food were heard by God, and every now and then even Lord Man became an alligator's dinner. Muir's engagement with nature in Florida had sharpened his thought. He was shifting from an anthropocentric view of nature that considered human beings to be the most significant entity in the universe to a Bio-centric view that considered all forms of life as having intrinsic value. After all, it was God, not Lord Man, who created nature and the system of divine harmony. Humans needed a good dose of humility before they arrogantly separated the useful from the useless in nature and the "good gifts" of God from the world's "evil" predators.

Even more problematic than nature's obstacles to Muir's travels was his encounter with the human condition and settlements he found in Florida in 1867. Muir's disdain for human civilization, as he experienced it, would be further reinforced in the next stage of his journey as he walked his way to Cedar Key and the Gulf of Mexico.

7

# CEDAR KEY: MALARIA, DELAY, AND DETOUR

*"inexorable leaden numbness"—John Muir, 1868*

Catching whiffs of salt air from the Gulf of Mexico miles before he came to Florida's west coast, John Muir strode into Cedar Key on October 23, his fifty-third day of travel. Just as a flower reminded him of botanizing with Merrill Moores, salt air reminded him of Dunbar, Scotland, nineteen years earlier, and provoked memories of his hometown. In his mind's eye, Muir recalled the "dulse & tangle & long winged gulls & the Bass Rock & the Firth of Forth & the old castle, schools, churches & long country rambles in search of bird nests." He marveled at this distant memory—now so vivid— writing, "How imperishable are all the impressions that ever vibrate one's life, we cannot forget anything."[365] Continuing in this vein, he wrote, "What dreams and speculative matter for thought arose as I stood on the strand, gazing out on the burnished, treeless plain!"[366] The memory of Scotland also awakened Muir's dream of traveling to South America—a dream he first had when reading Humboldt.

Muir planned to continue his travel, moving on to South America: the Orinoco, the Andes, and then down a tributary to the Amazon. Eventually, he hoped to go to Africa. How could he do this with no shipping vessels in the Cedar Key harbor? It was unlikely that any ships would come until a load of lumber sufficient for transport became available at the local mill. Muir thought about walking to Tampa or Key West and then getting a ship to Cuba. Or he could wait at Cedar Key, "like Crusoe, and pray for a ship."[367]

Cedar Key had a bustling lumber industry. Misnamed in 1852 by a group of settlers who thought the juniper trees were cedars, the village had 215 residents in thirty households according to an 1860 census and rose to 440 by 1870.[368] Originally located on Astena Otie Key, the village was founded initially as a resort for wealthy planters from Florida and Georgia. In 1846, David Levy Yulee established a 3,200-acre plantation, known as "Margarita," on the nearby Homosassa River. There, with a labor force of about a hundred slaves, he grew sugar and cotton.

In 1861, Yulee also used slaves to build his railroad. It was a monumental effort to construct the 155-mile railroad from Fernandina to Cedar Key through salt marshes, rivers, the spring-filled prairies outside Gainesville, and the pine hummocks leading into Cedar Key. Slaves chopped and slashed through tough, interlocking roots and vines, sweated in low swamp water, tried to avoid wild animals, alligators, and snakes, and contended with hostile Native Americans and anti-railroad landowners.[369] Muir appreciated the drudgery of this work, having dug out oak roots in Wisconsin. He noted that the cabbage palmetto had "a network of brown rusty looking scaly cables, which have to be chopped out inch by inch by the maker of fields & roads." The grubbing of oak roots in Wisconsin "is nothing compared with this toilsomeness & tediousness, the gangs of negro road hands make but slow progress in cutting through palmettos." Even a liberal allowance of whiskey did not speed progress.[370]

It was Yulee who chose Cedar Key rather than Tampa as the railroad's terminus. When the project was completed, the railroad was plagued by its shoddy construction; its right of way was too narrow; its embankments only ten-feet high rather than the required twelve feet; and, its cross ties were improperly laid.[371] It had just been completed when the Civil War broke out, threatening Yulee's investment and the landowner's interests that he ardently sought to protect.

During the Civil War, Union forces blockaded, attacked, and occupied Cedar Key. Marines in Union naval vessels destroyed Yulee's railroad Station No. 4 as well as the salt works and seized the Confederate ship *Curlew*, which attempted to run the blockade in June 1862. The Union occupation of Cedar Key persisted until 1865, with troops housed in the large two-story general store that became the Union barracks.

Yulee was arrested on 18 June 1865 and was sent to Fort Pulaski in Georgia. He denied having actively participated in the Confederate government, saying that his only concern was the welfare of his railroad. Yulee appealed for amnesty from President Andrew Johnson, who referred the case to Secretary of War Edwin Stanton. Though Stanton rejected Yulee's appeal, General Ulysses S. Grant wrote to Johnson on his behalf. On 22 March 1866, Yulee was released on parole.[372]

Yulee tried to re-establish the railroad, but he couldn't make his payments.[373] Since the railroad owned much of the town property at Cedar Key, bitter acrimony and lawsuits broke out as villagers sought to diversify services and economic growth beyond the cotton industry. This entailed raising taxes. These efforts included building a jail, a market, and a swine pen to attract farmers to their market.[374]

When Muir arrived at Cedar Key, African-American freedmen sought labor contracts for railroad work, for work on sugar or cotton plantations, and for work in the citrus orchards near Gainesville. Wages for farm labor stood at about $10 per month, whereas mostly white timber cutters made $20 to $30 per month.[375] Even with low wages, jobs were scarce; the planters had no money. Employment usually went to poor whites, such as the lumbermen. Consequently, there was significant unemployment among African-American freedmen in 1867. Florida's African-American population nearly equaled its white population, at 62,676 blacks to 77,747 whites. In 1870, about one out of four residents in Cedar Key was African

American.[376] Thus, this village was, as Fernandina had been, another source of potential turmoil and friction between freedmen and their white allies and Southerners with ties to the Confederacy. Local observers of Cedar Key, such as Eliza Hearn, were aware of these conditions.

Eliza Hearn, a devout local school teacher, had a dim view of the social and moral conditions of Cedar Key in 1867. Her diary, a repository of creative spelling, is full of complaints against the townspeople and the changes that took place in the social order during the era of Reconstruction. For example, Hearn was critical of African Americans' newfound civil liberties and of their unwillingness to remain deferential and compliant:

> Way Key is a sink of polution and Cedar Key is no better may the Lorde have marcy on them before it is to late is my humble prayer Oh the sad State of this once happy land the negures are permited to vote and tha do not behave as tha should the ablotion party has caused some insurrections in several places tha want to put them on equality with White men.[377]

Hearn reported that sixty thousand Floridian slaveholders had emigrated to South America. A victim of low wages herself, Hearn gave thought to leaving Cedar Key as well. "We want to sell and leave hear but there is no money in the country the people are suffering for bred and We have surfed our selves for I cannot get payed for our work God help us is my prayer."[378] Increasingly, lumber and fishing became the backbone of the economy; but, without a serviceable railroad, interior crops like cotton, pine lumber, and oranges could not get to market. Damage to the rolling stock and wharves was extensive, and repairs were slow. Despite the war's damages to the town, its citizens were making valiant efforts at a recovery centered primarily on the lumber business—although in 1867, lumber milling was in a temporary slump.[379]

Upon his arrival in Cedar Key on October 23, Muir sought work in a lumber mill outside of town on Way Key. The mill was owned, in part, by Richard W. B. Hodgson, who had arrived in Florida from Georgia in the 1850s. He and his wife, Sarah, lived on a knoll about a mile from Cedar Key, on Way Key. Their children were taught by Eliza Hearn.[380] The Hodgsons' spacious home, situated under live oak trees, had a lovely view, especially from its rooftop veranda, of the tidal flats and nearby Lime Key. On Muir's first night in town, Hodgson and his wife invited Muir to lodge with them. He characterized their hospitality as "unconstrained cordiality."

During his first few days with the Hodgsons, Muir heard that a lumber ship might be arriving soon to take cargo to Texas. He planned to be aboard that boat, and from Texas ship to the West Indies and thence to South America. In the meantime, he would work for the Hodgsons and board with their family.

On October 24, Muir's value as a machinist became evident to his new landlord and employer when he correctly balanced a pulley by turning it against a handmade tool. But before he could settle in to the Hodgsons' bunkhouse, he began to feel faint and dizzy.[381] He had contracted malaria, probably while sleeping outside in Savannah's St. Bonaventure Cemetery. While he was on a botany survey along the Cedar Key coast, painful headaches and fever had plagued him. To seek relief, he had plunged into the warm Gulf water. This provided some respite from the fever, but his illness persisted. Within the first few days of his illness, in addition to the fever and headaches that were bothering him, he experienced a sudden craving for lemons.

By the third day of his first attack of malaria, October 26, Muir could not eat—but his craving for citrus fruit intensified. He walked to the village to buy lemons, and entered the Parsons General Store, previously used to house Union troops. There, amidst the rattlesnake and alligator skins that were for sale, he found fresh lemons.[382] As he walked to the lumber camp in the middle of the afternoon, he passed out on the trail. Muir awoke to stars shining above him and found himself "at a loss to know which end of the trail to take." He guessed right and made his way to the lumber camp. "I rose, staggered, and fell, I know not how many times in delirious bewilderment," he wrote. Finally, he stumbled into camp, where the night watchman found him in a heap at the foot of the stairs and thought he was one of many drunken mill workers who weaved their way back from town each Saturday night. At first, the watchman refused to help Muir up the stairs and into bed. The exhausted Muir crawled up the stairs on hands and knees and "tumbled in [to bed] after a desperate struggle." He remained unconscious for "many days."

Fever, and "inexorable leaden numbness" overwhelmed him so that he missed the lumber schooner leaving for Texas. He tried to shake off his illness, but to no avail. "I did not fear any sickness, for I was never sick before, and was unwilling to pay attention to my cloudy feelings but yet heavier & more remorselessly pressed the growing fever, rapidly gaining upon my strength."[383]

Muir's Scottish stoicism almost did him in. He was moved from the barracks to the Hodgson home, "where I was nursed about three months, with unfailing kindness, and to the skill and care of Mr. and Mrs. Hodgson I doubtless owe my life." He was given "quinine and calomel—in sorry abundance— with other milder medicines." The fever became acute, with "night sweats, and my legs became like posts of the temper and consistency of clay on account of dropsy."[384] He was so ill and exhausted that he was unable even to speak.

After several days, when Hodgson asked Muir's attendant if her charge had spoken, the helper said that he hadn't. "Well, you must keep on pouring in quinine. That's all we can do," said Hodgson.[385] Muir remained ill and bedridden from late October until January 1868. This was a close call. Muir was certain that he owed his life to the Hodgson's care.

Muir remained grateful throughout his life for the kindness of the Hodgsons. In an 1898 trip to Savannah and then Miami, Muir visited the Hodgsons' house at Cedar Key. Discovering that the father and son had died, he learned that Sarah Hodgson was now a resident of Archer, Florida. He paid her a visit. Writing to his wife, Louie Strenzel, on 21 November 1898, Muir reported on the visit:

> I asked her if she knew me. She answered no, and asked my name. I said Muir. 'John Muir?' she almost screamed. 'My California John Muir? My California John?' I said, 'Why, yes. I promised to come back and visit you in about twenty-five years, and though a little late I've come.'[386]

It had been thirty-one years since they had last seen each other, and this encounter underscored how Sarah Hodgson had followed Muir's career and, in turn, how Muir had fulfilled his promise of a return visit out of a sense of gratitude for the Hodgsons' assistance during his illness.

Muir's recuperation was slow. When he was finally able to get out of bed, he spent long days outside under a "moss-draped live-oak," writing and revising his journal, especially the section on his time in the Bonaventure cemetery.[387]

In November, Muir was well enough to resume his correspondence with family and friends. He wrote to Jeanne Carr on November 8: "I am just creeping about getting plants and strength after my fever."[388] He thanked her for the letter she had sent him in Gainesville. "Somehow your letters always come when most needed," he wrote. He urged Carr to write him a long letter and forward it to New Orleans. "I shall have to go there for a boat to South America. I do not yet know which point in South America I had better go to. What do you say?"[389] Despite his battle with malaria, Muir was still thinking about the Orinoco and Amazon trip. He finally concluded the letter with his regret that he had not seen one of Carr's friends,

Miss Brooks, of the Bostwich plantation, about 130 miles outside of Savannah. He had passed the plantation and was not able to go back. Writing to his brother David, Muir requested $150 owed him by John Reid so that he could book passage to New Orleans.[390]

Muir's fever remained intermittent, and he had another bout of sickness in December. Writing on December 13, he reported to David, "I am still a prisoner of sickness." He had been feverish three days earlier, had been confined to bed and drenched with night sweats, and had been "insensible." He hoped that "my sound constitution will bear it all." To David, Muir reiterated his plans: "Hope of enjoying the glorious mountains and flower fields of S. America does much to sustain me."[391]

Muir began to investigate the Florida keys in a little skiff, noting juniper, long-leafed pine, and live oaks. The abundant juniper that he mentioned motivated the New Jersey Eberhard Faber Pencil Company to begin harvesting the trees. Muir particularly enjoyed the shorebirds, waders, and herons feeding in the tide-flats near his shade tree. The sharply pointed vegetable "cat" of the Spanish bayonet plant also drew his attention. "By one of these leaves a man might be as seriously stabbed as by an army bayonet, and woe to the luckless wanderer who dares to urge his way through these armed gardens after dark." The plants had no consideration for Lord Man.[392]

The strange and spiky plants of Florida, such as its fanged vines, briars, and bayonet plants, raised problems in Muir's thinking about a "benevolent" nature; so did his anxiety about alligators and, now, his experience with malaria. But the palmetto remained an example for him of nature's glory in Florida. The environment, together with its people, sharpened many ideas to which he was already predisposed. What was one to make of these experiences? The glory of the palmetto that shined in the sun like a royal crown was counterbalanced by the happiness of the alligator whose prayers and petitions

*"{Spanish bayonet} Fla"*

for food were heeded, and might include the dainty morsel of Lord Man. Muir's convalescence allowed him time to reflect on these and other important questions.

What was the meaning of the briars, the lethally sharp Spanish bayonet—and the bears, alligators, mosquitoes that suck the blood of Lord Man? Why were these regions swept by dangerous diseases? Was the world made especially for Lord Man when people drowned in its waters and were poisoned by its minerals, eaten by its predators, and stabbed by its thorny plants? While the coastal region of the keys was relatively healthy in comparison to inland Florida, Muir noted that no southern region was free from malaria, cholera, or yellow fever—afflictions "that come and go suddenly like storms prostrating the population and cutting gaps in it like hurricanes in woods."[393]

It was in the context of this imagery that Muir concluded it was presumptuous for anyone to think that the world was "made especially for man."

> A numerous class of men are painfully astonished whenever they find anything, living or dead, in all God's universe, which they cannot eat or render in some way what they call useful to themselves. They have precise dogmatic insight of the intentions of the Creator, and it is hardly possible to be guilty of irreverence in speaking of *their* God any more than of heathen idols. He is regarded as a civilized, law-abiding gentleman in favor either of a republican form of government or of a limited monarchy; believes in the literature and language of England; is a warm supporter of the English constitution and Sunday schools and missionary societies; and it is as purely a manufactured article as any puppet of a half-penny theater.[394]

Muir was not surprised that people who held views shaped by these presuppositions also held erroneous views of nature. Humans were conceited to think sheep are only "for us." It was presumptuous to assume, before the discovery of Pennsylvania oil, that whales were useful only for producing oil to light darkened stairways. Was iron only for hammers and ploughs? What about lead for bullets? Were such things "all intended for us?" And what about those parts of creation that feed on humans, such as lions, tigers, and alligators "that smack their lips over raw man?" In this vein he wrote:

> Why does water drown its 'Lord Man'? Why do so many minerals poison him? Why are so many plants and fishes deadly enemies? Why is the lord of creation [humankind] subjected to the same laws of life as his subjects? Oh, all these things are satanic, or in some way connected with the first garden.[395]

The questions drove the point home. Muir concluded:

> Now, it never seems to occur to these far-seeing teachers that Nature's object in making animals and plants might possibly be first of all the happiness of each one of them, not the creation of all for the happiness of one. Why should man value himself as more than a small part of the one great unit of creation?[396]

Yes, the universe would be incomplete without humankind, Muir thought, but it is also true that the universe would be incomplete without "the smallest transmicroscopic creatures that dwell beyond our conceitful eyes and knowledge."[397] Muir concluded that the creator made *homo sapiens* from the same material he has used to make every other creature, "however noxious and insignificant to us." These creatures are our fellow mortals—even the alligator; surely the palmetto.

> This star, our own good earth, made many a successful journey around the heavens ere man was made, and whole kingdoms of creatures enjoyed existence and returned to dust ere man appeared to claim them. After human beings have also played their part in Creation's plan, they too may

disappear without any general burning or extraordinary commotion whatever.[398]

Muir's encounter with Florida brought him low. He keenly felt his vulnerability. His brush with death gave him time to think, to rewrite his earlier reflections on death, and to sharpen his own thinking about humans and their relationship with nature. This strangely wonderful, tropical, and exotic "new" land of Florida, with its needle-like plants and animals of fang and claw provoked John Muir's deep reflection about the human condition and humanity's relationship to nature.

The human enterprise appeared to Muir to be fraught with arrogance and conceit. Humans had arrogated to themselves the title "Lord Man," an unmerited title because humans were vulnerable to predatory animals, thorny briars, blood-sucking mosquitoes, and lethal diseases. More than any place on his journey, including the St. Bonaventure cemetery, Florida caused Muir to sense his own vulnerability and come to keen insights. Here he came to understand that humans were but a small part of the planet's history—a small part of the universe. Plants and animals were an equal part of creation, deserving acknowledgment and respect from humans. They had their own reasons for existing. Those reasons were independent of human utilitarian purposes because they fit into a much larger plan of creation than human self-interest. Creation itself responded to laws that had been in existence longer than those established by states or by the actions of humans, whose presence on this planet was but a small part of the earth's history.

What Muir learned in Florida sharpened and deepened his view of nature and his worldview. He clearly is critical of an anthropocentric view of the human enterprise that placed human self-interest above all the created order, and, he affirmed a bio-centric view that all of creation worked within the context of a divine harmony having intrinsic value. All of these natural antipathies between creatures such as men and alligators are the product of a creator whose designs were not exclusively *for* human beings but *with* human beings in divine harmony with all of creation. In his walk through the South, Muir discovered a self at home in the wilderness as well as one vulnerable to a tropical environment. Muir's Florida education in perspective and insight shaped his environmental thinking, while, at the same time, a kindly, hospitable, and compassionate Southern family saved his life.

Muir's dream of traveling to South America remained active despite his malaria. Malaria was not just an individual problem, Muir discovered, but one that ravaged whole regions of the country and laid low large swaths of populations. Traveling to Florida forced Muir to confront his own limits and to recognize that there may well be some parts of the world just too hostile for an intrepid wanderer from northern climates. He noted as well that even its plant life threw up resistance to human civilization. Rather than abandon entirely his goal of visiting South America, Muir sought healing by leaving Cedar Key. There might yet be an opportunity to go to South America should his health recover. Perhaps a refreshing ocean voyage would help.

On New Year's Day 1868, Muir wrote Merrill Moores. Happy to have received a letter from his young friend, Muir described the shore life around Way Key with its hundreds of pelicans, bald eagles, and grey seabirds. He also underscored how dangerous the flora was and emphasized that it was nowhere near as easy to travel through Florida as it was to walk through Wisconsin. He warned Moores:

> [F]or if you left the path, the saw palmettos would saw you, and bamboo briers would hold you, prick you at the same time, and if you made out to heave and roll yourself through all of these fences you would soon find yourself sore with uncountable bayonet wounds, or entangled in a mesh of gum vines like a porpoise in a herring net.[399]

Muir wrote of a nature through which "you would have to go softly." In Florida, "Nature does not permit people to romp among her south flower fields as she does in those open ones of the North."[400]

Writing to his friends in Indianapolis on January 6, Muir voiced his longing to be in the North as a reprieve from heat and fever. "I wish I were among the storms and winds of the N for a while," he told them.[401] His letter underscored the strangeness of winds moving across unfamiliar plants and of the sight of Florida's unusual birds. Muir even charted his two months of illness. Developing a scale between "full health," represented by 0%, and "Death," represented by 100%; Muir recorded that he was 40% healthy most times, with occasional spikes of 80% and 60% when he felt closer to death.[402] He was not fully well even when he left Cedar Key.

On January 6, while situated on the rooftop veranda of the Hodgsons' house and watching the quiet, still waters of the Gulf, overhung with a magnificent cloud formation and lulled by hushed winds, Muir saw a "Yankee schooner," weaving its way through the twisting ship channel to the harbor of Cedar Key. It was the *Island Belle*, under command of Captain Parsons. Still reeling from the malaria, Muir decided on an unplanned detour to ship to Cuba rather than wait for a voyage to New Orleans. As he walked over to the harbor, Muir saw the ship's sailors filling water casks. He waited until they finished their work and then went with them to see the captain.

The *Island Belle* had a cargo of lumber for Cuba. Muir found that he could book passage to Cuba for $25, and the schooner would leave just as soon as she got a north wind. On the same day, Muir wrote the Merrills and Moores, "I mean to start for Cuba in two days. I am glad of this short opportunity of studying the sea."[403] He had to make a hasty departure. Gathering his plant press and satchel, he said his goodbyes to the Hodgsons, thanking them for their kind care,

150

about here when
I set out for
Cuba.

{ Two months of health line }

The mainland of Fla is more
sickly than the islets but no portion of
this coast nor of the flat border which
sweeps from Maryland to Texas is blessed
with the salubrity of climate, all the inhabitants
of this loved region whether black or white are liable
to be prostrated by the ever present fever
to say nothing of the plagues of Cholera
& Yellow fever, that come & go like storms
prostrating & cutting gaps in the population
like hurricanes in woods. The world we are told was
made for man. A presumption that
is totally unsupported by all the facts.

There is a very numerous class
of men who are cast into painful
fits of astonishment whenever they
find anything living or dead in all
Gods universe which they cannot
eat or in some way render what
they call useful to themselves

"{Two months of health line}"

Sketch in JMP 1:610 and JMP 23:110, John Muir Papers, Holt-Atherton Special Collections,
University of the Pacific Library. Copyright 1984 Muir-Hanna Trust

and promising to make a return visit within twenty-five years.[404] Perhaps Cuba could be his springboard to South America. Northern winds picked up, and in early January 1868, Muir was off to Cuba, a new land for a new year.

Florida, like the experience in the Bonaventure Cemetery, proved to be a critically important stage in Muir's thousand-mile walk. While his overall objective was South America, his only opportunity to get completely free of malaria seemed to be a passage to Cuba. The detour was necessitated by the fever itself.

How could an Edenic paradise such as wild nature be so lethal for Lord Man? Muir resolved the tension of this question by setting aside the received dominion theology of his father and constructing an environmental perspective that placed human beings within a broader biocentric design with a religious foundation.

Building on a foundation of God as creator, Muir dismantled the sin, redemption, utilitarian dominion theology of his father's heritage. He erected a new superstructure that was based on two premises. First, God's created order had equal claim and "rights" along with human beings. Second, human goals and purposes did not supersede the goals and claims of God's plans, designs, and laws, so evident in nature. What humans need to learn with these new principles, Muir wrote, is humility, something Muir had learned from his bout with malaria. Lord Man is not exempt from the design and laws, like magnetic forces, of nature itself. Humans could be eaten by alligators, poisoned by minerals, drowned by water, and susceptible to lethal diseases. Some regions were more conducive to human well-being than others. This may be one reason that Muir avoided cities with their plagues.

On the nature of death, Muir concluded that it was not to be feared as it, too, was part of a natural process. Muir believed that children needed to learn this important lesson of humility through exposure to nature rather than within the artificial walls of protection constructed by civilization. Lord Man needed nature to wean him away from the pride, conceit, and arrogance that valued nature and its resources as only a thing to meet his purposes and needs. Alligators, therefore, were not evil or satanic; that was a prejudice fostered by clerics and farmers who gave primacy to "useful" plants and animals. Rather, the alligator was a creature of God with its own definition of happiness, a being filling a role in the balance of nature, part of a "divine harmony." God's intention, in Muir's view, was the happiness of each of his creatures, even down to the simplest flower and the smallest microbe.

The malaria Muir battled in Cedar Key led first to a delay, and then to a detour that changed not just John Muir's goals, but his life direction and, more important, his thinking on the relationship between human beings and nature. Such adjustments in Muir's thinking provided a harbinger of his willingness to change his ideas in light of his experiences. His time in Florida sharpened the thinking that informed his vision regarding the intrinsic value of nature to teach human beings lessons about humility, death, balance, and "divine harmony." His experiences in Florida also taught him that some regions and places in nature are lethal to even the most devoted and well-informed travelers; one would do well to seek healthier climes. Muir would find this last lesson reinforced as he made his way to Cuba.

8

# CONVALESCENCE, CUBA, AND ONWARD TO YOSEMITE

*"but fortunately could not find passage at any near time for any South American Port."*
—*John Muir, 1868.*

Malaria hung on John Muir like a wet, hot, wool coat. When he sent the graph that chronicled his health to family and friends at home, he acknowledged that he was still depleted when he left Cedar Key. Malaria weighed him down with night sweats, low energy, and recurrent spikes of fever. He looked forward to his upcoming sea journey to get him out of the disease-ridden lowlands of Florida In fact, he wrote an indictment of the southern coastal areas from Maryland to Texas.

> [N]o portion of this coast ... is blessed with salubrity [sic] of climate. All the inhabitants of this (region) whether black or white are liable to be prostrated by the ever present fever to say nothing of the plagues of cholera & yellow fever that come & go like storms prostrating & cutting gaps in the population.[405]

His journey aboard the *Island Belle* would be a welcome change.

While he looked forward to seeing the natural world of Cuba, this trip also meant new cultural engagement with a people, a language, a religion, and a social and economic structure for which he had little preparation. His continuing poor health was also a detriment to his efforts.

As he continued to try to shake off malaria, Muir found his spirits brightening on the voyage from Cedar Key to Cuba's Havana harbor. The *Island Belle* "appeared to glory in her speed" through high winds and the foamy sea "& managed her full spread wings gracefully as a bird."[406] Captain Parsons, dubious of Muir's sea legs, thought it best that this obvious landlubber go to his quarters, lest he be washed overboard or become seasick. The captain said, "No landsman can stand this long."[407] Muir rejected the captain's suggestion. He wrote, "I had long waited in the woods for such a storm that now I would remain on deck & enjoy it."[408] Muir, who had a special affinity for storms, took note that the howl of the sea wind was different than that of the winds of Florida or the North. On this crossing, he wrote, "All (the storm) was inspired with Nature's perfection of beauty & harmony—every wave obedient & (harmonious) as the smoothest ripples of a forest lake..."[409] He thrilled in the "glorious sight" of phosphorescent waters lit up "like silver fire."[410] He found himself in a marvelous world.

Invigorated by the storm, Muir thought the trip much too short. The *Island Belle* made its way to the Cuban coastline, which was easily spied by the sailors, but, until the ship neared harbor, dim to him. In Cuba, he wrote, "A flock of white-plumaged ships" streamed out of the narrow Havana harbor under the lee of Morro Castle.

As the *Island Belle* drew up adjacent to the castle and dropped its sails, "she was boarded by a swarm of daintily dressed officials who were good-naturedly & good-gesturedly (*sic*) making all sorts of inquiries, while our busy captain, paying little attention to them, was giving orders to his crew."[411] Muir wanted to visit the flowery side of the Cuban harbor, but the captain urged him to go to town, promising him some fine plazas and gardens. Muir jumped into the boat to Havana and found himself there on Sunday, 12 January 1868, "the noisiest day of a Havana week." Church bells "clanged," vendors and pitchmen shrilly cried out their wares on a noisy wharf, hawkers for theaters and bullfights rang bells to attract paying spectators, and crowds roared approval for the finesse of the bullfighters in the stadium. The noise was deafening compared with the soft, southern silences of nature.

Still feeling malarial cravings, Muir made his way to the market to buy fruit. He noted with wonder the first pineapple he ever saw, and wandered through the narrow streets and sidewalks, "stunned with the babel (sic) of strange sounds and sights." Muir wrote that he "was glad to escape to our little schooner *Belle* again, weary and heavy laden with excitement and tempting fruits."[412] That evening he relished the harbor view from the ship, enjoying the "thousand lights" that "starred the great town."[413] The *Island Belle* became Muir's haven both for convalescence and from cultural engagement with Spanish and Cuban ways of life. Havana, with its noisiness, its labyrinthine streets, and its bustle were too much. Muir looked forward to the quiet wonder of nature on the opposite side of the harbor.

When he went ashore, Muir was confronted with a culture different from the Anglo-American culture in which he was reared. Language, religion, social class, social interaction, use (and abuse) of animals were all different. He found the sights, sounds, and smells irksome, whereas Capt. Parsons, noting his ship companion's curiosity, wanted to show Muir the town. Still weakened by malaria, Muir did not have the energy to engage a different culture; it was enough for him to study Cuba's plant life and shells. Except for short, uncomfortable visits to quiet plazas and botanical gardens, he remained on the ship, which provided him sanctuary from the noise and differences of Havana culture.

Muir's caution was in many ways shaped by his habitual avoidance of village and urban life in his walk through the American South. Moreover, he knew little or no Spanish and simply did not have the energy to learn it at that time. Had he genuinely engaged Cuban culture, it may well have enhanced rather than detracted from his personal growth and development. As it was, he was content with being an observer of Cuban plant life near the harbor, hoping that at some future date he could walk the island.

In the 1860s, Cuba was the richest and most populous of Spain's two remaining colonies in the Caribbean. Its economy depended on sugar and slavery, but the sugar economy had declined in the decade between 1850 and 1860. Cuban creoles had recently recovered their majority in the population at 57%, or a little over 468,000, while the island's slave population numbered 371,000, or 43% of its total population—its lowest number in the nineteenth century.[414] The financial panic of 1857 and foreign competition had closed down some four hundred sugar plantations between 1850 and 1860.[415]

Havana was also on the cusp of a ten-year civil war between defenders of the colonial regime and those who supported nascent Cuban nationalism; that war broke out in November 1868.[416] The recent US Civil War had encouraged creoles and white liberals to join ranks with blacks to promote abolitionism on the island. Slave uprisings had been ruthlessly repressed there in 1843. Cuba's Spanish government repelled annexation efforts by renegade US filibusters, and Spain also rejected official overtures from the US government to purchase Cuba in the 1850s.[417]

Through British pressure on the Spanish court, the trans-Atlantic slave trade came to an end in 1867. Spanish-born and native white economic leadership sought cheap labor abroad in the form of immigrants from Asia, especially China, and the indigenous peoples of Guatemala. There was a stark contrast between the aristocracy, their dependent slaves, and the free working populations. Havana became a bustling port of economic vitality as Cuba moved from a plantation society to an economy of trade and commerce. The city's white male population increased from 61,656 in 1846 to 91,625 in 1862.[418] Creole merchants sought to untangle their affairs from the mercantile trade restrictions placed on them by Spain. Muir entered Havana harbor during this period of economic liberalism. For example, he came to Havana harbor on a lumber ship from Florida; he left on a small fruiter carrying oranges for New York. Lax customs inspectors cared only about stowaway slaves, not about white passengers without papers. While not fully aware of this political context, Muir offers some insight in his journal as to the slackened governmental restraints on trade fostered by economic liberals in the Havana of early 1868.

Muir spent a month living on the *Island Belle*, but he ranged no more than ten to twelve miles beyond the outskirts of Havana and its harbor. As he gazed over his map of Cuba, he longed to ramble through the mountains from Havana in the West to the rugged and isolated Eastern parts of the island, but his health continued to be problematic. He wrote including his own editing, "but alas though out of Florida swamps, fever was yet weighing me earthward, & a mile of city walking was quite exhausting. The weather too was ~~fearfully~~ oppressively warm & sultry."[419] Four days later, after a dozen trial walks beyond Morro Castle, Muir concluded he was not well enough to venture into the interior regions of Cuba. "I was sadly compelled to see that no enthusiasm could enable me to walk to the interior," he wrote.[420]

Muir fell into a daily routine of being rowed to a distant beach, where he picked up shells and gathered flower specimens. He returned in the evening to fill his plant press, box his shells and regale the captain and the sailors with stories of his daily adventures amidst the cacti, flowers, and shells. Afterward, he spent a "dreamy" hour or so on deck and retired to "harbor wavelets tinkling outside close to my ear."[421]

As Muir recuperated, the captain prevailed upon him to go ashore in the evenings "on his side of the harbor." The two took a carriage to a distant plaza to walk among groves of trees and "magnificent flowers." Brass bands played in the plazas, with "lancer noted martial airs of the Spanish" filling the air. Muir noted, with a measure of appreciation, the fashionable promenades of the aristocracy during the cooler evenings. Describing the proud, aristocratic Cubans as "beautiful, rather small with features exquisitely moulded & set off with silks & broadcloth in excellent tastes," he found Cubans' treatment of animals repulsive. "I saw more downright brutal cruelty to mules and horses during the few weeks I stayed there than in my whole life elsewhere,"[422] he wrote. He found Cuban amusements, such as bullfighting, "coarse." He found the noise of the city intolerable, with its "brainsplit bellringing" and "the most lancing & artificial music."[423] While he did comment occasionally on Cuban social mores, and on the aristocracy and African-Cuban stevedores, his primary focus of attention remained with the plants he encountered on his daily excursions.

Of Cuban society and the town of Havana, Muir noted that the aristocracy had long wagon tongues and long traces for their horses as a show of their status. He appreciated the well-watered and well-kept plazas, but was critical of the crooked and narrow streets and sidewalks. Of the African-Cuban stevedores he wrote, "I saw the strongest & the very ugliest negroes in Havana that I met in my whole walk." Even the *Island Belle* sailors admired the strength and muscle of the Cuban stevedores.[424]

There is no record in Muir's journal regarding emerging social tensions between supporters of Spanish authority and Cuban nationalists. There is likewise no mention of the emerging realities of civil war. When Muir dreamed, he dreamed of the safety of the harbor and the haven of the ship.[425]

What Muir did comment on was the flora of the Havana region through which he passed during his month's stay. He contrasted the fragile flora of temperate regions, where human feet, cities, and farm animals trampled and eradicated wild plants, with the armed, spiky plants of the tropics that resisted human encroachment.[426] In his journal he wrote, "But the armed & united plants, vigorous offspring of tropic light, hold plantfully their rightful Kingdoms and never since the first appearance of the great biped lord, have they never, or yet, suffered defeat."[427]

A five-minute walk outside of Havana led Muir to "the undisturbed settlements of Nature," which were rich in vines, cacti, and grasses. Muir loved the wildflowers of the seaside fields and he characterized them as "a happy band, closely joined in splendid array."[428] Long and short vines covered several hundred yards in complex weavings and unions. Cacti were also notable. Some were small, spiny, singular plants tucked away between rocks; others stood tall, like trees, wide at the top and with foot-wide trunks. Cubans planted trees for use as fences, along with the dramatically flowering agave and the deadly Spanish bayonet. While walking along some low rocks one afternoon, Muir jumped back, startled by what he thought was a great snake. Instead, it was the sinuous flow of a cactus, slung low to the ground. This plant, like its reptile counterpart, "possessed many a fang," wrote Muir. He noted that the cactus lay prostrate, "as though under the curse of Eden."[429] Cuba's plants adapted and protected themselves well from careless human encroachment.

From a distance, on that same day, Muir thought he saw two small poplars. Instead, they turned out to be agaves in flower, the first he had ever seen, and so he sketched one in his journal.

The agave's twenty-five-foot flower spike grew in just a few weeks, but, in Muir's judgment, this "unquiet effort" was no more notable in nature than the growth of a grass panicle.[430] As impressive as the tall agave flower was, Muir found delight in hardy, small, resilient flowers. As Muir collected shells along Cuba's rocky shore, noting the flow of waves and breakers, he saw a "little plant with closed flowers" in the hollow of a brown, wave-washed rock. "'Surely,' said I, as I stopped over it for a moment, before the oncoming of another

*Agave in flower*

wave, 'surely you cannot be living here!'"[431] It was. Its roots were wedged into coral rock and seemed to flourish despite the crashing waves. Muir admired the plant's rugged adaptation to its challenging environment and noted that nature's complexity was like the abundant revisions of a writer, with cross-outs, word alterations, and additions that made the original draft unintelligible (not unlike some parts of Muir's original journal).

Reflecting on his Cedar Key revisions and their similarities to adaptive behaviors of the plant kingdom, Muir wrote:

> Our limited powers are similarly perplexed and overtaxed in reading the inexhaustible pages of nature, for they are written over and over uncountable times, written in characters of every size and color, sentences composed of sentences, every part of a character a sentence. [432]

Muir continued emphasizing the grand unity of every bit of nature: "There is not a fragment in all nature, for every relative fragment of one thing is a full harmonious unit in itself. All together form the one grand palimpsest of the world."[433] Fascinated by the complexity of nature, Muir paid little attention to the complexity of the historical, economic, religious, social, and political environments found in the cities and villages through which he passed. For Muir, it was enough to discover the unity within the complexity of nature.

Muir's singular focus on nature was his great gift. He chose to be critical rather than to understand the cultural and human environment that intruded upon this Eden. His emerging goal involved engagement with a wild Eden in order to save civilized "Lord Man" from himself—by connecting him with his evident limitations and his arrogant pride. He believed that Lord Man needed both a natural vision that "all things were hitched together" and a chastening humility to save himself from egocentric agendas formed out of a false view of his God-decreed superiority and self-centered utilitarianism. Lord Man's common good seldom considered the interests of the flowers, the animals, the trees, the landscape, the lakes, the rivers, the oceans, the air, or even Lord Man's enemies, the predators such as wolves, bears, panthers, and alligators.

As Muir continued to convalesce on the ship, he freed himself from having to come to grips with Cuban culture. It became his goal to recuperate fully, so that he could travel to South America and fulfill his dream. He wrote in his journal that even though he still had not regained his health, "I made up my mind to push on to South America while my stock of strength (such as it was) lasted."[434] He visited several shipping agencies, but he did not find passage to South America. He wrote in his journal, "but fortunately could not find passage at any near time for any South American Port."[435] When did this word "fortunately" creep into the narrative? This is clearly a retrospective entry, written some time after Muir better understood both his weakened state and the imminent threats of tropic disease that might engulf him if he pushed on to South America and Africa.[436]

Muir regretted the limitations that his health had imposed upon him while he was in Cuba. "It seemed hard to leave Cuba thus unseen, un-walked," he wrote, "but sickness forbade my stay & I had to comfort myself with hopes of returning to its [Cuba's] waiting treasures in full health at some other time & immediately prepared for departure."[437] Penciling in a revision to his journal, he provided an account of his decision to go to California rather than to South America.

While resting in a Havana plaza, he found a discarded, but recent New York newspaper with shipping advertisements for "cheap passage" to California.[438] None of the California ships stopped in Cuba. The *Nebraska* was scheduled to leave New York, to go around the horn of South America and to receive passengers on the west side of Panama. If Muir could get to New York, he might book passage to the eastern port at

Panama, take a rail route across that country, and meet up with the *Nebraska* on the Pacific side of Panama. Timing was critical.

Captain Parsons provided assistance, pointing out a trim, fast schooner loaded with oranges bound for New York. Muir had to see the ship's captain right away because the vessel was due to ship out soon. Jumping into a dinghy, he crossed the narrow bay to the fruiter. The Dutch captain agreed to give Muir passage for $25.[439]

The ship was scheduled to sail the next morning. Muir had to get his papers in order at the American consulate. His packing was an easy task; finding the consul was not. Short on time, Muir left Cuba without papers. After bidding Captain Parsons goodbye, Muir boarded the fruiter to await the morning's inspection by Spanish authorities. Fortunately, Spanish officials did not board the ship; they simply glanced at the captain's paperwork and accepted his word that no escaped slave stowaways were on board. The captain assured the officials that he had "not a d---d one." "All right, then, farewell!" said the Spaniard. "A pleasant voyage to you!"[440]

The inspection near Morro Castle was perfunctory; Muir hid out of sight until the vessel beat its way against strong northern winds out of the harbor. This lax customs policy saved Muir from an embarrassing arrest. In another context, this decision to leave without papers could have been perilous. Muir thought he might have been spared the humiliation and financial hardship of an arrest because of the good luck he had enjoyed throughout his life.

The voyage northward through the Gulf Stream gave Muir ample opportunity for observation and reflection on the seas and the winds. He enjoyed "clinging to a small chip of a ship like ours when the sea is rough & long."[441] As the seas rose, so did the "grandeur & beauty" of the ocean scenery. Muir loved the buoyant rhythm of the little schooner riding up and down the large swells with comet-tailed spumes of foam and water trailing off the wave tops. The glossy sea country forbade the growth of trees and walkers could not stride upon its waters.[442] In a fantasy of imaginative creativity, Muir wondered what it would be like to walk the ocean, to study its plant life and currents, to sleep in wild weather in a bed of phosphorescent wave foam or briny scented seaweeds, to follow the courses of flying fish trailing luminescent pathways in the night and to walk across the glossy plain in calms.[443] It was an extraordinary set of images. Muir had discovered yet another wilderness to think about—that of a walker on the ocean.

But alas! Humans are limited to walking on land; even some regions of land prevent an easy or healthy walk.

> [A] little portion of the land is all that is allowed freely to man & if he among other journeys on forbidden paths ventures trespassingly among the icelands or hotlands, or up in air in balloon bubbles on the ocean in ships or down into it in smothering diving bells—in all such little adventures, man is punished in terms which clearly tell him that he is in a country which, ... he was never designed for though how far our star may finally be subdued none can tell.[444]

The tropics may have been a region for which he was never designed; now he was sailing his way northward to seek yet another welcoming home in nature. The sea had its charms, but since his trek across the Cumberland Mountains, Muir had thought that Yosemite would be a better choice.

After finding the shallow, transparent, calm waters off Florida as different from dull-colored "ordinary" water as mountain air was to town smoke, he wondered why the ship didn't run aground. He was also impressed by the sight of a squadron of flying fish swimming and flying away from a dolphin that was in hot pursuit. As the dolphin closed in, the fishes' tight organization gave way to scattered confusion. Muir saw so much life in these oceans. Surely, the sea was not a wasteland, as some suggested. As land animals, he thought, humans know so little of the land. So too, humans knew little about the oceans. Civilized people gave only "turbid glances" through "our commercial eyes" and thus, the limited knowledge humans had of the oceans was "comparatively worthless."[445] In Muir's view, "the sea is as full of life as the land."[446]

Off the coasts of the Carolinas, the fruiter carrying Muir met with stiff headwinds. Waves drenched its cargo of oranges. Loose oranges on the ship's deck and in its cargo hold rolled around, with the ship's rocking and pitching making for dangerous footing. A portion of the cargo spoiled. Flying fish avoided the ship at day as they flew from wave top to wave top, but at night they fell among the oranges. Sailors ate some of the fish and entertained themselves by collecting others as curiosities for friends on land. A large, black Newfoundland dog pounced on the fish as if they were toys, and he found them good eating as well. Muir hung out above the bowsprit enjoying the light show as the schooner crashed through waves of phosphorescent glow. Drawn again to nature's light and energy, he spent hours gazing forward into the wind. "Every fishes pathway, every crested wave was most gloriously illumined,"[447] he wrote.

On the twelfth day of its voyage, the schooner sailed to within sight of "the big ship metropolis," New York. Having become accustomed to the perpetual green of the tropics, Muir now found the leafless trees along the coast strange. As it was now February 1868, snow covered the ground. A blast of frosty air blew onto the ship in the Sandy Hook area, and sailors rummaged through their wardrobes to find winter clothing. Muir found the feeling of the chill air on his skin "delicious."

Scurrying into New York harbor, the little schooner outraced all other vessels, and, at evening, the ship was "grinding & wedging" against ice fields on the Hudson River, coming into its moorage at nine o'clock.[448] The following morning, a wagonload of rotten oranges, along with the ship's sailors and Muir, were dropped off at the market. Muir wrote the last entry of his original journal: "[A]ll the purposes of our sail from Cuba accomplished."[449]

New York was just the beginning of Muir's new life, because it afforded passage to Yosemite's golden hills, poppy-filled fields, and clear mountain streams with ouzels dipping in and out of cataracts together with the magnificent "range of light." Muir would spend the next thirty years residing in California and traveling to remote wilderness areas before returning to the South in 1898. [450]

Muir remained on the schooner in New York, as he had stayed on the boat in Cuba, until he could make arrangements for his passage to California. The *Nebraska* would depart for California in ten days, and passage from the western Isthmus port cost only $40. This, Muir could afford. Forced to take a cheaper steerage fare on another vessel to the eastern port of Panama at Aspinwall-Colon, Muir would cross the isthmus by rail and pick up the *Nebraska* on the western side for passage to California.

For the next few days he ambled through the city, not knowing anyone and feeling lost. "I felt completely lost in the vast throngs of people, the noise of the streets, and the immense size of the buildings,"[451] he wrote. Having trekked, guided by a compass, through southern forests and swamps, he worried that if he stopped to explore Central Park, he might not find his way back to his ship. He wrote that he would like to explore the city if it were clear of its inhabitants.[452] When he went to purchase maps of California, the clerk persuaded him to buy a large bundle. The salesman suggested that once Muir reached California, he could sell the maps to recent arrivals at a high price and make a tidy profit. Since Muir determined to travel light on his trip westward, the maps proved to be "a very large, awkward bundle," but they were the only significant baggage he carried beyond his plant press and his rubberized satchel.

Though Muir found himself relieved to leave New York, his passage to Aspinwall-Colon became a misery. Brutal confinement in steerage contrasted starkly with his exhilarating passage in the fruiter. Meals were disgusting. "Never before had I seen such a barbarous mob, especially at meals,"[453] he wrote. He had only a half-day "to ramble" about the tropical forests of Panama before getting on the train, but the train's passage through tropical forest and scenery along the Chagres River delighted Muir. "The riotous exuberance of great forest trees, glowing in purple, red, and yellow flowers, far surpassed anything I had ever seen, especially of flowering trees, either in Florida or Cuba."[454] Of his emotional response, he wrote, "I fairly cried for joy and hoped that sometime I should be able to return and enjoy and study this most glorious of forest to my heart's content."[455] At the western port he boarded the *Nebraska*, a much more comfortable ship than the first vessel, which steamed its way north to San Francisco Bay, arriving on 1 April 1868. Muir sought the quickest way out of the city to make his way to Yosemite. His thousand-mile walk through the South was now formally at an end, and the next chapter of his life was opening before him.

Muir had partially recovered from malaria while in Cuba. He had found haven from both his illness and prevailing cultural challenges in the sanctuary of the ship *Island Belle*. At a time of personal vulnerability, he reconsidered his dream of travel to South America. Then he changed course— temporarily, he thought—to recover in the cold and frost of the North and in the sunshine and high-mountain air of the Sierra Nevada in California.

Muir's change of course proved life-shaping in that he found not only a home in California but also a purpose. Muir's experience in Cuba redirected his travel objectives. The tropics were not helping him heal, that he knew. Healing would come with a different environment. While nature afforded numerous examples of adaptation to difficult environments, such as the small flower Muir had found on the Cuban wave-washed rocks, tropical environments could be deadly to humans. Admitting this fact, Muir changed his plans and concluded that he was "fortunate" in not being able to book passage to South America while he was in Cuba.

What he learned from Cuba was similar to that which he discovered in Florida: He would make better progress in his convalescence if he traveled to a cooler climate. The discovery of shipping schedules, written in English, in a Cuban plaza was fortuitous, and his recollection of the Yosemite pamphlet provided an alternative to the Orinoco and more exposure to tropical heat and disease. Muir demonstrated hard-won flexibility in fine-tuning one of his most cherished goals. He never gave up the dream of visiting South America and Africa; he chose only to postpone that dream's fulfillment.

Muir's three months' convalescence in Cedar Key and Cuba altered his plans. He found the tropics too hostile and alien for his health and well-being. Sea voyages, rest, and good sense prevailed over his ambitious dreams of walking through South America and the interiors of Africa. In the settings of both Cedar Key and Cuba, Muir discovered his limits and revised his goal of travel to South America. His prudent judgment prevailed as adventure and curiosity gave way to his eventual discovery of a home. This adjustment entailed a serious consideration for his health and well-being along with ample inspiration from nature itself.

# CONCLUSION

John Muir's "fortunate" detour to Yosemite from South America in 1868 changed his life and his influence on the American environmental movement. It was a momentous detour, one that Muir himself began to understand perhaps as early as his first summer in the Sierras. The convalescence in Cuba had given him a sober perspective on his limitations and an option for his future.

Yet it was the walk, and what Muir experienced in the South in 1867 and 1868, that proved critical in the development of his thoughts about nature, humanity's relation to nature, death, and the importance of wilderness. In fact, the groundwork for Muir's contribution to environmental thinking was laid during his transformative thousand-mile walk.

While books inspired his dreams to visit South America and even Africa, his passion for travel also sprang from his strong, innate curiosity and his scientific goals in botany. Given John Muir's talents as a self-taught student of literature and a mechanical genius, along with his open-ended faith, love of science, affection for fieldwork, strong physical constitution, and unique intellectual gifts, his life course could have gone many directions as a young adult.

Travel had been a path to escape the boredom, harsh discipline and tedium of schooling in Scotland, and farm work in Wisconsin. After his eye accident and injury, Muir found that travel provided relief from the stifling constraints of factory life. His walk through the South was purposeful in that his most important goal, even greater than reaching South America, was the collecting and identification of plants wholly new to him. The walk became the means by which his study of plants broadened to deeper environmental thought and reflection toward a unified environmental ethic that viewed all of creation—including plants deemed useless weeds and predatory animals such as the alligator—as having rights. Through the discipline of writing almost daily entries of his observations and reflections, Muir honed his writing skills. His elegant, keen, and perceptive writing eventually drew the attention of influential intellectuals and publishers so that Muir's ideas, germinating and coming to fruition on the walk, would gain currency among publishers, politicians, and industrial and cultural leaders.

A determination "to see anew" spurred Muir's walk to a strange country with strange plants, strange winds, and a culture to which Muir had never before been exposed. The experience shaped the formation of his identity and his environmental thought. He learned about himself on this journey; he learned about death; he learned about "Lord Man's" limits in wild places; and he gained a new vision that was to inform him for the rest of his life. This vision informed his thought and gave force to his writings.

The journey afforded him the time and the opportunity to solidify a worldview that challenged the human-centric, dominion-oriented, and utilitarian perspective informed by traditional orthodox Christian faith for farming communities and urban populations. During his walk, Muir came to the conclusion that nature and nature's laws operated independent of human egotism.

Muir did not kick God out of nature, but he saw God's purposes working out within nature for purposes and ends that exceeded simple human self-interest. Embedded in nature, the flowers, the animals, and the rocks themselves had purposes and reasons for being in which "All was harmony divine;" or, as Muir would write later, "when we try to pick out anything by itself, we find it hitched to everything else in the universe."[456] He saw a fundamental equality between the natural and the human. Humans were *not* to arrogate "dominion" over nature in a hierarchy; humans were to live harmoniously with nature, wherein positive and negative forces, like those of magnetic poles, balanced. Muir recognized that humans would do well to understand their limits within this context. Humans could even be food for predators. Indeed, in Muir's words God heard the prayers and petitions of the alligator for food, even if that food might be "Lord Man." Were a war to break out between humans and bears, Muir wrote, he sympathized with the bears. "Useful" animals, such as horses, cattle, and sheep, did not simply exist for human comfort; they had their own independent purposes for being. Muir rejected the division of nature into the categories of "useful" and "useless." The distinction between a weed and a pretty, domesticated flower in a trimmed, artificial garden was, Muir thought, an egocentric and invidious distinction. All flowers had reasons for being and all had their own beauty. Every plant, animal, and rock fulfilled its own purpose, and a clear and keen observer would do well to think hard about that purpose before destroying, killing, or ripping one out for the sake of convenience or self-interest.

Muir saw the sacred in nature. Borrowing the language of Milton, he saw the "glory" in the light bouncing off a palmetto, he saw trees waving in the wind as "signs of worship," and, referencing scripture, he followed Solomon's wisdom and Jesus' teaching to "consider the lilies of the field." Initially, Muir viewed nature as an undefiled Eden.

In his five-day stay in St. Bonaventure Cemetery, in Savannah, Georgia, Muir thought about death in unconventional ways. One lesson he learned was that plants, coupled with the weather, eventually grow over gravestones, which themselves erode. While Muir was sleeping amidst a community of the dead, he was greeted each morning with sunlight, bird songs, vines, and mosses rapidly encroaching on the headstones. This cemetery was an abode of life, not of death. Society taught children to fear death, Muir said, but let a child go into the wild and soon a correct perspective would be learned. Death is natural, not to be feared. There is no reason for melancholy, for even in cemeteries life abounds, if you have the wits to see it.

Thus, for Muir, nature and wilderness were critically important for human beings. Nature showed human beings the smallness of their perspective. Engagement with nature disciplined humanity with lessons in humility. Children educated in nature would see the balance of life and death and would be unafraid to die. But even engagement in nature could not completely change the influence of culture on John Muir.

Muir's experiences with Southern and Cuban cultures show the extent to which he reflected the norms and folkways of his nineteenth-century society. While he had made his peace and was, therefore, not caught up in the politics of the Civil War, he, nevertheless, came to the conclusion that violence in war and against animals was a denial of life and something to be avoided. In his conversations with Southerners, he tended to change the subject, or he simply listened to those caught up in the Reconstruction politics of the day. More often than not, he found himself impatient with the ideological cant that informed Southern judgments on issues regarding freedmen, race, civil liberties, and congressional, military reconstruction. He was equally uninterested in local politics, but he listened to those who sought his open ears.

In dealing with and recuperating from malaria, Muir was forced to confront his own limits. Rather than push on to South America from Cuba or New Orleans in his debilitated state, Muir demonstrated adaptability, and because of this change in plans, Muir would find even more flowers, compelling geology, and a "range of light" in the Sierras. Here he would remain and ramble for more than thirty years, still pursuing his passion to study botany. His scientific interests expanded to geology in his examination of the Sierra Nevada Mountains and pursuing his great contribution to environmental thought in educating Americans that "all things are hitched together." He would argue forcefully for the preservation of wilderness in order that Americans learn both a sense of their limits and how they fit into the great scheme of things. This would be Muir's life purpose in his newfound home in California. The thousand-mile walk prepared the way for this thought and work. One cannot understand Muir's life direction without understanding the influence of his time in the South.

John Muir struggled with the issue of race. All too often, though he was always careful in his analysis of nature, he was susceptible to specious fears and generalizations about "robber negroes." He used language common to his day, such as "Afric," and "Nig," and he sometimes replaced these words with the more genteel "Negro."

Along with most others of his time, Muir often equated the clean, orderly, educated, and technically advanced with the aristocratic. He clearly preferred the plantation houses of Athens, Georgia, and Gainesville, Florida, with their educated residents, to the homey, rough-hewn folk culture of mountainous North Carolina. Because the sheriff's home in Murphy was clean, neat, and tidy surrounded with flowers and vines, Muir saw it as a positive sign of cultural advancement. And in Cuba he compared the dress, appearance, and manner of the Spanish aristocracy with the appearance of the stevedores along the Havana wharves, whom he depicted as strong, yet ugly.

Muir was puzzled by the African-American couple whose naked child came out of the mud near Gainesville, Florida. Evidently they were unemployed freedmen trying to get by. It was difficult for him to understand why parents would bury their child in the mud. They may have heard, seen, and feared Muir, a white man, and thus hidden their child. Or, since the child had no clothing, mud may have been his best protection against mosquitoes, which plagued everyone in that part of Florida. Muir commented on the event with a confused distaste and then went to the biblical analogy of Adam coming up from the mud.

Thus, Muir's astute understanding of nature was not always complemented with an equal understanding of civilization, community life, social structures, or the political, economic, and cultural contexts within which he found himself. In his personal interactions, Muir was sociable and gregarious, and he enjoyed the company of all classes and peoples regardless of their political views or prejudices. Nature, not human beings or their constructions, was his abiding interest.

Once Muir had established his conviction that nature is sacred, then inculcating the ethic of its responsible presservation or restrained use for the common good becomes a moral imperative. Even before his thousand-mile walk, Muir suggested to his brother-in-law, David Galloway, that a favorite part of his family's farm be fenced in and preserved.[457] The grandeur of Yosemite provoked another effort at preservation. Once Muir arrived in Yosemite and began to apply the lessons of his Southern walk to his study of both plant life and the glacial origins of Yosemite Valley, he found his true home and vocation. After four years in Yosemite, when his writings about nature began to be known, Muir wrote to his mother, "My life work is now before me plain enough. & it is full of hard labor & abundant in all kinds of pure reward—Nature[.] God asks much & gives much & if we only are pure in heart we will see him in all times, & in all lands."[458] Muir had found his purpose, informed by insights gained on his thousand-mile walk through the South.

What does Muir's walk mean to those who live in the present? First, Muir presents a challenge to the view of nature that elevates the utilitarian above the sacred, the hierarchical above the equalitarian and interdependent, and the human-centric above the biocentric (which includes a just, but balanced perspective on humankind's interests). The thousand-mile walk solidified Muir's vision and worldview. Sustained travel, more than just superficial tourism, helped to forge in the young Muir deeper perspectives, flexibility, adaptability, and a more open heart to that which needed changing. He found his path not as a mechanic/inventor, nor a minister, nor a college professor. The walk gave him the time and experience to define life in his own terms rather than to subscribe to the ones prescribed by society. In so doing, he helped the American public and his readership to see nature as he did, with new eyes. John Muir's thousand-mile walk laid the foundation for the way in which he viewed his experience in California and his first summer in the Sierras. The walk intensified and transformed his vision.

Muir valued direct experience with nature, and the reading public came to value his writings. Though a vivid writer, Muir did not relish time in his "scribble den;" he understood and lamented the gap between direct experience and the narration of that experience.

> Books and talks and articles about Nature are at least little more than advertisements, hurrah invitations, dinner bells. Nothing can take the place of absolute contact, of seeing and feeding at God's table for oneself. The cold and perishing cannot be warmed by descriptions of fire and sunshine, nor the hungry fed with books about bread. The Lord himself must anoint eyes to see, my pen cannot. One can only see by loving; love makes things visible and all labor light. Nobody can be ambitious to do anything wonderful, when God's wonders are in sight. Every day we should all pray, 'O Lord, open Thou mine eyes.'[459]

Muir's restored eyesight led to a walk that opened his eyes. The walk gave him a renewed vision, a worldview, a vocation, and a moral imperative.

The thoughts that were a product of Muir's thousand-mile walk present a challenge to those of the present day who view nature as a warehouse of resources rather than a sacred, unified, and interdependent web of connections constituting the fabric of life and well-being. Muir came to view nature in equalitarian and interdependent terms rather than with a hierarchical and utilitarian perspective. In the creator's eyes, the rights of the alligator were every bit as important as the rights of human beings, according to Muir. This meant that nature should be viewed from a biocentric perspective, where everything in nature has intrinsic value rather than an anthropocentric point of view, which places humanity at the center of creation's purpose. These lessons could best be learned in the wilderness. Wilderness would need to be set aside for the sake of humanity's soul and well-being.

As John Muir engaged in his study of plants and reflected upon his experiences, he consistently expressed gratitude for the loveliness of the natural world. Temporary blindness provided Muir with an experience of what it would mean not to see nature. His gratitude for the welcoming arms of oaks, the sunlight glinting off palmetto fronds, and the wonder in the discovery of new plants, flowers, and vines resonates throughout his journal entries. The sense of joy, gratitude, and wonder with each discovery brightens up his prose. A reader can share in that delight with Muir.

By reading Muir's account of his walk, one can see how he set aside his father's dogmatic vision of life without throwing out a faith in God. John Muir found a way to see the hand of God in nature that challenged the agrarian, anthropocentric, and hierarchical presuppositions that informed much of nineteenth-century thought and theology about nature and creation. In so doing, he moved toward an alternative and fresh theological perspective on the value of nature as a good in itself because it was created by God. This vision provided a spiritual foundation for the preservation and conservation of nature, a value to which he remained committed for the rest of his life. Informed by empirical views of nature, Muir provided a spiritual and emotive rationale for its protection as a wilderness to remain untrammeled by utilitarian and selfish interests. In following Muir's journey closely, a reader may find his or her eyes opened to this vision. As Muir himself pointed out, books about food cannot feed a hungry person— but by reading about another's experiences and reflections, one can gain fresh, new insights that one might not otherwise have considered.

As the walk helped to solidify Muir's vision and worldview as a young adult, it can demonstrate the value of a time of pilgrimage or moratorium in young people's lives that helps clarify their purposes and goals. Youthful travel that engages a person in nature or other cultures or that serves human needs can be as transformative to their thinking as it was to John Muir's. Travel, careful observation, and written reflection like that which Muir did on the walk and even in his travels to Canada can help forge deeper perspectives, a sense of direction or purpose, flexibility, and a broader vision of life, just as it did for Muir.

Concerned adults would do well to encourage younger adults to pursue avenues of service, travel, study, and reflect ion before they engage vocational responsibilities. Young adulthood is an optimum time to discover one's true gifts and vocation, not the ones prescribed by social obligations. Muir's walk suggests that a significant quest, with disciplined curiosity and written reflection, can be a pathway toward a life of contribution and purpose.[460]

In my own role as a professor traveling with students to Central America for their five-month immersion in language, culture, and life with rural families in Honduras, I have seen a transformation similar to what took place during Muir's walk—in their thinking, their worldview, their passion, and a deepening sense of purpose in their lives. As co-founder of the Krista Foundation for Global Citizenship, which encourages young adults to embark on a sustained period of service in their twenties, I have also witnessed young adults finding both their passion and a vision very different from that which they might have pursued had they remained at home. Their perspectives can broaden and deepen. They can gain confidence and demonstrate adaptability and flexibility. By "going out," they are really "going in."

Muir's walk through the South in 1867 and 1868 was significant in the development of his environmental thought and ethics. In regaining his sight, he envisioned an integrated relationship between himself and nature. He developed new thoughts about nature's glory and grandeur, about a unity and harmony that holds all things together. He learned how nature's vitality trumps the constructs humans put on death: gravestones, morbid thoughts, and funeral rites. He concluded that it was human ego, self-interest, and pride that divided nature into artificial and arbitrary categories. "Useful" and "useless" were simply human constructions. Nature was neither good nor evil; it simply fulfilled a set of natural laws and a divine plan. Ultimately, Muir's journey helped inform his vision, work, and ethics.

Through understanding the significance of John Muir's walk, engaging his thought and reflections, and joining in his discovery, wonder, and gratitude, we too may find our own thinking and behavior changing. We too may be able to transcend conventional ways of thinking about wilderness and nature, embrace gratitude for the gifts of nature, comprehend how all things are linked together, and more richly value our lived experience in harmony with all things natural.

*John Muir, c.1872 at 34 years.*

# Select Bibliography

*Primary Sources*

*Manuscripts and Microform or Digitized Images of Manuscripts:*
   The John Muir Papers [JMP] are available in a 51-reel, 53-fiche microfilm and microform collection containing all the collected John Muir Papers edited by Ronald H. Limbaugh and Kirsten E. Lewis, published by Chadwyck-Healey, Inc. (Alexandria VA, 1986) available in 1986 by the Holt-Atherton Center for Western Studies, University of the Pacific, Stockton, California, hereinafter cited as JMP. I have used the microfilm edition of the JMP through the University of Montana Library and the Library at the University of California, Berkeley as well as at the Holt-Atherton Collection at the University of the Pacific. The Holt Atherton Collection also has a digitized copy of Muir's original journal of his walk to the Gulf that is found in JMP: reel 23 frames 21–146. This format allowed for magnification of images to read more carefully the texts and Muir's revisions.
   The Muir Family Papers and the Papers of Jeanne C. Carr, both relevant to this study, are available at The Huntington Library in San Marino, California. I also consulted libraries and special collections at the following institutions and depositories:

Eckstrom Library, Rare Books and Special Collections, University of Louisville, Louisville, Kentucky.
Filson Historical Society, Louisville, Kentucky.
William T. Young Library, University of Kentucky Libraries, Lexington, Kentucky.
John C. Hodges Library, University of Tennessee, Knoxville, Tennessee.
Fentress County Historical Society, Jamestown, Tennessee.
Tennessee State Library and Archives, Newspaper Collection, Knoxville, Tennessee.
Roane County Archives and Historical Research Center, Kingston, Tennessee.
Cherokee County Museum, Murphy, North Carolina.
Union County Historical Society, Blairsville, Georgia.
Smithgall Woods Natural Conservation Area, Helen, Georgia.
Hall County Library, Gainesville, Georgia.

Hargrett Rare Book and Manuscript Library, University of Georgia
Libraries, Athens, Georgia.
Augusta Museum of History, Augusta, Georgia.
Georgia Historical Society, Savannah, Georgia.
Smathers Libraries, University of Florida, Gainesville, Florida.
Payne's Prairie Preserve State Park, Gainesville, Florida.
Levy County Courthouse, Bronson, Florida.
Cedar Key Historical Society Museum, Cedar Key, Florida.
Cedar Key Public Library, Cedar Key, Florida.

Contemporary Imprints and Reprinted Sources:
Badé, William Frederic. *The Life and Letters of John Muir*. 2 vols. Boston
and New York: Houghton Mifflin, 1923.
Bokum, Herman. *The Tennessee Handbook and Immigrant's Guide*.
Philadelphia: J.B. Lippincott, 1868.
Burns, Robert. *Poems and Songs*. Edited by James Kinsley. London:
Oxford University Press, 1971.
-----*The Songs of Robert Burns*. London: Bell and Daldy, 1863.
Butler, James Davie. "The Calypso Borealis: Botanical Enthusiasm."
*Boston Recorder* 51 (21 December 1866): 1.
Dick, Thomas. *The Christian Philosopher or, The Connection of Science
with Religion*. Hartford, Connecticut: Robinson and Pratt, 1834.
Engberg, Robert, and Donald Wesling, editors. *John Muir, to Yosemite
and Beyond, Writings from the Years, 1863 to 1875*. Salt Lake City:
University of Utah Press, 1999.
Gisel, Bonnie Johanna, editor. *Kindred & Related Spirits, the Letters of
John Muir and Jeanne C. Carr*. Foreword by Ronald H. Limbaugh. Salt
Lake City: University of Utah Press, 2001.
Graydon, Ellen D. "John Muir," 14 Nov [1942?]. [Linnie Marsh] Wolfe
Papers, Holt-Atherton Special Collections, University of the Pacific,
Stockton, California.
[Hearn], Eliza. *Diary of Eliza Horn, Way Key, East Florida, 1867-1869*.
Historical Records Survey, Works Progress Administration.
Jacksonville FL: State Office, 1937, typescript of original available at
Cedar Key Public Library, Cedar Key, Florida.
Hunhner, Leon. *David L. Yulee, Florida's First Senator* [n.d.] Smathers
Libraries, Special Collections, University of Florida, Gainesville,
Florida.
Lamartine, Alphonse de. *The Stone-Mason of Saint Point, a Village Tale*.
Translated from the French. New York: Harper & Brothers, 1851.

*Louisville and Its Defenses*. Washington DC: US Engineers, 1865. Special Collections, Eckstrom Library, University of Louisville, Louisville, Kentucky.

Marsh, I.M. *Bonaventure, a Poem* (1860), Georgia Historical Society, Savannah, Georgia.

Milton, John. *Paradise Lost, a Poem*. Boston: Crosby & Ainsworth, 1867.

Muir, John. "Address to the Sierra Club." *Sierra Club Bulletin* 1/7 (January 1896): 271–85.

-----"The Calypso Borealis: Botanical Enthusiasm," *Boston Recorder* #51 (December 21, 1866), 1.

-----*John Muir, the Eight Wilderness-Discovery Books*. Introduction by Terry Gifford. Seattle WA: The Mountaineers, Diadem Books, 1992. Contains eight of Muir's published writings: *The Story of My Boyhood and Youth; A Thousand Mile Walk to the Gulf; My First Summer in the Sierra; The Mountains of California; Our National Parks; The Yosemite; Travels in Alaska*; and *Steep Trails*.

-----*John Muir's Last Journey, South to the Amazon and East to Africa, Unpublished Journals and Selected Correspondence*. Edited by Michael P. Branch. Washington DC: Island Press, 2001.

-----*Letters to a Friend, Written to Mrs. Ezra S. Carr, 1866-1879* [1915]. New York: Cosimo Classics, 2006.

-----*The Story of My Boyhood and Youth*. Boston and New York: Houghton Mifflin, 1913.

-----*The Story of My Boyhood and Youth*. Foreword by Vernon Carstensen. Madison: University of Wisconsin Press, 1965.

-----*The Story of My Boyhood and Youth*. Foreword by David Quammen. San Francisco: Sierra Club Books, 1988.

-----*A Thousand-Mile Walk to the Gulf*. Edited by William Frederic Badé, with illustrations. New York: Houghton Mifflin, 1916.

-----*A Thousand-Mile Walk to the Gulf*. Foreword by Colin Fletcher. San Francisco: Sierra Club Books, 1991.

Park, Mungo. *Travels in the Interior Districts of Africa*. Edited with an introduction by Kate Ferguson Marsters. Durham NC: Duke University Press, 2000.

*Purse's Directory of the City of Savannah together with a Mercantile and Business Directory*. Savannah GA: Purse and Son, 1866.

*Savannah City Directory, 1867*. Savannah GA: N.J. Darrrell & Co., 1867.

*Search for Yesterday, A History of Levy County, Florida*. Bronson FL: Levy County Archives Committee, 1977.

Thompson, Georgia Franklin. *A Tour of Central Florida and the Lower West Coast* [November 22, 1865–December 21, 1865]. Report to Col.

T. W. Osborn, Spring 1866. Original in George A. Smathers
Libraries, Gainesville, Georgia, 1999. Online:
http://web.uflib.ufl.edu/spec/pkoneg/thompson/gftdiary3.html.
See reprints of Thompson's published articles in *The Tallahassee
Sentinel*, 19, 30 April 1867; 3 May 1867, "Observations in Tropical
Florida," Online beginning at:
http://uflib.ufl.edu/spec/pkyonge/thompson/tts1.html.
Subsequent documents are found at tts2, tts3, tts4, and tts5.

Von Humboldt, Alexander, and Aime Bonpland. *Personal Narrative of
Travels to the Equinoctial Regions of America, during the Years 1799–
1804*. Translated from the French and edited by Thomasina Ross. 3
vols. London: George Bell & Sons, 1908.

Witherspoon, T.D. *The Appeal of the South to Its Educated Men*. Memphis
TN: n.p., 1867.

Wolfe, Linnie Marsh. *John of the Mountains, the Unpublished Journals of
John Muir*. Madison: University of Wisconsin Press, 1979.

Wood, Alphonso. *Class-Book of Botany: Being Outlines of the Structure,
Physiology, and Classification of Plants; with a Flora of the United States
and Canada* [1845]. New York: A.S. Barnes & Company, 1863, 1880.

Yulee, Charles Wickliff. *Senator David Yulee*. [n.d.] Smathers Libraries,
Special Collections, University of Florida, Gainesville, Florida.

Young, J.H. *Tourist's Pocket Map of the State of Tennessee Exhibiting its
Internal Improvements, Roads, Distance & c*. Philadelphia: S. Augustus
Mitchell, 1835.


*Census and Population Compilations:*

Andriot, Donna, editor. *Population Abstract of the United States*.
Woodbridge CT: Gale Group, 2000.

Kieber, John E., editor. *The Encyclopedia of Louisville*. Lexington:
University Press of Kentucky, 2001.

*Population of the United States in 1860: compiled from the original returns of
the Eighth Census under the direction of the Secretary of the Interior, by
Joseph C.G. Kennedy*. Vol. 1, Population. Washington DC:
Government Printing Office, 1864.

*The Statistics of the Population of the United States, Compiled from the
original returns of the Ninth Census (June 1, 1870) under the direction of
the Secretary of the Interior, by Francis A. Walker*. Vol. 1, Population.
Washington DC: Government Printing Office, 1872.

*Statistics of the Population of the United States at the Tenth Census (June 1,
1880)*. Washington DC: Government Printing Office, 1883.

Newspapers:

Kingston, Tennessee
  *East Tennessean*, 1867.
Athens, Georgia
  *Southern Banner*, 1867.
  *Southern Watchman*, 1867.
Augusta, Georgia
  *Daily Chronicle and Sentinel*, 1867.
  *Daily Press*, 1867.
  *Tri-Weekly Constitutionalist*, August–October, 1867.
  *Weekly Chronicle and Sentinel*, September–October, 1867.
  *Weekly Constitutionalist*, 2 October 1867.
  *Weekly Loyal Georgian*, 10 August 1867–15 February 1868.
Savannah, Georgia
  *Business Circular*, 13 April 1867.
  *Colored Tribune*, 25 March–22 April, 1867.
  *Daily News and Herald* 4 October 1867; 5–14 October, 1867.
  *The Savannah Daily Republican* 20 August–14 October 1867.
Fernandina, Florida
  *Express*, 1867.
  *Fernandina Courier*, 1866–67.
  *The News*, 1867.
  *Florida Mirror*, 1868.
Gainesville, Florida:
  *New Era*, 1867.


*Secondary Works*

Andriot, Donna, editor. *Population Abstract of the United States.*
  Woodbridge CT: Gale Group, 2000.
Ash, Stephen V. *Middle Tennessee Society Transformed, 1860–1870, War
  and Peace in the Upper South.* Knoxville: University of Tennessee
  Press, 2006.
Badé, William Frederic. *The Life and Letters of John Muir.* 2 vols. Boston:
  Houghton Mifflin, 1923–24.
Bass, Bernard M. *Bass & Stogdill's Handbook of Leadership, Theory,
  Research and Managerial Applications.* 3rd edition. New York:
  Macmillan, 1990.
Bethell, Leslie, editor. *Cuba, a Short History.* New York: Cambridge
  University Press, 1993.

Branch, Michael P., editor. *John Muir's Last Journey, South to the Amazon and East to Africa, Unpublished Journals and Selected Correspondence.* Washington DC: Island Press, 2001.

Brownstone, David A. *Facts About American Immigration.* New York: H.W. Wilson, 2001.

Cohen, Michael P. *The Pathless Way, John Muir and American Wilderness.* Madison: University of Wisconsin Press, 1984.

Coulter, E. Merton. *William G. Brownlow, Fighting Parson of the Southern Highlands* [1937]. Reprinted with introduction by Stephen V. Ash. Knoxville: University of Tennessee Press, 1999.

Daloz, Laurent A. Parks, Cheryl H. Keen, James P. Keen, and Sharon Daloz Parks. *Common Fire, Lives of Commitment in a Complex World.* Boston: Beacon Press, 1996.

Dees, Jesse Walter, and Vivian Flannery Dees. *"Off the Beaten Path," the History of Cedar Key, Florida, 1843–1990.* Chiefland FL: Rife Publishing, March, 1990.

Dorman, Robert L. *A Word for Nature, Four Pioneering Environmental Advocates, 1845–1913.* Chapel Hill: University of North Carolina Press, 1998.

Dorsey, James E. *The History of Hall County Georgia.* 2 vols. Gainesville GA: Magnolia Press, 1991.

Earl, John. *John Muir's Longest Walk: John Earl, a Photographer, Travels His Journey to Florida.* Garden City NY: Doubleday & Company, 1975.

Emmons, Robert A., et al. *The Psychology of Gratitude.* New York: Oxford University Press, 2004.

-----*Thanks! How the New Science of Gratitude Can Make You Happier.* Boston: Houghton Mifflin, 2007.

Fishburne, Jr., Charles Carroll. *The Cedar Keys in the 19th Century* [1993]. Cedar Key FL: Cedar Key Historical Society, 2004.

-----*The Cedar Keys in the Civil War and Reconstruction, 1861–1876.* Cedar Key FL: Sea Hawk Publications, 1982.

Fisher, Noel C. *War at Every Door, Partisan Politics & Guerrilla Violence in East Tennessee, 1860–1869.* Chapel Hill: University of North Carolina Press, 1997.

Ford, Angela Lee. *Screven & Jenkins Counties.* Charleston SC: Arcadia Publishing, 1999.

Freel, Margaret Walker. *Our Heritage, The People of Cheokee County, North Carolina.* Ashville NC: Miller Publishing, 1956.

Freytag, Ethel, and Glena Keis Ott, *A History of Morgan County, Tennessee.* [n.p.]: Specialty Printing, 1971.

Gardner, Howard. *Leading Minds: An Anatomy of Leadership.* New York: Harper Collins, 1996.

Gisel, Bonnie J. with images by Stephen J. Joseph. *Nature's Beloved Son, Rediscovering John Muir's Botanical Legacy.* Berkeley CA: Heyday Books, 2008.

Gott, Richard. *Cuba, a New History.* New Haven CT: Yale University Press, 2004.

Groce, W. Todd. *Mountain Rebels, East Tennessee Confederates and the Civil War, 1860–1870.* Knoxville: University of Tennessee Press, 1999.

Hall, Jere, and Jock B. Shelby. *Valley of Challenge and Change, Roane County, Tennessee, 1860–1900.* Knoxville: East Tennessee Historical Society, 1986.

Hartman, David W., and David Coles. *Biographical Rosters of Florida's Confederate and Union Soldiers.* 6 vols. Wilmington NC: Broadfoot Publishing, 1999.

Hays, Tony. *No Man's Land, Civil War and Reconstruction in Hardin County.* Chattanooga TN: Kitchen Table Press, 1996.

Heifetz, Ronald. *Leadership without Easy Answers.* Cambridge MA: Belknap Press, Harvard University, 1998.

Herr, Kincaid A. *The Louisville & Nashville Railroad, 1850–1942.* Louisville KY. L.&N. Magazine, [1943].

Hildreth, Charles H. and Merlin D. Cox. *History of Gainesville, 1854–1979.* Gainesville FL: Alachua Press, 1981.

Hines, Edward Warren. *Corporate History of the Louisville & Nashville Railroad Company and Roads in its System.* Louisville KY: J.P. Morton, [1905?].

Hodges, T.R. "Early Cedar Key Days." *Tampa Sunday Tribune,* Sunday, 21 February 1954, 12ff.

Holmes, Steven J. *The Young John Muir, an Environmental Biography.* Madison: University of Wisconsin Press, 1999.

Hull, Augustus Longstreet. *Annals of Athens, Georgia, 1801–1901.* Danielsville GA: Heritage Papers, 1906.

Hunhner, Leon. *David L. Yulee, Florida's First Senator.* (n.p. n.d.) Smathers Libraries, Special Collections, University of Florida, Gainesville, Florida.

Kavanaugh, Celeste H. *David Levy Yulee: A Man and His Vision.* 2nd edition. Fernandina FL: Amelia Island Museum of History, 1995.

Klein, Maury. *History of the Louisville & Nashville Railroad.* New York: Macmillan, 1972.

Knight, Franklin W. *Slave Society in Cuba during the Nineteenth Century.* Madison: University of Wisconsin Press, 1970.

Lord, Jr., Mills M. *David Levy Yulee, Statesman and Railroad Builder.* Gainesville FL: University of Florida, 1940.

Miller, James J. *An Environmental History of Northeast Florida.* Gainesville: University Press of Florida, 1998.

Miller, Rod. *John Muir, Magnificent Tramp.* New York: Tom Doherty Associates, 2005.

Miller, Sally M., editor. *John Muir in Historical Perspective.* New York: Peter Lang, 1999. A collection of thirteen scholarly articles based on papers read at a 1996 conference on John Muir at the University of the Pacific, Stockton, California.

-----*John Muir, Life and Work.* Albuquerque: University of New Mexico Press, 1993. A collection of fourteen scholarly articles based on a 1990 conference on Muir held at the University of the Pacific, Stockton, California.

Perez, Jr., Louis A. *Cuba Between Reform & Revolution.* 2nd edition. New York: Oxford University Press, 1995.

Perkins, Donald E. *History of the Perkins Family of Perkins, Georgia.* Privately published, 1979. Georgia Historical Society, Savannah, Georgia.

Rowe, H.J. *History of Athens and Clarke County.* Athens GA: The McGregor Company, 1923.

Sands, Sarah G. Cox. *History of Monroe County, Tennessee, From the Frontier Days to the Space Age.* Baltimore: Gateway Press, 1982.

Severance, Ben. H. *Tennessee's Radical Army, The State Guard and Its Role in Reconstruction, 1867-1869.* Knoxville: University of Tennessee Press, 2005.

Seymour, Randy. *Wildflowers of Mammoth Cave National Park.* Lexington: University Press of Kentucky, 1997.

Stanley, Millie. *The Heart of John Muir's World, Wisconsin, Family and Wilderness Discovery.* Madison WA: Prairie Oak Press, 1995.

Sutherland, Daniel E., editor. *Guerrillas, Unionists, and Violence on the Confederate Home Front.* Fayetteville: University of Arkansas Press, 1999.

Sweet, Frank. *Yulee's Railroad.* Palm Coast FL: Backintyme Press, 2000.

Thomas, Frances Taliaferro. *A Portrait of Historic Athens & Clarke County.* Athens: University of Georgia Press, 1992.

Thompson, Arthur William. *David Yulee, a Study of 19th Century American Thought and Enterprise.* Ann Arbor MI: University Microfilms, 1954.

Turner, Frederick. *John Muir, Rediscovering America.* Cambridge MA: Perseus Publishing, 1985.

Van Vugt, William E. *Britain to America, Mid-Nineteenth-Century Immigrants to the United States.* Urbana: University of Illinois Press, 1999.

Wilkins, Thurman. *John Muir, Apostle of Nature.* Norman: University of Oklahoma Press, 1995.

Williams, Dennis C. *God's Wilds, John Muir's Vision of Nature.* College Station: Texas A&M University Press, 2002.

Wolfe, Linnie Marsh. *Son of the Wilderness, the Life of John Muir* [1945]. Foreword by Steven J. Holmes. Madison: University of Wisconsin Press, 2003.

Worcester, Donald C. *A Passion for Nature, The Life of John Muir.* New York: Oxford University Press, 2008.

Yulee, Charles Wickliff. *Senator David Yulee.* (n.p. n.d.) Smathers Libraries, Special Collections, Gainesville, Florida.

Scholarly Articles

Callicott, J. Baird. "Genesis and John Muir." *ReVision* 12/3 (Winter 1990): 31–48.

Cason, Roberta F. "The Loyal League in Georgia." *The Georgia Historical Quarterly* 20 (June 1936): 125–53.

Coulter, E. Merton. "Aaron Alpeoria Bradley, Georgia Negro Politician during Reconstruction Times." Parts I, II and III, *Georgia Historical Quarterly* 51/1 (March 1967): 15–41; 51/2 (June 1967): 154–74; and 51/3 (September 1967): 264–306.

——. "Slavery and Freedom in Athens, Georgia, 1860-1866." *Georgia Historical Quarterly* 49 (September 1965): 264–306.

Fishburne Jr., Charles C. "Eliza Hearn and Life on the Way Key, 1867–1973." *Search for Yesterday, a History of Levy County.* Bronson FL: Levy County Archives Committee, October 1982.

Grimm, D.L. et al. "Counting Your Blessings: Positive Memories Among Grateful Persons." *Current Psychology: Developmental, Learning, Personality, Social* 23 (2004): 52–67.

Limbaugh, Ronald H. "The Nature of John Muir's Religion." *The Pacific Historian* 29/2 and 3 (Summer/Fall 1985): 16–29.

Russ, Jr., William A. "Radical Disfranchisement in Georgia, 1867-1871." *The Georgia Historical Quarterly* 19 (September 1935): 175–209.

Shofner, Jerrell H. "Andrew Johnson and the Fernandina Unionists," *Prologue: The Journal of the National Archives* (Winter 1978): 211–24.

Stanley, Millie. "John Muir in Wisconsin." *The Pacific Historian* 29/2 and 3 (Summer/Fall 1985): 7–15.

Stoll, Mark. "God and John Muir, A Psychological Interpretation of John Muir's Journey from the Campbellites to the 'Range of Light'" in *John Muir, Life and Work*. Edited by Sally M. Miller. Albuquerque: University of New Mexico Press, 1993.

Dissertations, Thesis and Unpublished Materials

Adler, Joseph Gary. "The Public Career of Senator David Yulee." PhD dissertation, Cleveland OH: Case Western Reserve, 1973.

[Anon.] "Hodgson Hill in Cedar Key," Unpublished Manuscript. Cedar Key Historical Society, Cedar Key, Florida, [n.d.].

Caudle, Everett W. "Postbellum Race Relations in Gainesville, Florida, a Study of Social, Economic, and Institutional Arrangements," Undergraduate Honors Paper. Submitted to Merlin G. Cox, University of Florida, Gainesville, Florida, 1986.

Knetsch, Joe. David Levy Yulee and the Development of Antebellum Florida. Typescript. Amelia Island Museum of History, 23 April 1998.

Mann, Jesse T. "Fernandina: A City in Turmoil, 1863–1888," MA thesis. Tallahassee FL: Florida State University, 1971.

Millirons, Martha Woobright. "A Bibliographical Checklist of Tennessee Imprints in Small Towns, 1867–1876." MA thesis, Knoxville: University of Tennessee, August, 1965.

Stafford, Hanford Dozier. "Slavery in a Border City: Louisville, 1790–1860," Ph.D thesis, Lexington: Young Library, University of Kentucky, 1982.

Stein, Leslie Reicin. "David Levy Yulee and Florida Territorial Politics." MA thesis. Tampa FL: University of South Florida, March 1973. Copy available at Smathers Libraries, Special Collections, University of Florida, Gainesville, Florida.

Trefille, John R. "Reconstruction in Augusta, Georgia, 1865–1868." MA thesis. Chapel Hill: University of North Carolina, 1979.

# Notes

[1] The John Muir Papers [JMP] are available in a 51-reel, 53-fiche microfilm collection containing all the collected John Muir Papers, edited by Ronald H. Limbaugh and Kirsten E. Lewis, published by Chadwyck-Healey, Inc. (Alexandria, Virginia, 1986), available in 1986 by the Holt-Atherton Center for Western Studies, University of the Pacific, Stockton, California, hereinafter cited as JMP. The papers are also in digitized format through the University of the Pacific's Holt Atherton John Muir Papers Collection Web site: [http://digitalcollection.pacific.edu/cdm4/browse. php? Pacific.CISOROOT=/muirjournals]. I have used the microfilm edition of the JMP through the University of Montana Library and the Library at the University of California, Berkeley, as well as at the Holt-Atherton Collection at the University of the Pacific. The key biographies of John Muir used in this study, along with his manuscripts, are: Donald Worster, *A Passion for Nature, The Life of John Muir* (New York: Oxford University Press, 2008); Bonnie Gisel with images by Stephen J. Joseph, *Nature's Beloved Son, Rediscovering John Muir's Botanical Legacy* (Berkeley, California: Heyday Books, 2008); Dennis C. Williams, *God's Wilds, John Muir's Vision of Nature* (College Station, Texas: Texas A & M University Press, 2002), Steven J. Holmes, *The Young John Muir, an Environmental Biography* (Madison: University of Wisconsin Press, 1999); Frederick Turner, *John Muir, Rediscovery of America* (Cambridge MA: Perseus Press, 1985); Michael P. Cohen, *The Pathless Way, John Muir and American Wilderness* (Madison: University of Wisconsin Press, 1984); Sally Miller, ed., *John Muir, Life and Work* (Albuquerque: University of New Mexico Press, 1993); Sally Miller, ed., *John Muir in Historical Perspective* (New York: Peter Lang, 1999); and Linnie Marsh Wolfe, *Son of the Wilderness, the Life of John Muir* [1945] (Madison: University of Wisconsin Press, 2003).

[2] John Muir to Mrs. Ezra S. Carr, [6 April 1867] in John Muir, *Letters to a Friend Written to Mrs. Ezra S. Carr* (New York: Cosimo Classics, 2006) 15–19. Hereinafter cited as Muir, *Letters*.

[3] John Muir to Mrs. Ezra S. Carr, [April 1867] in Muir, *Letters*, 19–20.

[4] John Muir to Mrs. Ezra S. Carr, "The Hallow," 21 January 1866 in Muir, *Letters*, 1.

[5] JMP 23:59.

[6] John Muir to Betty Averell, 2 March 1911, Michael P. Branch, ed., *John Muir's Last Journey, South to the Amazon and East to Africa, Unpublished Journals and Selected Correspondence* (Washington DC: Island Press, 2001) 15–16.

[7] John Muir, *A Thousand-Mile Walk to the Gulf*, ed. William Frederic Badé, with illustrations (New York: Houghton Mifflin, 1916). For a readily available edition see, John Muir, *A Thousand-Mile Walk to the Gulf*, Frederick William Badé edition, (San Francisco: Sierra Books, 1991). In 1908, Muir worked with his autobiographical materials, reviewed and revised his journals, and began dictating his life story at E.H. Harriman's lodge on Pelican Bay, Klamath Lake, Oregon. Muir began the process of transcribing the journal for publication. Typescript copies of these autobiographical materials are known as the "Pelican Bay manuscripts." Eventually, the journal was published with the title, *A Thousand-Mile Walk to the Gulf*, edited by William Frederic Badé, in 1916, two years after Muir's death. This study is based on the original journal available on microfilm and in digitized format, the 1908 transcriptions known as the Pelican Bay manuscripts, and the Badé edition of the published work. It is also based on research in the John Muir Papers, deposited at the University of Pacific's Holt Atherton Collection in Stockton, California. I have also consulted libraries in the numerous states, towns and villages through which Muir passed in 1867 and 1868. I followed his route through the Southern states with a 2007 research trip. Of course, much has changed since 1867, but there are scattered portions of undeveloped nature left that remind one of the plants, foliage, creatures, and vistas John Muir witnessed. These experiences, together with examination of relevant family papers, letters, manuscripts, sketches, maps, and photographs provide a portrait of John Muir in a formative period of his life when his passion for wilderness became inflamed and his environmental thought and ethics grew as he encountered the new experience of walking in the tropics.

[8] John Muir, *The Story of My Boyhood and Youth* (Boston: Houghton Mifflin, 1913) 53. Muir dictated stories about his boyhood and youth beginning in 1908 to Thomas Price, secretary to E.H. Harriman, the railroad magnate, who urged Muir to begin writing his story. Price typed

pages of transcripts of Muir's dictation, which became known as the Pelican Bay manuscripts since this was done at Harriman's Lodge on Pelican Bay, on Klamath Lake, Oregon. Muir may well have returned to his earliest autobiographical writings early in 1887 as he began to draw away from active involvement in his orchards at Martinez, California. Muir later retrieved the notebooks of his first summer in the Sierra Nevada Mountains and had them published in a volume in 1911. He had recopied all of these Sierra journals in 1887. The originals have been lost. See Steven J. Holmes, *The Young John Muir, an Environmental Biography* (Madison: University of Wisconsin Press, 1999), Appendix A, 253–59 and John Muir, *My First Summer in the Sierra* (Boston: Houghton Mifflin, 1911). He worked hard on the Pelican Bay materials between 1910 and 1911, finishing a manuscript for publication in July 1911, two years after the death of Harriman. Published installments of *The Story of My Boyhood and Youth* appeared in 1912 in the *Wisconsin Alumni Monthly* and the *Atlantic Monthly*. Houghton Mifflin published this autobiography in 1913 when Muir was seventy-five. As in most autobiographies, Muir selected memories that reinforced what he knew he had become. His first goal was to trace back to his childhood his love of nature, but he also wrote about his love of the outdoors through walks, Saturday adventures in the countryside, travel, and the ways he sought to escape the confinement of "civilization," whether it was in school, home, university, or factory. At the end of his first chapter, for example, Muir wrote, "Wildness was ever sounding in our ears, and Nature saw to it that besides school lessons and church lessons some of her own lessons should be learned, perhaps with a view to the time when we should be called to wander in wildness to our heart's content" (Muir, *Boyhood and Youth*, 49–50). If one consults his earliest letters and writings, this clear-cut direction is not always so clear. Certainly there were emerging interests in nature and travel, such as many growing boys experience, but Muir was also drawn to mechanics and invention; he spent long hours in the early morning reading a wide array of literature; a professorship could loom in the future. As is true of every human being, there were numerous forces at work in his life. Yet he both experienced and thought about travel.

[9] Muir, *Boyhood and Youth*, 54.

[10] Ibid., 57.

[11] Ibid., 57–58.

[12] Linnie Marsh Wolfe, *Son of the Wilderness, the Life of John Muir* [1945], (Madison: University of Wisconsin Press, 2003) 24–25, and Muir, *Boyhood and Youth*, 58–59.

[13] Wolfe, *Son of the Wilderness*, 25, and Muir, *Boyhood and Youth*, 59.

[14] Muir, *Boyhood and Youth*, 59.

[15] Ibid., 61.

[16] Ibid., 63–64.

[17] William E. Van Vugt, *Britain to America, Mid-Nineteenth Century Immigrants to the United States* (Urbana: University of Illinois Press, 1999) 8.

[18] Mark Stoll, "God and John Muir, A Psychological Interpretation of John Muir's Journey from the Campbellites to the 'Range of Light,'" in Sally M. Miller, ed., *John Muir, Life and Work* (Albuquerque: University of New Mexico Press, 1993) 66, and Wolfe, *Son of the Wilderness*, 4.

[19] Wolfe, *Son of the Wilderness*, 5.

[20] Ibid., 7.

[21] Ibid., 8, and Donald Worster, *A Passion for Nature, The Life of John Muir* (New York: Oxford University Press, 2008) 20.

[22] Wolfe, *Son of the Wilderness*, 9.

[23] Ibid., 8.

[24] Muir, *Boyhood and Youth*, 31.

[25] Ibid., 10.

[26] Ibid., 24, 43–44.

[27] Ibid., 24–26.

[28] Ibid., 28–29.

[29] Ibid., 43–44.

[30] Ibid.

[31] Ibid.

[32] Ibid., 54.

[33] Ibid., 77.

[34] Cecelia Galloway, Reminiscence, 23 March 1944, JMP 51 (Linnie Marsh Wolfe Papers) 00133-00157, and Muir, *Boyhood and Youth*, 240.

[35] Muir, *Boyhood and Youth*, 241.

[36] Ibid., 242.

[37] Ibid., 243.

[38] Ibid., 246.

[39] Ibid., 254–55.

[40] Wolfe, *Son of the Wilderness*, 56-57.

---

[41] Muir, *Boyhood and Youth*, 262.

[42] Ibid.

[43] Ibid., 269.

[44] Wolfe, *Son of the Wilderness*, 59.

[45] Daniel Muir to John Muir, Buffalo, 25 January 1861, JMP 1:87–89.

[46] Robert Burns, "Epistle to John Lapraik, an Old Scottish Bard," *The Poems of Robert Burns* (London: Bell and Daldy, 1863) 169.

[47] Philip Sheldrake, *Living Between Worlds, Pilgrimage and Journey in Celtic Spirituality* (Boston: Cowley Publications, 1995), chaps. 5 and 6; Oliver Davies, Thomas O'Laughlin, and James Mackey, eds., *Celtic Spirituality*, Introduction by Oliver Davies (New York: Paulist Press, 1999) 19; Thomas O'Loughlin, *Journeys on the Edge* (Maryknoll NY: Orbis Books, 2000); Philip Edwards, *Pilgrimage and Literary Tradition* (Cambridge, England: Cambridge University Press, 2005); and, Hew Ainslie and Thomas Lotto, *A Pilgrimage to the Land of Burns* [1822], reprint (Whitefish MT: Kessinger Publishers, 2006).

[48] Robert Burns, "To James Smith" *The Poems of Robert Burns* (London: Bell and Daldy, 1863) 62.

[49] John Milton, *Paradise Lost, a Poem* (Boston: Crosby & Ainsworth, 1867) [IV:237–48], 81–82.

[50] Milton, *Paradise Lost* [V:192–96], 108.

[51] Milton, *Paradise Lost* [V:153–54], 107.

[52] John Muir to Wanda Muir, 1893, qtd. in William Frederic Badé, ed., *The Life and Letters of John Muir*, 2 vols. (Boston: Houghton Mifflin, 1923) 1:30.

[53] Dennis C. Williams, *God's Wilds, John Muir's Vision of Nature*, (College Station: Texas A & M University Press, 2002) 24–25; Holmes, *Young John Muir*, 58–64; Worster, *Life of John Muir*, 36–40; and Stoll, "God and John Muir," Miller, ed., *John Muir*, 66–68, 73, 74–75.

[54] Milton S. Griswold, Reminiscence, 30 March 1917, JMP 51 [Badé Papers]: 01017-01023.

[55] Alphonso Wood, *Class-Book of Botany: Being Outlines of the Structure, Physiology, and Classification of Plants; a Flora of the United States and Canada* (New York: A.S. Barnes & Company, 1880) Title page. Muir's 1862 edition of this text may be found in John Muir's personal library, Holt Atherton Department of Special Collections, University of the Pacific Library, Stockton, California.

[56] Wood, *Class-Book of Botany*, 10.

[57] Ibid., 9.

[58] Bonnie Gisel with images by Stephen J. Joseph, *Nature's Beloved Son, Rediscovering John Muir's Botanical Legacy*, (Berkeley, California: Heyday Books, 2008) 64. This is a scholarly and beautiful book containing full-page images of plant specimens collected by Muir in his herbariums. For twentieth-century photography re-tracing of Muir's 1867 walk, with excerpts from Muir's published journal edited by Badé, see John Earl, *John Muir's Longest Walk: John Earl, a Photographer, Traces His Journey to Florida* (New York: Doubleday, 1975).

[59] Muir, *Boyhood and Youth*, 259–60.

[60] Mungo Park, *Travels in the Interior Districts of Africa Performed under the Direction and Patronages of the African Association in the years 1795, 1796, and 1797* [1799], edited with and Introduction by Kate Ferguson Marsters, (Durham NC: Duke University Press, 2000) 67.

[61] Alexander von Humboldt, *Personal Narrative of Travels to the Equinoctial Regions of America, During the Years 1799–1804*, translated from the French and edited by Thomasina Ross, 3 vols. (London: George Bell & Sons, 1907) 1:x.

[62] Michael P. Branch, ed., *John Muir's Last Journey, South to the Amazon and East to Africa, Unpublished Journals and Selected Correspondence* (Washington DC: Island Press, 2001).

[63] Qtd. in Wolfe, *Son of the Wilderness*, 107.

[64] Ibid.

[65] Ibid.

[66] Burns, *Poems*, "Epistle to John Lapraik," 169.

[67] Frederick Turner, *John Muir, Rediscovery of America* (Cambridge MA: Perseus Press, 1985) 91.

[68] Linnie Marsh Wolfe, *Son of the Wilderness, the Life of John Muir* [1945], (Madison: University of Wisconsin Press, 2003) 62.

[69] Ibid., 63.

[70] Ibid.

[71] Eveline [Merrill] to John Muir, Lone Rock, [Wisconsin], 17 July 1861, JMP 1:219–21.

[72] John Muir to Mr. and Mrs. Pelton, c. [fall?] 1862, JMP 1:252.

[73] John Muir to Frances M. Pelton, 27 March 1862, JMP 1:201.

[74] Frances M. Pelton to John Muir, Middlefield, Massachusetts, 11 July 1862, JMP 1:219–21.

[75] John Muir to Sarah and David Galloway, Madison, Wisconsin, 1862, JMP 1:250.

[76] John Muir to David Galloway, 12 June [1863], Madison, Wisconsin, JMP 1:297.

[77] John Muir to Mr. and Mrs. [Ambrose] Newton, [Middlefield, Massachusetts], Fountain Lake [or, Geddo], Wisconsin, 2 August 1863, JMP 1:308.

[78] [Ann Gilrye Muir] Mother, Portage City, Wisconsin, 16 May 1863, JMP 1:289.

[79] John Muir to David [M. Galloway], Madison, Wisconsin, 8 June, 1863, JMP 1:292; qtd. in William Frederic Badé, ed., *The Life and Letters of John Muir*, 2 vols. (Boston: Houghton Mifflin, 1923) 1:97.

[80] John Muir to Sarah and David Galloway, Madison, Wisconsin, 1 June 1863, JMP 1:291. and Badé, *Life and Letters*, 197.

[81] Badé, *Life and Letters*, 1:97–98.

[82] Wolfe, *Son of the Wilderness*, 84.

[83] Badé, *Life and Letters*, 1:98.

[84] John Muir to Emily Pelton, Fountain Lake, 27 February 1864, McGregor, [Iowa], 7 July 1863, Badé, *Life and Letters*, 1:98–101.

[85] Wolfe, *Son of the Wilderness*, 87.

[86] John Muir to David and Sarah Galloway, [Madison, Wisconsin, July 1863], JMP 1:306–307, and Badé, *Life and Letters*, 1:111.

[87] John Muir to Daniel Muir, Fountain Lake, Wisconsin, 20 December 1863, JMP 1:327.

[88] JMP 1:327.

[89] John Muir to Emily Pelton, Fountain Lake, 1 March 1864, Badé, *Life and Letters*, 1:116. The only record of this trip was a herbarium discovered by William Frederic Badé when he compiled his letters and published them together with a Muir biography in 1923. The herbarium provided place names and dates.

[90] Badé, *Life and Letters*, 1:117–18.

[91] Ibid., 1:119.

[92] Ibid., 1:120.

[93] Ibid., 1:129.

[94] Wolfe, *Son of the Wilderness*, 96–97.

[95] John Muir to [Jeanne C.] Carr, Trout's Mill, [Canada], 13 September 1865, JMP 1:380, and Bonnie Johanna Gisel, ed., *Kindred & Related Spirits, The Letters of John Muir and Jeanne C. Carr* (Salt Lake City: The University of Utah Press, 2001) 21.

[96] Bonnie Gisel's scholarly editing of this correspondence has underscored the critical importance of Jeanne C. Carr's sponsorship in his life. Gisel, ed. *Kindred & Related Spirits*, 3–6, 21–28, and 65–70.

[97] JMP 1:380.

[98] Gisel, ed., *Kindred & Related Spirits*, 22.

[99] Qtd. in Turner, *John Muir*, 203–04.

[100] Qtd. in Wolfe, *Son of the Wilderness*, 78–79.

[101] Gisel, ed., *Kindred & Related Spirits*, 30, and JMP 1:380.

[102] Badé, *Life and Letters*, 1:120–21. See also, John Muir, Autobiographical sketches, 1906, JMP 45:11015–17.

[103] Badé, *Life and Letters*, 1:121, "The Calypso Borealis: Botanical Enthusiasm," *Boston Recorder*, 21 December 1866, 1., and Gisel, ed., *Kindred and Related Spirits*, 40-42 and 42-43.

[104] JMP 1:380.

[105] JMP 1:381.

[106] Jeanne C. Carr to John Muir, Sauk City, Wisconsin, 24 September [1865] in Gisel, ed., *Kindred & Related Spirits*, 33.

[107] Gisel, ed., *Kindred & Related Spirits*, 33.

[108] Ibid., 33–34.

[109] John Muir to Jeanne Carr, "The Hollow," 21 January 1866, JMP 1:407–08.

[110] John Muir to Jeanne Carr, "The Hollow," 21 January 1866 in Gisel, ed., *Kindred & Related Spirits*, 34–35.

[111] Gisel, ed., *Kindred & Related Spirits*, 35–36.

[112] Wolfe, *Son of the Wilderness*, 97.

[113] Qtd. in Wolfe, *Son of the Wilderness*, 98.

[114] John Muir to Daniel Muir, Jr., Indianapolis, Indiana, 7 May 1866, JMP 1:432.

[115] JMP 1:432.

[116] John Muir to Jeanne C. Carr, [April, 1867], in Gisel, ed., *Kindred & Related Spirits*, 50. The first part of this letter is missing and refers to Muir having read about Yosemite: "I read a description of the Yosemite Valley

last year and thought of it most every day since. You know my tastes better than any one else."

[117] John Muir to Sarah Muir Galloway, Indianapolis, Indiana, May 1866, JMP 1:444.

[118] JMP 1:444.

[119] Ibid.

[120] Jeanne C. Carr to John Muir, Madison, Wisconsin, 12 October [1866], in Gisel, ed., *Kindred & Related Spirits*, 37, and JMP 1:461.

[121] JMP 1:461, and Gisel, ed., *Kindred & Related Spirits*, 38.

[122] John Muir to Jeanne C. Carr, Osgood & Smith, [Indianapolis, Indiana], [October, 1866] in Gisel, ed., *Kindred & Related Spirits*, 38–39, and JMP 1:463.

[123] JMP 1:463-464.

[124] Wolfe, *Son of the Wilderness*, 101–02.

[125] Wolfe, *Son of the Wilderness*, 102.

[126] John Muir to Daniel H. Muir, [Indianapolis, Indiana], 19 November 1866, JMP 1:465–70.

[127] JMP 1:467–70.

[128] Jeanne C. Carr to John Muir, Madison, Wisconsin, 12 October [1866] in Gisel, ed., *Kindred & Related Spirits*, 39–40.

[129] John Muir, Autobiographical Sketches, dictated 1906, Pelican Bay, Oregon, JMP 45:11021–22. and Gisel, ed., *Kindred & Related Spirits*, 44-46.

[130] Qtd. in Wolfe, *Son of the Wilderness*, 104, and John Muir to Jeanne C. Carr, [Indianapolis], Sunday, 6 April [1867] in Gisel, ed., *Kindred & Related Spirits*, 45.

[131] Mary Hark to John Muir, Oakville, Canada, 3 April 1867, JMP 1:513–16.

[132] Jeanne C. Carr, Madison, Wisconsin, 15 March 1866, in Gisel, ed., *Kindred & Related Spirits*, 43.

[133] Gisel, ed., *Kindred & Related Spirits*, 43–44.

[134] John Muir to Jeanne C. Carr, Ind[ianapolis], 3 April 1867 in Gisel, ed., *Kindred & Related Spirits*, 44, and John Muir to Jeanne C. Carr, [Indianapolis] Sunday, 6 April [1867] in Gisel, ed., *Kindred & Related Spirits*, 45.

[135] John Muir, Autobiographical Sketches, Pelican Bay, Oregon, 1906, JMP 45:11023.

[136] Jeanne C. Carr to John Muir, Madison, 15 April [1867], in Gisel, ed., *Kindred & Related Spirits*, 48–49.

[137] Qtd. in Wolfe, *Son of the Wilderness*, 104.

[138] John Muir to Jeanne C. Carr, [April, 1867] in Gisel, ed., *Kindred & Related Spirits*, 50.

[139] John Muir to Jeanne C. Carr, Indianapolis, 2 May 1867 in Gisel, ed., *Kindred & Related Spirits*, 51–52.

[140] John Muir, Autobiographical Sketches, Pelican Bay, Oregon, c.1907, JMP 45:11024–25.

[141] John Muir to Jeanne C. Carr, Indianapolis, 9 June 1867, Bonnie Johanna Gisel, ed., *Kindred & Related Spirits, The Letters of John Muir and Jeanne C. Carr* (Salt Lake City: The University of Utah Press, 2001) 52.

[142] John Muir to Merrills & Moores, Indianapolis, 4[6?] March 1867, JMP 1:492. In this letter to the local families who welcomed him into their homes, Muir reports that he has lost an eye in an accident, "Yesterday in connecting a machine belt I thrust a pointed file through the outer membrane and as I received the liquid of the first bruise upon my fingers felt that not a single flower, no more of lovely scenery, not any more of beauty would ever pass the portal of my right eye. It is lost." Muir then goes on to report that "For weeks I have daily [studied] maps in locating a route through the southern states, the West Indies, South America, and Europe—a botanical journey studied for years, and so my mind has long been in a glow with the visions of the glories of a tropical flora, but, alas, I am half blind."

[143] John Muir to Jeanne C. Carr, 3 April [1867], in Gisel, ed., *Kindred & Related Spirits*, 44.

[144] Alphonse de Lamartine, *The Stone-Mason of Saint Point*, trans. from the French, (New York: Harper & Brothers, 1851) 41.

[145] Lamartine, *The Stonemason*, 43.

[146] John Muir to Jeanne C. Carr, [April, 1867], in Gisel, ed., *Kindred & Related Spirits*, 49.

[147] John Muir to Jeanne C. Carr, [Indianapolis], [April, 1867], in Gisel, ed., *Kindred & Related Spirits*, 50.

[148] John Muir to [James Davie] Butler, Indianapolis, 27 April [1867], JMP 1:544.

[149] John Muir to Jeanne C. Carr, Portage, 1–12 August 1867, JMP 1:560-61.

[150] Ibid.

[151] Linnie Marsh Wolfe, *Son of the Wilderness, the Life of John Muir* [1945], (Madison: University of Wisconsin Press, 2003) 106.

[152] Wolfe, *Son of the Wilderness*, 106.

[153] John Muir to [Moores], transcription, Portage, July [1867], JMP 1:570.

[154] John Muir to [Moores], transcript, July [1867], JMP 1:570. Muir also wrote of his enthusiasm for the botanical journey to Jeanne Carr, "I am enjoying myself exceedingly. The dear flowers of Wisconsin are incomparably more numerous than those of Canada or Indiana. With what fervid, unspeakable joy did I welcome those flowers that I have loved so long!" John Muir to Jeanne C. Carr, [Portage City, August 1867] Gisel, ed., *Kindred & Related Spirits*, 53–54.

[155] Wolfe, *Son of the Wilderness*, 108.

[156] Ibid.

[157] Qtd. in Wolfe, *Son of the Wilderness*, 109.

[158] John Muir to [Jeanne C.] Carr, Indianapolis, 30 August 1867, JMP 1:587–88, and Gisel, ed., *Kindred & Related Spirits*, 57.

[159] JMP 1:588.

[160] Donna Andriot, ed., *Population Abstract of the United States* (Woodbridge CT: Gale Group, 2000) 180.

[161] John Muir to Daniel H. Muir, Indianapolis, Indiana, 1 September 1867, JMP 1:590.

[162] JMP 1:590.

[163] John Muir, *A Thousand-Mile Walk to the Gulf*, edited by William Frederic Badé, (New York: Houghton Mifflin, 1916) 1; JMP 45:11467-68; JMP 23:21–22; and, digitized copy of Journal, JMP 23:3.

[164] John Muir to Jeanne C. Carr, Among the Hills of Bear Creek, 7 miles S.E, of Burkesville, Kentucky, 9 Sept[ember] [1867], JMP 1:591, and Gisel, ed., *Kindred & Related Sprits*, 57–58.

[165] JMP 23:21. For online access to the John Muir Journals, see the Web site at the Holt-Atherton Collection at the Special Collections Library of the University of the Pacific, Stockton, California: Journal no. 3, January–May 1869, Twenty Hill Hallow, image no. 2, http://digitalcollections.pacific.edu/cdm4/browse.php?CISOROOT=/muirjournals.

[166] JMP 23:21–22. John Muir, in editing his journal at a later time, crossed out this section. Thus, this statement was not included in Badé's edition of the journal. Muir edited his journal either while recovering from malaria at Cedar Key or at a later point in his life, possibly while in Yosemite in 1870 or Pelican Bay, Oregon, while working on his journals and his autobiographical materials together with the dictation he provided in 1906–1908. Most of these editing marks are in pencil. Thus, the original comments tend to be in ink and the cross-outs and edited passages are written in pencil. Michael Cohen (1984) argues that there is reason to believe the entire journal was re-written or re-copied after the walk when Muir was in Yosemite (Michael P. Cohen, *The Pathless Way, John Muir and American Wilderness* [Madison: University of Wisconsin Press, 1984] 3–4). Stephen J. Holmes (1999) takes issue with Cohen, and in an extended Appendix B commented that acknowledging Muir's tendency to let days pass before making entries, "the journal as a whole, however, seems to be original." As to when Muir made his revisions and editing, "my hunch is that it was not until after he was struck down with malaria at Cedar Key (on the Gulf coast of Florida) that he went back to fill in the uncompleted parts" (Steven J. Holmes, *The Young John Muir, an Environmental Biography* [Madison: University of Wisconsin Press, 1999] Appendix B, 261–63). I rely on the microfilm and digitized copy of the Muir journal throughout the book, and, when necessary, identify the published edition of Muir's journal as the Badé edition. William Frederic Badé was Muir's literary executor and edited Muir's original journal. He was forthright in his use of Muir materials in the publication of the posthumously published journal made into a book, *A Thousand-Mile Walk to the Gulf*, ed. William Frederic Badé, with illustrations (New York: Houghton Mifflin, 1916). First, he used the original journal with its penciled revisions and followed Muir's lead in making changes for publication. Second, Badé used a type written copy of the journal, dictated to a stenographer at Pelican Bay known by scholars at the Pelican Bay manuscript. The editor wove materials from this manuscript into the publication. The Pelican Bay manuscript "shows many significant omissions and additions." Third, Badé used two separate accounts of Muir's experience in Savannah. Fourth, Badé included a previously published article in *The Overland Monthly* (July 1872) on "Twenty Hill Hollow." Muir, *A Thousand-Mile Walk*, Badé edition (1916),

xxv. The original journal ended with Muir arriving in New York City before his trip to Panama and then onto California.

[167] JMP 23:22.

[168] JMP 23:22.

[169] Muir, *Thousand-Mile Walk*, Badé ed., 2.

[170] John E. Kieber, ed., *The Encyclopedia of Louisville* (Lexington: University Press of Kentucky, 2001) 634, and *Louisville and Its Defenses* (Washington DC: US Engineers, 1865) Special Collections, Eckstrom Library, University of Louisville, Louisville, Kentucky.

[171] JMP 23:22. In using material from the original journal, I have retained the use of Muir's strikeovers to show the reader the direction of his revision done at a later time. Muir's edited words are in parentheses.

[172] JMP 1:593, and Gisel, ed., *Kindred & Related Spirits*, 58.

[173] Muir, *Thousand-Mile Walk*, Badé ed., 2, and JMP 23:22.

[174] JMP 23:23.

[175] From September 2 to September 9 he covered, by his estimation, 170 miles or about 18.8 miles a day. Gisel, ed., *Kindred & Related Spirits*, 58.

[176] JMP 1:591.

[177] JMP 23:23.

[178] JMP 23: 23, and Muir, *Thousand-Mile Walk*, Badé ed., 3.

[179] JMP 23: 23-24, and Muir, *Thousand-Mile Walk*, Badé ed., 4.

[180] JMP 23:23, and Muir, *Thousand-Mile Walk*, Badé ed., 5.

[181] JMP 23:24, and Muir, *Thousand-Mile Walk*, Badé ed., 4–6.

[182] JMP 23:25.

[183] Randy Seymour, *Wildflowers of Mammoth Cave National Park* (Lexington: University Press of Kentucky, 1997) 146–206.

[184] JMP 23:26, and Muir, *Thousand-Mile Walk*, Badé ed., 7–9.

[185] Muir, *Thousand-Mile Walk*, Badé ed., 9, and JMP 23:26.

[186] Muir, *Thousand-Mile Walk*, Badé ed., 10–11, and JMP 23:27.

[187] Muir, *Thousand-Mile Walk*, Badé ed., 11–12.

[188] JMP 23:28.

[189] Ibid. Muir, *Thousand Mile Walk*, Badé ed., 13.

[190] JMP 23:28–29.

[191] JMP 1:591–92, and Gisel, ed. *Kindred & Related Sprits*, 58.

[192] John Muir, *A Thousand-Mile Walk to the Gulf*, ed. William Frederic Badé, with illustrations (New York: Houghton Mifflin, 1916) 16.

[193] Muir, *Thousand-Mile Walk* (Badé ed.) 24.

[194] E. Merton Coulter, *William G. Brownlow, Fighting Parson of the Southern Highlands* [1937], (Knoxville: University of Tennessee Press, 1999) chap. 14, 325 ff.

[195] Herman Bokum, *The Tennessee Handbook and Immigrant's Guide* (Philadelphia: J.B. Lippincott, 1868) 6.

[196] Martha Woobright Millirons, *A Bibliographical Checklist of Tennessee Imprints in Small Towns, 1867–1876*, (master's thesis, Knoxville: University of Tennessee, August 1965) 12. This characterization refers to Millirons's reading of T.D. Witherspoon, *The Appeal of the South to Its Educated Men* (Memphis TN: n.p. 1867), one of only fourteen imprints listed in 1867 from the region.

[197] Stephen V. Ash, *Middle Tennessee Society Transformed, 1860–1870, War and Peace in the Upper South* (Knoxville: University of Tennessee Press, 2006) chap. 10, 226–53; Coulter, *Brownlow*, chap. 14; Daniel E. Sutherland, ed., *Guerillas, Unionists and Violence on the Confederate Homefront* (Fayetteville: University of Arkansas Press, 1999); Noel C. Fisher, *War at Every Door, Partisan Politics and Guerilla Violence in East Tennessee* (1997); and, Tony Hays, *No Man's Land, Civil War and Reconstruction in Hardin County* (Chattanooga TN: Kitchen Table Press, 1986).

[198] JMP 23:29.

[199] JMP 23:29–30. This story is a penciled addition to the original journal and may well be a recollection written at a later point in either the journey or even as late as 1908–10 when Muir was working on his biographical materials, for in this section, he alludes specifically to contents of the bag and the books he carried in his dictation to Harriman's stenographer. In Version "D," adapted from his autobiography written between 1910 and 1913, he wrote, "I carried only a plant press and a little bag on my back; wealth of a kind few would be likely to care for. The bag, made of thin rubber cloth, contained only a change of underclothing, comb brush, towel, and three small books, —Burns' Poem, Milton's Paradise Lost and New Testament." John Muir, Walk to Mexico c.1910–13, JMP 48:13438.

[200] JMP 23:31.

[201] Ibid.

[202] Muir, *Thousand-Mile Walk* (Badé ed.) 21.

[203] Ibid., 22.

[204] Ibid., 23–24, and JMP 23:31.

[205] Muir, *Thousand-Mile Walk* (Badé ed.) 23 and JMP 23:31.

[206] JMP 23:31.

[207] Muir, *Thousand-Mile Walk* (Badé ed.) 23-24 and JMP 23:31.

[208] Muir, *Thousand-Mile Walk* (Badé ed.) 23–24. JMP 23:31. "And he [Solomon] spake of trees, from the cedar tree that is in Lebanon even unto the hyssop that springeth out of the wall: he spake also of beasts, and of fowl, and of creeping things, and of fishes. *The Holy Bible, King James Version*, 1 Kgs 4:33.

[209] Muir, *Thousand-Mile Walk* (Badé, ed.) 25.

[210] Ibid. This section is clearly a revision as later edited by both Muir and Badé. Even John Muir was unhappy with his original rendering of the story because he wrote a note to himself in pencil "Poorly told. Give this story in full." JMP 23:33. This penciled note with brackets is written in a slightly heavier hand and appears to be written well after the trip was finished when Muir was working on his autobiographical materials, possibly in 1908. Other penciled revisions with a thinner and more even hand may have been done at the end of the American leg of the trip while convalescing in Florida from malaria. Badé accepts Muir's revisions and produced a work more appropriate for the elderly 70-year-old Muir than the 29-year-old Muir. In the original journal the dialogue is less specific and the points more cryptic. The substance of the argument remains largely intact.

[211] Muir, *Thousand-Mile Walk* (Badé ed.) 25.

[212] Ibid., 26.

[213] JMP 23:33.

[214] Ibid.

[215] Ibid.

[216] Ibid.

[217] This story was not developed in the original journal. There is a penciled insertion: "(Tell story of guerillas)." Badé's edition provides a full treatment of this story in Muir, *Thousand-Mile Walk* (Badé ed.) 27–29.

[218] JMP 23:33–34; Ethel Freytag and Glena Keis Ott, *A History of Morgan County, Tennessee*, (n.p.: Specialty Books, 1971) 25–30; *Population of the United States in 1860: compiled from the original returns of the Eighth Census under the direction of the Secretary of the Interior, by Joseph C.G. Kennedy*, vol. 1, Population, (Washington DC: Government Printing Office, 1864) 466 and 469; and, *The Statistics of the Population of the United States, Compiled from the original returns of the Ninth Census (June 1, 1870) under the direction of the*

*Secretary of the Interior, by Francis A. Walker,* vol. 1, Population (Washington DC: Government Printing Office, 1872) 266–67.

[219] JMP 23:34.

[220] Recent studies on gratitude have underscored how helpful this virtue is when contending with obstacles, opposition, pain, sorrow, or the tough passages in life. Robert A. Emmons *et al., The Psychology of Gratitude* (New York: Oxford University Press, 2004); Robert A. Emmons, *Thanks! How the New Science of Gratitude Can Make You Happier* (Boston: Houghton Mifflin, 2007) chap. 1; and, D. L. Grimm, *et al.,* "Counting Your Blessings: Positive Memories Among Grateful Persons," *Current Psychology: Developmental, Learning, Personality, Social,* 23 (2004): 52–67.

[221] JMP 23:34, and *Ninth Census* (1870) 1:267.

[222] JMP 23:34–35.

[223] JMP 23:35, and *Eighth Census* (1860) 1:62, 466–67; *Ninth Census* (1870) 1:263, 266, 267, 371; and, *Statistics of the Population of the United States at the Tenth Census (June 1, 1880),* (Washington DC: Government Printing Office, 1883) 1:333, 337.

[224] JMP 23:35.

[225] Ibid.

[226] Ibid.

[227] Muir, *Thousand-Mile Walk* (Badé ed.) 36–37.

[228] JMP 23:36.

[229] Muir, *Thousand-Mile Walk* (Badé ed.) 37.

[230] JMP 23:37.

[231] Ibid.

[232] Ibid., and Muir, *Thousand-Mile Walk* (Badé ed.) 38–39.

[233] JMP 23:38.

[234] Margaret Walker Freel, *Our Heritage, the People of Cherokee County, North Carolina* (Ashville NC: Miller Publishing, 1956) 52–53.

[235] JMP 23:39 and Muir, *Thousand Mile Walk* (Badé ed.) 43.

[236] JMP 23:38.

[237] John Muir, *A Thousand-Mile Walk to the Gulf,* ed. William Frederic Badé, with illustrations (New York: Houghton Mifflin, 1916) 43, and JMP 23:39.

[238] JMP 23:39.

[239] *Ninth Census* (1870) 1:103.

[240] JMP 23:39.

---

[241] Ibid.

[242] Muir, *Thousand-Mile Walk* (Badé ed.) 44–45, and JMP 23:39.

[243] Muir, *Thousand-Mile Walk* (Badé ed.) 44, and JMP 23:39.

[244] JMP 23:40, and Muir, *Thousand-Mile Walk* (Badé ed.) 46.

[245] JMP 23:40, and Muir, *Thousand-Mile Walk* (Badé ed.) 47.

[246] Debra H. Davis and Larry Davis, slide presentation, Wildflowers II, 14 September 2007, Georgia State Department of Natural Resources, Smithgall Woods Natural Conservation Area, Helen, Georgia.

[247] Muir, *Thousand-Mile Walk* (Badé ed.) 47, and *Ninth Census* (1870) 1:103.

[248] JMP 23:40–41, Muir, *Thousand-Mile Walk* (Badé ed.) 48, and "Wills and Deeds of Hall County Georgia," Court of Ordinary, Will Book A, 1837–67 & 1868–90 Hall County Library, Gainesville, Georgia.

[249] James E. Dorsey, *The History of Hall County, Georgia* 2 vols. (Gainesville GA: Magnolia Press, 1991) 1:166.

[250] Dorsey, *History of Hall County*, 1:167, and 26 July 1865, Athens, Georgia *Southern Watchman*.

[251] Dorsey, *History of Hall County*, 1:169.

[252] Dorsey, *History of Hall County*, 1:170, and 2 October 1867, *Southern Watchman*.

[253] Dorsey, *History of Hall County*, 1:176.

[254] JMP 23:40–41.

[255] Muir, *Thousand-Mile Walk* (Badé ed.) 50–51.

[256] JMP 23:28.

[257] JMP 23:43, and Muir, *Thousand-Mile Walk* (Badé ed.) 78–79.

[258] Augustus Longstreet Hull, *Annals of Athens, Georgia, 1801–1901*, (Danielsville GA: Heritage Papers, 1906) 328 and *Eighth Census* (1860) 1:74, and *Ninth Census* (1870) 1:100. Athens continued to grow to more than 7,483 in 1880 *Tenth Census* (1880) 1:121.

[259] Muir, *Thousand-Mile Walk* (Badé ed.) 52, and JMP 23:44.

[260] Qtd. in Frances Taliaferro Thomas, *A Portrait of Historic Athens & Clarke County* (Athens: University of Georgia Press, 1992) 106.

[261] Hull, *Annals of Athens*, 323–24.

[262] H.J. Rowe, *History of Athens and Clarke County* (Athens GA: The McGregor Company, 1923) 11–15.

[263] JMP 23:44.

[264] JMP 23:47.

[265] JMP 23:48-49.

[266] Ibid.

[267] JMP 23:49.

[268] John R. de Trefille, "Reconstruction in Augusta, Georgia, 1865–1868," (master's thesis, Chapel Hill: University of North Carolina, 1979) 16–21.

[269] Trefille, 18–19, and JMP 23:49–50.

[270] JMP 23:49–50.

[271] JMP 23:51, and Muir, *Thousand-Mile Walk* (Badé ed.) 56–57.

[272] JMP 23:51. The author's revisions are in brackets. Muir's revisions are in cross-outs and parentheses.

[273] Ibid.

[274] JMP 23:51 and Muir, *Thousand-Mile Walk* (Badé ed.) 59.

[275] Donald E. Perkins, *History of the Perkins Family of Perkins, Georgia*, (Privately published: Georgia Historical Society, Savannah, Georgia, 1979) 90–91.

[276] Muir, *Thousand-Mile Walk* (Badé ed.) 59, and JMP 23:51–52.

[277] JMP 23:51.

[278] JMP 23:52.

[279] Angela Lee Ford, *Screven & Jenkins Counties* (Charleston SC: Arcadia Publishing, 1999) 21, and Central of Georgia Railroad Company, map #224-48-04434, Georgia Historical Society, Savannah, Georgia.

[280] Muir, *Thousand-Mile Walk* (Badé ed.) 61.

[281] Muir, *Thousand-Mile Walk* (Badé ed.) 63. The original journal made only a penciled edited comment as a reminder for a more fully developed story that ended up in the Badé edition. The short comment was: "Electricity my hobby." This fuller story may well have been added in Muir's 1908 working with his autobiographical materials when the consequences of electricity were more pervasive and evident.

[282] JMP 48:13439. Muir, *Thousand-Mile Walk* (Badé ed.) 64. This document detailing Muir's arrival is among the autobiographical sketches Muir was working on in 1908 and from 1910–13. He may have had access to his journal and used the penciled revisions and notes as memory prompts to fill out the details in an otherwise cryptic entry in the original journal. Muir worked over the Savannah and Bonaventure cemetery material numerous times. There are evidences of several different kinds of revision in the original journal. His dictation in 1908 added detail to his

original account for it is through these materials that we learn of his time of arrival, the Adams Express Company and how he discovered the road to Bonaventure.

[283] *Ninth Census* (1870) 1:100.

[284] JMP 23:53.

[285] JMP 23:53; JMP 48:13440 and JMP 48:13473.

[286] JMP 48:13440.

[287] JMP 23:54.

[288] JMP 48:13440.

[289] JMP 23:54-55 and Muir, *Thousand-Mile Walk* (Badé ed.) 68-69.

[290] Frederick Turner, *John Muir, Rediscovery of America* (Cambridge MA: Perseus Press, 1985) 143.

[291] JMP 48:13473-4.

[292] I.M. Marsh, *Bonaventure, a Poem*, (1860), courtesy of the Georgia Historical Society, Savannah, Georgia.

[293] Some of the revisions of his journal wove their way into the original journal in the form of penciled editing, cross-outs and re-writes. Portions of these re-writes were evidently composed after Muir contracted malaria in Florida. He likely was exposed to malaria in his stay in Savannah and the Bonaventure cemetery. The experience was very important in Muir's self understanding. Even late in life, Muir was re-writing this significant section of his life experience in the thousand-mile walk. JMP 23:55–57; JMP 45:11475–85.

[294] JMP 23:57. Muir crossed out this section when he revised his manuscript journal. This cross-out may have been at the end of the journey in 1867 or much later while in Yosemite, or maybe in 1908, or while working on his autobiographical materials between 1910 and 1913. It is difficult to determine when these revisions took place. The Bonaventure story, even in the original journal has two different beginnings. It does seem that the first two or three pages of the journal are nearly contemporary entries. Much of the fuller development and reflection appears to be written well after Muir contracted malaria while in Cedar Key in mid-October 1867.

[295] JMP 23:-58.

[296] John Muir to Jeanne C. Carr, September–October, 1867, Bonnie Johanna Gisel, ed.,, *Kindred and Related Spirits, The Letters of John Muir and Jeanne C. Carr*, Salt Lake City: The University of Utah Press, 2001) 59.

[297] Ibid.

[298] JMP 23:58.

[299] Ibid.

[300] JMP 23:58-59.

[301] Ibid.

[302] JMP 23:56–57.

[303] JMP 23:59.

[304] "Lord Man" was Muir's term of critique for humans who viewed Nature with prideful arrogance in seeking to exploit its resources or viewing nature as simply a warehouse to meet narrow and selfish human needs. "Lord Man" often abused nature due to indifference and ignorance, if not short-sighted hostility. In Muir's view, these prideful abusers little understood how nature's web of life was so critical for human well being.

[305] JMP 23:62.

[306] JMP 48:13445.

[307] JMP 23:63, and JMP 48:13472.

[308] JMP 23:63.

[309] JMP 23:64.

[310] JMP 48:13445-13446.

[311] JMP 48:13446.

[312] JMP 48:13446–47.

[313] JMP 48:13447.

[314] Ibid.

[315] Ibid.

[316] JMP 23:70.

[317] JMP 23:71, and John Muir, *A Thousand-Mile Walk to the Gulf,* ed. William Frederic Badé, with illustrations (New York: Houghton Mifflin, 1916) 88.

[318] James J. Miller, *An Environmental History of Northeast Florida* (Gainesville: University Press of Florida, 1998) 163–64.

[319] Jerrell H. Shofner, "Andrew Johnson and the Fernandina Unionists," *Prologue, the Journal of the National Archives* (Winter 1978): 211–13.

[320] Charles C. Fishburne, *The Cedar Keys in the Civil War and Reconstruction, 1861–1876* (Cedar Key FL: Sea Hawk Publications, 1982) 21ff. See also Frank W. Sweet, *Yulee's Railroad* (Palm Coast FL: Backintyme Press, 2000); Joseph Gary Adler, *The Public Career of Senator David Yulee*

(PhD diss., Cleveland OH: Case Western Reserve, 1973); Joe Knetsch, *David Levy Yulee and the Development of Antebellum Florida.* Typescript. [for Amelia Island Museum of History 23 April 1998]; Mills M. Lord, Jr., *David Levy Yulee, Statesman and Railroad Builder* (Gainesville: University of Florida, 1940); Arthur William Thompson, *David Yulee: A Study of 19th Century American Thought and Enterprise* (Ann Arbor MI: University Microfilms, 1954); Charles Wickliff Yulee, *Senator David Yulee* (n.d.) Smathers Libraries, Special Collections, University of Florida, Gainesville, Florida; Leon Hunhner, *David L. Yulee, Florida's First Senator* (n.d.) Smathers Libraries, Special Collections, University of Florida, Gainesville, Florida; and, Celeste H. Kavanaugh, *David Levy Yulee: A Man and His Vision,* 2nd ed., (Fernandina FL: Amelia Island Museum of History, 1995).

[321] US Bureau of Census, *Ninth Census* (1870) 98; Jesse T. Mann, "Fernandina: A City in Turmoil, 1863–1888," (master's thesis, Florida State University, 1971) 82–85; and, Shofner, "Andrew Johnson" (1978): 211–24.

[322] Shofner, "Andrew Johnson," (1978): 218.

[323] Ibid.

[324] Qtd. in Shofner, "Andrew Johnson," (1978): 218.

[325] JMP 23:71, and Muir, *Thousand-Mile Walk* (Badé ed.) 89.

[326] JMP 23:71–72, and Muir, *Thousand-Mile Walk* (Badé ed.) 90.

[327] JMP 23:72, and Muir, *Thousand-Mile Walk* (Badé ed.) 90.

[328] JMP 23:72, and Muir, *Thousand-Mile Walk* (Badé ed.) 91.

[329] JMP 23:73.

[330] JMP 23:75, and Muir, *Thousand-Mile Walk* (Badé ed.) 93.

[331] JMP 23:74, and Muir, *Thousand-Mile Walk* (Badé ed.) 92.

[332] JMP 23:75, and Muir, *Thousand-Mile Walk* (Badé ed.) 93.

[333] JMP 23:76, and Muir, *Thousand-Mile Walk* (Badé ed.) 95–96.

[334] JMP 23:77, and Muir, *Thousand-Mile Walk* (Badé ed.) 96-97.

[335] JMP 23:78, and Muir, *Thousand-Mile Walk* (Badé ed.) 98.

[336] JMP 23:78, and Muir, *Thousand-Mile Walk* (Badé ed.) 98–99.

[337] JMP 23:78–79, and Muir, *Thousand-Mile Walk* (Badé ed.) 99.

[338] JMP 23:80, and Muir, *Thousand-Mile Walk* (Badé ed.) 100.

[339] JMP 23:80, and Muir, *Thousand-Mile Walk* (Badé ed.) 101.

[340] JMP 23:80.

[341] "Biocentric" is an adjective that "centers in life; regarding or treating life as a central fact;" or, where "all living things as having intrinsic value." See *The Oxford English Dictionary,* 2nd ed., reprint 2002, complete text

reproduced micrographically (Oxford: Oxford University Press, 1989) 137, and http://www.merriam-webster.com/dictionary/biocentric. "Anthropocentric" is an adjective that "regards man as the central fact of the universe to which all surrounding facts have reference" and "considers human beings as the most significant entity in the universe." See *Oxford English Dictionary* (2002) 57, and Merriam-Webster Dictionary, online edition at http://www.merriam-ebster.com/dictionary/anthropocentric.

[342] Shofner, "Andrew Johnson," (1978): 217–21.

[343] JMP 23:87–88, and Muir, *Thousand-Mile Walk* (Badé ed.) 110.

[344] JMP 23:82, and Muir, *Thousand-Mile Walk* (Badé ed.) 103–07. The published edition of Muir's journal includes an anecdote about an attempted robbery by a young black man. In this story Muir bluffs his way out of the robbery due to a ruse where he pretends to have a hidden gun in his pocket. In the story both men are afraid of one another. Muir's original journal does not carry the story, but it was included in the 1916 account. Since it was not in the original journal, I have chosen to omit the story. See JMP 23:81–82 and Muir, *Thousand-Mile Walk* (Badé ed.) 103–04.

[345] JMP 23:83, and Muir, *Thousand-Mile Walk* (Badé ed.) 106–07.

[346] Ibid.

[347] JMP 23:83, and Muir, *Thousand-Mile Walk* (Badé ed.) 107.

[348] JMP 23:84.

[349] Ibid., and Muir, *Thousand-Mile Walk* (Badé ed.) 107.

[350] US Bureau of Census, *Ninth Census* (1870) 97.

[351] James E. Dorsey, *The History of Hall County, Georgia*, 2 vols. (Gainesville GA: Magnolia Press, 1991), 1:166–69; Charles H. Hildreth and Merlin D. Cox, *History of Gainesville, 1854–1979* (Gainesville GA: Alachua Press, 1981) 54-56; Historic Gainesville Incorporated, "A History of Gainesville, Florida," http://www.afn.org/~hgi/gnvhistory.html. Excerpted from Ben Pickard, ed., *Historic Gainesville, A Tour Guide to the Past* (Gainesville, FL, Historic Gainesville Inc, 1991).

[352] JMP 23:84, and Muir, *Thousand-Mile Walk* (Badé ed.) 108.

[353] JMP 23:87, and Muir, *Thousand-Mile Walk* (Badé ed.) 109.

[354] JMP 23:88, and Muir, *Thousand-Mile Walk* (Badé ed.) 110.

[355] JMP 23:88, and Muir, *Thousand-Mile Walk* (Badé ed.) 111.

[356] JMP 23:88 and Muir, *Thousand-Mile Walk* (Badé ed.) 111, and David W. Hartman and David Coles, *Biographical Rosters of Florida's Confederate*

and *Union Soldiers*, 6 vols., (Wilmington NC: Broadfoot Publishing, 1999) 2:825.

357 JMP 23:89–90, and Muir, *Thousand-Mile Walk* (Badé ed.) 113–14.

358 JMP 23:91, and Muir, *Thousand-Mile Walk* (Badé ed.) 115–16.

359 JMP 23:94.

360 JMP 23:94, and Muir, *Thousand-Mile Walk* (Badé ed.) 118–19.

361 JMP 23:94–95, and Muir, *Thousand-Mile Walk* (Badé ed.) 121.

362 JMP 23:94–95, and Muir, *Thousand-Mile Walk* (Badé ed.) 121–122.

363 JMP 23:95, and Muir, *Thousand-Mile Walk* (Badé ed.) 122.

364 JMP 23:96, and Muir, *Thousand-Mile Walk* (Badé ed.) 122.

365 JMP 23:97, and John Muir, *A Thousand-Mile Walk to the Gulf*, ed. William Frederic Badé, with illustrations (New York: Houghton Mifflin, 1916) 124.

366 JMP 23:97, and Muir, *Thousand-Mile Walk* (Badé ed.) 124.

367 Muir, *Thousand-Mile Walk* (Badé ed.) 124.

368 US Bureau of Census, *Ninth Census* (1870) 98; Jesse Walter Dees and Vivian Flannery Dees, *"Off the Beaten Path": The History of Cedar Key, Florida, 1843–1990* (Chiefland, FL: Rife Publishing, 1990); Charles Fishburne, Jr., *The Cedar Keys in the Civil War and Reconstruction, 1861–1876* (Cedar Key FL: Sea Hawk Publications, 1982); Charles Carroll Fishburne, Jr., *The Cedar Keys in the 19th Century* (Cedar Key FL: Cedar Key Historical Society, 2004) 60; "Hodgson Hill in Cedar Key," unpublished Mss (Cedar Key FL: Cedar Key Historical Society); and Frederick Turner, *John Muir, Rediscovery of America* (Cambridge MA: Perseus Press, 1985) 150, 375n.

369 Dees and Dees, *"Off the Beaten Path"* 46.

370 JMP 23:66.

371 Dees and Dees, *"Off the Beaten Path"*, 42–44.

372 Ibid., 56.

373 Ibid., 60.

374 Ibid. 56–59.

375 Everett W. Caudle, "Postbellum Race Relations in Gainesville, Florida, a Study of Social, Economic, and Institutional Arrangements," Undergraduate Honors Paper submitted to Merlin G. Cox (Gainsville: University of Florida, 1986) 31.

376 *Ninth Census* (1870) 98.

377 Eliza Hearn, [11 July 1867], *Diary of Eliza Horn* [sic], *Way Key, East Florida, 1867–1869*, typescript copy, (Jacksonville FL: Historical Records

Survey, Works Progress Administration, State Office, deposited in Cedar Key Public Library, Cedar Key, Florida, 1937) 8.

[378] Hearn, [31 December 1867], *Diary*, 10.

[379] Dees and Dees, *"Off the Beaten Path,"* 63–64.

[380] Charles C. Fishburne, Jr., "Eliza Hearn and Life on the Way Key, 1867–1973," *Search for Yesterday, a History of Levy County* (Bronson, Florida: Levy County Archives Committee, October 1982) chap. 12, 24.

[381] JMP 23:99, and Muir, *Thousand-Mile Walk* (Badé ed.) 72.

[382] JMP 23:99.

[383] Ibid.

[384] JMP 23:100–01.

[385] JMP 23:99–100, and Muir, *Thousand-Mile Walk* (Badé ed.) 129.

[386] Qtd. in Turner, *John Muir*, 315.

[387] Revision and added reflection on the Bonaventure experience probably comes from this period, especially when the reader notes a shift from immediate present tense to past tense in the text.

[388] John Muir to Jeanne C. Carr, Bonnie Johanna Gisel, ed., *Kindred & Related Spirits, The Letters of John Muir and Jeanne C. Carr* (Salt Lake City: The University of Utah Press, 2001) 60.

[389] John Muir to Jeanne C. Carr, 8 November [1867], Gisel ed., *Kindred & Related Spirits*, 60.

[390] John Muir to David Gilyre Muir, 8 November [1867], [Cedar Keys, Florida], JMP 1:600.

[391] John Muir to David Gilyre Muir, 13 December [1867], JMP 1:603.

[392] JMP 23:105, and Muir, *Thousand-Mile Walk* (Badé ed.) 133.

[393] Muir, *Thousand-Mile Walk* (Badé ed.) 136.

[394] JMP 23:110–11, and Muir, *Thousand-Mile Walk* (Badé ed.) 136.

[395] JMP 23:111–12.

[396] Ibid., and Muir, *Thousand-Mile Walk* (Badé ed.) 138-139.

[397] JMP 23:112-113.

[398] JMP 23:113, and Muir, *Thousand-Mile Walk* (Badé ed.) 140.

[399] John Muir to Merrill Moores, 1 January [18]68, JMP 1:605.

[400] Ibid.

[401] John Muir to [Merrills & Moores], 3 January 1868, JMP 1:608–610.

[402] John Muir to [Merrills & Moores], 3 January 1868, Ced[ar] Key, [Florida], JMP 1:608–610, and JMP 23:110.

[403] John Muir to [Merrills and Moores], 3 January [18]68, Cedar Keys, [Florida], JMP 1: 610.

[404] Muir, *Thousand-Mile Walk* (Badé ed.) 143–45.

[405] JMP 23:110.

[406] JMP 23:115.

[407] JMP 23: 116.

[408] Ibid.

[409] Ibid.

[410] Ibid.

[411] JMP 23:117.

[412] JMP 23:118.

[413] Ibid.

[414] Louis A. Perez, Jr., *Cuba Between Reform & Revolution*, 2nd ed. (New York: Oxford University Press, 1995) 113.

[415] Perez, *Cuba, Between Reform & Revolution*, 113.

[416] Leslie Bethell, ed., *Cuba, a Short History* (New York: Cambridge University Press, 1993) 21; Perez, *Cuba Between Reform & Revolution*, 112–21; Franklin W. Knight, *Slave Society in Cuba During the Nineteenth Century* (Madison: University of Wisconsin Press, 1970) chap. 7; and Richard Gott, *Cuba, A New History* (New Haven CT: Yale University Press) 64–74.

[417] Gott, 65–67.

[418] Perez, *Cuba, Between Reform & Revolution*, 117.

[419] JMP 23:119.

[420] JMP 23:119, and Muir, *Thousand-Mile Walk* (Badé ed.) 151. Muir's original journal text is the following: "I was sadly compelled to see that no ~~attainable pitch of~~ enthusiasm~~tic alacrity~~ would ~~enable me to excite the needful amount of power in my muscles to~~ carry me to the interior ~~amid insurmountable fatigue~~ & so was compelled to limit my researches within 10 or 12 miles of Havana." JMP 23:119-120.

[421] Muir, *Thousand-Mile Walk* (Badé ed.,), 153 and JMP 23:122.

[422] Muir, *Thousand-Mile Walk* (Badé ed.,), 156 and JMP 23:126.

[423] JMP 23:122–23.

[424] JMP 23:140.

[425] JMP 23:122.

[426] JMP 23:127.

[427] JMP 23:127.

[428] JMP 23:128.

[429] JMP 23:130–31.

[430] JMP 23:138.

[431] Muir, *Thousand-Mile Walk* (Badé ed.) 162–63, and JMP 23:134.

[432] Muir, *Thousand-Mile Walk* (Badé ed.) 164, and JMP 23:135–37.

[433] JMP 23:135–37, and Muir, *Thousand-Mile Walk* (Badé ed.), 164.

[434] JMP 23:140.

[435] Ibid.

[436] Ibid. The word "fortunately" appears in the original journal. (JMP 23:140) The original inked entry has him not finding passage to any "American" port, and the word "South" is added as a penciled revision along with an encircled X, suggesting a desire to expand this section. Since this section comes after many revisions he made in Cedar Key, it is likely this journal was revised some time later in his life, either in his first years in California or even as late as 1908 when he was dictating his autobiography and working on autobiographical materials, including this journal. Muir had a tendency to revise in pencil; it is difficult to know when he decided that abandoning his dream to go to South America was fortunate. Likely, after experiencing the healthy and visual delights of Yosemite, he decided that not going to South America was indeed "fortunate." After all, he did know the outcome of Mungo Park's trek through Africa that led to Park's death by his persistent, yet failed attempt to trace the route of the Niger River when most of the men of his expedition fell away by disease. Park disappeared in Africa in 1805. (Kate Ferguson Marsters, "Introduction," *Travels in the Interior Districts of Africa by Mungo Park* [Durham NC: Duke University Press, 2000] 8) He also thought that if his health improved in California he then would be free to travel to South America. Muir made a plan to go to the frosts of New York to ship passage to California and, perhaps, find a more suitable climate to restore his health, which is indirectly suggested by the word "frosts." (JMP 23:140) Frosts are not conducive to mosquitoes and malaria. California was his new goal. He wrote, "there thought I, I shall find health & sunshine & new Kingdoms of plants & all that is surpassingly grand in mountain." (JMP 23:140) The crossed out revision suggests that Muir had already felt the sunshine and seen the mountains when he wrote this passage but in revision sought to leave out the detail to lend credibility to the Cuba narrative since presumably he had no experience with Yosemite in January 1868, having only read about it and being reminded of it by Jeanne Carr.

He had not yet felt its sunshine or seen its "surpassingly grand" mountains.

[437] JMP 23:140.

[438] Ibid.

[439] JMP 23:141.

[440] Ibid and Muir, *Thousand-Mile Walk* (Badé ed.) 172.

[441] Ibid.

[442] JMP 23:142.

[443] Ibid.

[444] JMP 23:142-143 and Muir, *Thousand-Mile Walk* (Badé ed.) 179.

[445] JMP 23:144 and Muir, *Thousand-Mile Walk* (Badé ed.) 182.

[446] Muir, *Thousand-Mile Walk* (Badé ed.) 182.

[447] JMP 23:145.

[448] JMP 23:146.

[449] JMP 23:146.

[450] Frederick Turner, *John Muir, Rediscovery of America* (Cambridge MA: Perseus Press, 1985) 315.

[451] Muir, *Thousand-Mile Walk* (Badé ed.) 186.

[452] Ibid.

[453] Muir, *Thousand-Mile Walk* (Badé ed.) 187.

[454] Ibid.

[455] Muir, *Thousand-Mile Walk* (Badé ed.) 187–88.

[456] John Muir, *My First Summer in the Sierra* [1911], (New York: Barnes and Noble, 206) 123.

[457] John Muir, "Address to the Sierra Club," *Sierra Club Bulletin* 1,7 (January 1896): 271–85, and Holmes, *The Young John Muir*, 159–60.

[458] John Muir to Ann Gilyre Muir, 27 September [18]72, Yosemite Valley, Muir Family Papers, Huntington Library, San Marino, California.

[459] Qtd. in "John Muir" by Ellen D. Graydon, 14 Nov [1942?], [Linnie Marsh] Wolfe Papers, Holt-Atherton Special Collections, University of the Pacific, Stockton, California.

[460] For example, current studies of young adulthood and youthful development suggest that there is a connection between travel and leadership development, but this is an area that remains relatively underdeveloped as a field of scholarship. Laurent A. Parks Daloz, Cheryl H. Keen, James P. Keen, and Sharon Daloz Parks, *Common Fire, Lives of Commitment in a Complex World* (Boston: Beacon Press, 1996) 38, 108–09;

Howard Gardner, *Leading Minds, Anatomy of Leadership* (New York: Harper Collins, 1995) 248–49; and Bernard M. Bass, *Bass & Stogdill's Handbook of Leadership, Theory, Research, and Managerial Applications*, 3rd edition (New York: Macmillan, 1990) 813–14.

# INDEX

Emerson, Ralph Waldo, 41, 55,
60
Emory River, Tennessee, 81, 82
Erie Canal, 8
East Central Tennessee, 73
Europe, 10, 25, 202n
Eye injury, 1 30, 49-50, 51, 171,
202n
Evening primrose, 68
Fentress County, Tennessee, 75
Fentress County Courthouse, 75
Fernandina, Florida, 2, 114, 117,
118-120, 122, 128, 130, 134,
139, 140, 212n, 213n
Ferns, 37, 43, 49, 57, 58, 68, 77,
79, 82, 83, 96, 120
Florida, 2, 61, 62, 100, 107, 114,
115, 116, 117, 118, 121, 123,
125, 127, 128, 131, 134, 136,
138, 139, 142, 145, 147, 149,
150, 153, 155, 156, 159, 166,
169, 175, 204n, 207n, 211n,
212n
Florida Central Railroad, 118,
139, 141
Florida Keys, 145
Flying fish, 166, 167
Fort Butler, 88
Fort Winnebago, 8-9
Foster, Stephen, 64
Fountain Lake Farm, 9, 17, 32,
36, 57
France, 10
Free labor, 94
Freedmen, 74, 93, 95, 102, 114,
118, 119, 140, 141, 175
Freedman's Bureau, Georgia, 92
French marigolds, 91
Gaines, Gen. Edmund P., 130
Gainesville, Georgia, 70, 92, 93,
214n

Gainesville, Florida, 118, 128,
129-130, 134, 139, 140, 144,
175, 215n
Gainesville Academy, 130
Galloway, David, 32, 33, 34, 35,
36, 57, 58, 83, 176
Galloway, Jean Millar (mother
of David Galloway), 58
Galloway, Sarah (Muir), 32, 34,
35, 36, 46, 57, 58, 60, 83
Gentian, fringed, 91
Geology, 4, 23, 25, 26, 30, 34, 39,
64-65, 70, 174
Georgia, 2, 61, 62, 86, 87, 90, 92,
93, 94, 95, 98, 99, 100, 101,
114, 115, 117, 118, 139, 142
Georgia farmers, 91
Georgia, University of, 95
Georgian Bay, Lake Huron,
Canada, 37
Germany, 10
Ghosts, 101
Gilyre, David (grandfather), 7
11-12, 14, 18
Gilyre, Ann (mother), 7, 11, 12,
25, 60
Gilyre family, 11
Glasgow, 8, 10
Glasgow Junction, Kentucky, 64,
69
God (Almighty, Creator, Great
Architect, King, Lord,
Providence, Spirit), 1, 3, 14,
19, 21, 22, 24, 27, 32, 40, 43-
44, 46, 49, 50, 51-52, 55, 56,
58, 61, 81, 85, 96, 98, 108, 115,
124, 125, 128, 130, 132, 135,
135, 136, 137, 141, 147, 153,
154, 163, 172, 173, 176, 179
"God's Inventions," 1, 51-52, 59
Gold, 87

# Index

# Index

Muscadine grapes, 92, 100, 108
"My Old Kentucky Home," 64
Native Americans, 87-88, 93,
 136, 139

Nature
Anthropocentric View, 127, 137,
 145, 149, 153, 213n-172, 178,
 179, 180, 214n
Beauty of, 9, 35, 37, 41, 47-48, 49,
 64, 67, 69, 72, 78, 81-82, 83,
 85-86, 89, 90, 96, 105, 108,
 109, 111, 121-123, 131-132,
 132, 156, 165, 167, 169, 202n,
Biocentric View, 2, 127, 137, 145,
 149, 153, 154, 173, 176, 177,
 178, 180, 213n-214n ;
 Dominion view, 123, 136,
 153, 172-173 ; "God's
 Inventions," 1, 51-52, 59
Muir's Views of, 1-2, 9, 21, 23,
 24, 35, 39, 41, 43-44, 47-48, 49,
 61, 64, 70-71, 81-81, 82, 96, 96-
 98, 104-105, 108-109, 114, 115,
 116, 117, 121-123, 123-124,
 127, 132, 135-136, 145-149,
 151, 153-154, (on storms) 156,
 160-161, 161-163, 163-164,
 165-167, 169, 171, 173, 174-
 175, 176, 177, 180, 195n, 213n-
 214n
Utilitarian View, 2, 69, 70, 75, 85,
 108-109, 117-118, 121, 124,
 127, 135, 137, 147, 149-150,
 163-164, 167, 172, 173, 176,
 177, 178, 180, 212n

Nebraska, 164, 165, 168, 169
New Orleans, Louisiana, 144,
 145, 151, 153, 174

New Testament, 11, 13, 22, 23, 24,
 60, 107, 132, 206n
New York City, 8, 159, 164, 165,
 168, 169, 205n 218n
New York investors, 119
New York newspaper, shipping
 news, 164
Niagara Falls, 37
Niger River, 218n
Nodding pogonia, 68
North Carolina, 2, 70, 72, 73, 83,
 85, 90, 110, 175
Northern sympathizers, 141
Northerner, 72, 94
Oaks, 4, 64, 67, 69-70, 72, 79, 82,
 100, 105, 110, 139, 142, 144,
 145
Oconee County, Georgia, 96
Ogeechee River, Georgia, 102
Ohio River, 59, 60, 61, 64
Oklahoma, (Indian Territory),
 88
Old South, 74
Old Testament, 22, 35 ;
 Proverbs, 35
Oranges, 167
Orinoco River, 2, 25, 138, 144,
 170
Osgood, Smith and Co.,
 (Indianapolis), 45, 48, 92
"Outlaw to society," 113
Palmetto(s), 64, 102, 104, 108,
 120-121, 122, 131, 132, 136,
 139, 145, 148, 173 ; Cabbage,
 122, 139 ; Saw, 102, 150
Palm grove(s), 131, 134
Panama, 164, 165, 168, 169, 205n
Paradise Lost, a Poem (Milton),
 21-22, 60, 123, 132
Pardeeville, Wisconsin, 18

231